VCP VMware® Certified Professional vSphere™ 4 Study Guide

(Exam VCP410)

Robert Schmidt

New York Chicago San Francisco
Lisbon London Madrid Mexico City
Milan New Delhi San Juan
Seoul Singapore Sydney Toronto

ISBN: Book p/n 978-0-07-163366-6 and CD p/n 978-0-07-163369-7
of set 978-0-07-163368-0

MHID: Book p/n 0-07-163366-9 and CD p/n 0-07-163369-3
of set 0-07-163368-5

Sponsoring Editor Timothy Green	**Copy Editor** Bob Campbell	**Illustration** ContentWorks, Inc.
Editorial Supervisor Patty Mon	**Proofreader** Paul Tyler	**Art Director, Cover** Jeff Weeks
Project Manager Molly Sharp	**Indexer** J & J Indexing Services	**Cover Designer** Peter Grame
Acquisitions Coordinator Meghan Riley	**Production Supervisor** George Anderson	
Technical Editor Rick Scherer	**Composition** ContentWorks, Inc.	

This book is dedicated to my wife and daughters for putting up with me while I was writing it.

CONTENTS AT A GLANCE

CONTENTS

PREFACE

The vSphere Suite is the latest iteration of VMware's enterprise-class virtualization products. It introduces a large number of new features that help to further leverage virtualization in production Datacenters. The VMware VCP410 exam tests your ability to install, configure, and manage a full-scale vSphere environment. This book will help you to prepare for the exam and to understand how you can better leverage vSphere in your production environment.

The objective of this study guide is to prepare you for the VCP410 exam by familiarizing you with the technology or body of knowledge tested on the exam. This exam, combined with the official VMware course, will allow you to achieve the VCP certification. Because the primary focus of the book is to help you pass the test, we don't always cover every aspect of the related technology. Some aspects of the technology are only covered to the extent necessary to help you understand what you need to know to pass the exam, but we hope this book will serve you as a valuable professional resource after your exam.

In This Book

This book is organized in such a way as to serve as an in-depth review for the VCP410 exam for both experienced virtualization professionals and newcomers to VMware's virtualization technologies. Each chapter covers a major aspect of the exam, with an emphasis on the "why" as well as the "how to" of working with and supporting VMware's vSphere suite of products.

On the CD

For more information on the CD-ROM, please see the Appendix "About the CD-ROM" at the back of the book.

Exam Readiness Checklist

At the end of the Introduction you will find an Exam Readiness Checklist. This table has been constructed to allow you to cross-reference the official exam objectives with the objectives as they are presented and covered in this book. The checklist also allows you to gauge your level of expertise on each objective at the outset of your studies. This should allow you to check your progress and make sure you spend the time you need on more difficult or unfamiliar sections. References have been provided for the objective exactly as the vendor presents it, the section of the study guide that covers that objective, and a chapter and page reference.

In Every Chapter

We've created a set of chapter components that call your attention to important items, reinforce important points, and provide helpful exam-taking hints. Take a look at what you'll find in every chapter:

- Every chapter begins with **Certification Objectives**—what you need to know in order to pass the section on the exam dealing with the chapter topic. The Objective headings identify the objectives within the chapter, so you'll always know an objective when you see it!

- **Exam Watch** notes call attention to information about, and potential pitfalls in, the exam. These helpful hints are written by authors who have taken the exams and received their certification—who better to tell you what to worry about? They know what you're about to go through!

- **On the Job** notes describe the issues that come up most often in real-world settings. They provide a valuable perspective on certification- and product-related topics. They point out common mistakes and address questions that have arisen from on-the-job discussions and experience.

- **Inside the Exam** sidebars highlight some of the most common and confusing problems that students encounter when taking a live exam. Designed to anticipate what the exam will emphasize, getting inside the exam will help ensure you know what you need to know to pass the exam. You can get a leg up on how to respond to those difficult-to-understand questions by focusing extra attention on these sidebars.

- The **Certification Summary** is a succinct review of the chapter and a restatement of salient points regarding the exam.

- ■ The **Two-Minute Drill** at the end of every chapter is a checklist of the main points of the chapter. It can be used for last-minute review.

- ■ The **Self Test** offers questions similar to those found on the certification exams. The answers to these questions, as well as explanations of the answers, can be found at the end of each chapter. By taking the Self Test after completing each chapter, you'll reinforce what you've learned from that chapter while becoming familiar with the structure of the exam questions.

Some Pointers

Once you've finished reading this book, set aside some time to do a thorough review. You might want to return to the book several times and make use of all the methods it offers for reviewing the material:

- ■ *Re-read all the Two-Minute Drills*, or have someone quiz you. You also can use the drills as a way to do a quick cram before the exam. You might want to make some flash cards out of 3 × 5 index cards that have the Two-Minute Drill material on them.

- ■ *Re-read all the Exam Watch notes and Inside the Exam elements*. Remember that these notes are written by authors who have taken the exam and passed. They know what you should expect—and what you should be on the lookout for.

- ■ *Re-take the Self Tests*. Taking the tests right after you've read the chapter is a good idea, because the questions help reinforce what you've just learned. However, it's an even better idea to go back later and do all the questions in the book in one sitting. Pretend that you're taking the live exam. When you go through the questions the first time, you should mark your answers on a separate piece of paper. That way, you can run through the questions as many times as you need to until you feel comfortable with the material.

ACKNOWLEDGMENTS

I would like to thank the following people:

The team at McGraw-Hill, especially Megg Morin and Meghan Riley for their help and support during the writing process and for helping to keep me on track. Thanks go to Molly Sharp also for help in keeping the project running smoothly throughout.

I would also like to thank my technical editor, Rick Scherer, for all of the suggestions he made to help keep the book accurate.

INTRODUCTION

Welcome to the *VCP VMware® Certified Professional vSphere™ 4 Study Guide (Exam VCP410)*. This book will provide you with a thorough understanding of all of the technologies that make up VMware's vSphere product and will help to prepare you for the VCP410 exam. This book closely follows the exam objectives from the VMware VCP Blueprint. It is designed to allow you to study each exam objective and be prepared for the types of questions that will be asked about the objective, This book will cover the wide range of subjects that are required to pass the VCP410 exam and will give you the knowledge you need to be confident that you will pass the exam.

A large number of companies are starting to realize the potential savings they can achieve through virtualization, and VMware is currently the leader of the pack when it comes to virtualization. Because of this, the VCP certification is a very sought-after credential to have near the top of your résumé.

Test Structure

The VCP exam is a computer-based multiple-choice exam. All of the questions will present you with a question or scenario, and you will be expected to pick the best answer from a list. Some of the questions will have multiple answers and the question will tell you how many correct answers you should pick. Some of the questions will have an accompanying graphic that you can look at to help answer the question. For these types of questions there will be an Exhibit button that will bring up a separate window with the graphic.

Question Types

There are two main question types on the VCP exam: knowledge based and performance based. Knowledge-based questions will ask something that is a fact. An example of a knowledge-based question is:

How many virtual CPUs can a virtual machine have under vSphere?

A. 1

B. 2

C. 4

D. 8

Generally for these types of questions, you will either know the answer or you won't. Performance-based questions pose a scenario where you must determine what will happen or determine the best course of action. An example of a performance-based question is:

What will happen to a virtual machine that is powered on in an HA cluster if there are not sufficient failover resources to meet failover requirements?

A. It will be powered on.

B. It will not be powered on.

C. If admission control is set to "Allow VMs to be powered on even if they violate availability constraints," the VM will be powered on.

D. If admission control is set to "Do not allow VMs to be powered on even if they violate availability constraints," the VM will be powered on.

Study and Testing Strategies

The VCP exam is difficult but not unreasonably so. The questions are designed to test your knowledge and do not use language tricks like double negatives. I have taken a large number of certification exams, and I have found that the following strategies worked very well:

1. Review the table of contents of this book to get a decent understanding of the scope of the exam. The amount of material that is covered can seem daunting, but once you have a grasp of the entire body of knowledge, you can start breaking it down into manageable parts.

2. Read through each chapter of the book. Each chapter covers a different aspect of vSphere. Take notes while you read through the chapter. Taking notes will help you to remember important facts and will make it easier to answer fact-based questions on the exam. Once you have read the chapter, review the certification summary and attempt to answer the sample questions at the end of the chapter.

3. Find a way to get hands-on experience. There is no replacement for hands-on experience with vSphere. The appendix of this book details how to set up a virtual lab on a single workstation that you can use to get additional hands-on experience.

4. Review the material on the included CD. There is a sample exam included on the CD that will closely resemble the types of questions you will see on the exam. There is also a flash card deck included on the CD that you can use to help you to memorize the many facts associated with the vSphere product.

Once you have studied and feel confident, you will be ready to take the exam. The following is some general advice for taking the exam:

- The exam has a time limit. Remember that the exam has a time limit, but don't be too concerned about it. The vast majority of people who take the VCP exam finish with plenty of time to spare.

- Read each of the questions carefully. Once you have read the question, take a second and see if you can come up with the answer before looking at the choices. If you can come up with the answer before looking at the choices and then you find that answer in the choices, you will be more certain that you have a correct answer.

- If you cannot think of the correct answer to a question, try to rule out any answers that are obviously not correct and make an educated guess. There will usually be at least one answer that is obviously not the correct answer, and by ruling it out, you will increase your odds of guessing the correct answer.

- Answer every question. For this exam an unanswered question is counted as incorrect. If you don't know the answer, make your best educated guess.

- Mark any question you are not sure about. The exam allows you to mark questions to review later. It is possible that other questions may spark the answer for a previous question, and if it is marked, you will be able to get back to it easily.

- Do not skip any question planning to come back to it later. Instead of skipping a question make your best educated guess and mark the question for review. It is possible you will not have time to come back to the question, so you do not want to leave it blank.
- Relax. The most important advice I ever received for taking an exam was to relax. If you have studied for the exam and you are familiar with the product, you will be fine.

Registering for the Exam

VMware exams are administered by Sylvan Prometric and Pearson VUE. They have testing centers located all over the world, and you can register for the exam by going to their web site:

- www.prometric.com
- www.pearsonvue.com

When signing up for the exam, you will need to provide your name, e-mail address, and contact information. They will find a testing center that is close to you and confirm that the site and testing time and date will work for you. They will then send you a confirmation e-mail listing the exam, date, time, and location for the exam.

Taking the Test

Here are a few final tips for sitting the exam:

- Bring two forms of ID with you to the testing center.
- They will provide you with scratch paper, so do not bring any of your own.
- Eat something before you sit for the exam. You do not want to be distracted by being hungry.
- Arrive at the testing center early. This will help to reduce the stress you feel before the exam, and you can often start the exam earlier than your assigned time.
- Finally, remember that this is just a test.

Exam VCP410

Exam Readiness Checklist

Official Objective	Study Guide Coverage	Ch #	Beginner	Intermediate	Expert
Plan, Install, and Upgrade VMware ESX/ESXi					
Install VMware ESX/ESXi on local storage	ESX Server Installations	3			
Upgrade VMware ESX/ESXi	Upgrading to ESX Server 4.0	3			
Secure VMware ESX/ESXi	Configuring Basic ESX Server Security	3			
Identify vSphere Architecture and Solutions	ESX and ESXi Server Architecture	3			
Configure ESX/ESXi Networking					
Configure Virtual Switches	Understand and Configure Virtual Switches	5			
Configure vNetwork Distributed Switches	Understand and Configure vNetwork Distributed Switches	5			
Configure VMware ESX/ESXi Management Network	Understand and Configure the ESX/ESXi Management Network	5			
Configure ESX/ESXi Storage					
Configure FC SAN Storage	Configure FC SAN Storage	6			
Configure iSCSI SAN Storage	Configure iSCSI SAN Storage	6			
Configure NFS Datastores	Configure NFS Datastores	6			
Configure and Manage VMFS Datastores	Configure and Manage VMFS Datastores	6			

Exam Readiness Checklist

Official Objective	Study Guide Coverage	Ch #	Beginner	Intermediate	Expert
Install and Configure vCenter Server					
Install vCenter Server	vCenter Server Installation	4			
Manage vSphere Client Plug-ins	Install Additional vCenter Modules	4			
Configure vCenter Server	Configure and Manage vCenter Server	4			
Configure Access Control	Configure Access Control through vCenter Server	4			
Deploy and Manage Virtual Machines and vApps					
Create and Deploy Virtual Machines	Create and Deploy Virtual Machines	7			
Manage Virtual Machines	Manage Virtual Machine Configurations	7			
Deploy vApps	Deploy and Manage vApps	7			
Manage Compliance					
Install, Configure, and Manage VMware vCenter Update Manager	Configure and Manage VMware vCenter Update Manager	8			
Establish and Apply ESX Host Profiles	Establish and Apply ESX Host Profiles	8			
Establish Service Levels					
Create and Configure VMware Clusters	Create and Configure VMware Clusters	9			
Enable a Fault-Tolerant Virtual Machine	Enable a Fault-Tolerant Virtual Machine	9			
Create and Configure Resource Pools	Create and Configure Resource Pools	9			

Exam Readiness Checklist

Official Objective	Study Guide Coverage	Ch #	Beginner	Intermediate	Expert
Migrate Virtual Machines	Migrate Virtual Machines	9			
Back Up and Restore Virtual Machines	Back Up and Restore Virtual Machines	9			
Perform Basic Troubleshooting and Alarm Management					
Perform Basic Troubleshooting for ESX/ESXi Hosts	Basic Troubleshooting for ESX/ESXi Hosts	10			
Perform Basic Troubleshooting for VMware FT and Third-Party Clusters	Basic Troubleshooting for VMware FT and Third-Party Clusters	10			
Perform Basic Troubleshooting for Networking	Basic Troubleshooting for Networking	10			
Perform Basic Troubleshooting for Storage	Basic Troubleshooting for Storage	10			
Perform Basic Troubleshooting for HA/DRS and VMotion	Basic Troubleshooting for HA/DRS and VMotion	10			
Create and Respond to vCenter Connectivity Alarms	Create and Respond to vCenter Connectivity Alarms	10			
Create and Respond to vCenter Utilization Alarms	Create and Respond to vCenter Utilization Alarms	10			
Monitor vSphere ESX/ESXi and Virtual Machine Performance	Monitor vSphere ESX/ESXi and Virtual Machine Performance	10			

1

Introduction to the VMware Certified Professional Exam for vSphere

W elcome to the *VCP VMware® Certified Professional vSphere™ 4 Study Guide (Exam VCP410)*. This book will help to guide you through understanding all of the technologies that are covered on the VCP exam. In this chapter I will give you a brief overview of the vSphere suite of technologies and the various versions that are available. This overview will give you a good base of understanding to prepare you to move deeper into the individual technologies of vSphere in later chapters.

CERTIFICATION OBJECTIVE 1.01

Introduction to vSphere

vSphere is the latest virtualization product suite from VMware. It is designed to allow administrators to deploy highly available large-scale virtual environments that span the entire corporate network. It contains features that allow rapid deployment of virtual environments, centralized management of those virtual environments, and the ability to back up and restore those environments for disaster recovery and high availability. In this section I will describe the features that are available in vSphere and discuss the different editions that can be purchased.

vSphere Features and Editions

The vSphere suite has a number of available features. In this section I will list these features and give a brief overview of each one. I will then talk about the different editions of vSphere and list the features that are available in each edition. You may not understand these features at this point, but they will become clearer as we cover them in detail in later chapters. The important thing to remember at this stage is which features are available in each edition of vSphere.

vSphere Features

vSphere has a large number of available features. The following is a list of these features and a basic description of each one.

vSMP Support

vSMP is the ability to create a virtual machine that has two or more virtual CPUs.

Editions of vSphere allow up to eight-way vSMP. In most production environments it would be very rare to see a virtual machine that would need eight-way vSMP. As physical servers become more powerful the use of eight-way vSMP will become more common.

Thin Provisioning

Thin provisioning is a vSphere technology that is used to reduce storage requirements for virtual machines.

Update Manager

Update Manager is a patch and update management utility for both ESX Servers and the virtual machines running on them.

Update Manager is a very powerful utility. As ESX Server farms grow in size and as more servers become virtualized, it can become very difficult to keep them updated. Update Manager will help administrators to perform these updates and reduce the number of weekends they need to spend on the job.

VMSafe

VMSafe is a method of providing increased security for virtual machines by allowing third-party security products to operate at the virtualization layer on ESX Servers.

High Availability (HA)

High Availability, or HA, as it is generally called, is the ability of vSphere to restart virtual machines on a new physical server if the physical server they were on experiences a failure.

Data Recovery

Data Recovery is a method of backing up and restoring virtual machines.

Hot Add

Hot Add is a vSphere feature that allows additional CPU or memory resources to be added to a running virtual machine without any disruption to the virtual machine.

Fault Tolerance

Fault Tolerance is the ability of vSphere to eliminate virtual server downtime by maintaining a shadow copy of a virtual machine that is activated when the original virtual machine experiences a failure.

on the
Job

Fault Tolerance can be a very good selling point to management for deploying vSphere. It can easily give a virtual machine that requires extremely high availability all of the benefits of server clustering without any of the expense.

vShield Zones

vShield Zones is the ability of vSphere to help enforce corporate security policies at the application level.

VMotion

VMotion is the ability of vSphere to move a running virtual machine from one physical server to another without any interruption to the virtual machine.

Storage VMotion

Storage VMotion is the ability of vSphere to move the files that comprise a running virtual machine from one SAN location to another without any interruption to the virtual machine.

Distributed Resource Scheduling (DRS)

Distributed Resource Scheduling (DRS) is the ability of vSphere to move running virtual machines from one physical server to another without any interruption to the virtual machine to balance the utilization across multiple physical servers.

Distributed Power Management (DPM)

Distributed Power Management (DPM) is the ability of vSphere to conserve energy by selectively turning off Hosts when they are not needed and turning them back on when they are needed.

vNetwork Distributed Switch

A vNetwork Distributed Switch allows the administrator to define virtual networking at the vCenter Datacenter level instead of at the ESX Server level.

Host Profiles

Host Profiles are a method for capturing the configuration of an existing ESX Server and using that information to quickly deploy additional ESX Servers.

vSphere Editions

vSphere is available in a number of different editions. Each edition has the ability to run a subset of the available vSphere features.

vSphere Essentials

vSphere Essentials is the most basic vSphere package available. It is designed for smaller companies that do not require the more extensive functionality of other editions. It supports the following functionality:

- Six cores per processor
- Four-way vSMP support
- 256GB of memory per physical server
- Thin provisioning
- Update Manager
- VMSafe

vSphere Essentials Plus

vSphere Essentials Plus is the next higher edition of vSphere. It is designed for companies that require slightly more functionality than is available in vSphere Essentials. It has all of the functionality of vSphere Essentials with the addition of

- High Availability
- Data Recovery

vSphere Standard

vSphere Standard is an entry-level edition of vSphere. It supports the following functionality:

- Six cores per processor
- Four-way vSMP support
- 256GB of memory per physical server
- Thin provisioning
- Update Manager
- VMSafe
- High Availability

vSphere Advanced

vSphere Advanced is a mid-level edition of vSphere. It has all of the functionality of vSphere Standard with the addition of

- Twelve cores per processor
- Data Recovery
- Hot Add
- Fault Tolerance
- vShield Zones
- VMotion

vSphere Enterprise

vSphere Enterprise is a more fully functional edition of vSphere. It has all of the functionality of vSphere Advanced with the addition of

- Storage VMotion
- Distributed Resource Services
- Distributed Power Management

vSphere Enterprise Plus

vSphere Enterprise Plus is the most fully functional version of vSphere. It supports all of the functionality available in vSphere. This includes all of the functionality of vSphere Enterprise with the addition of

- vNetwork distributed switches
- Host profiles

TABLE 1-1   Comparison of vSphere Editions

Edition	High Availability	Data Recovery	Hot Add	Fault Tolerance	vShield Zones	VMotion	Storage VMotion	DRS	dvSwitches	Host Profiles
Essentials										
Essentials Plus	✓	✓								
Standard	✓									
Advanced	✓	✓	✓	✓	✓	✓				
Enterprise	✓	✓	✓	✓	✓	✓	✓	✓		
Enterprise Plus	✓	✓	✓	✓	✓	✓	✓	✓	✓	✓

Note: The following features are available in all versions of vSphere: Thin provisioning, Update Manager, VMSafe, and Storage APIs. Every version of vSphere supports a maximum of 4-way vSMP and 256GB of memory for ESX/ESXi Servers, except for Enterprise Plus which supports 8-way vSMP and has no limit on ESX/ESXi memory.

INSIDE THE EXAM

Choosing the Right Edition of vSphere

It is important to be able to determine the correct edition of vSphere to use for a given situation both for the exam and in real life. At first glance it looks as if it would be easiest to recommend that your clients just use Enterprise Plus to get all of the functionality of vSphere. Unfortunately, most companies

need to consider costs and will want to use the least expensive edition that meets their functionality requirements. You should expect to see questions on the exam that will test your knowledge of which features are available in which editions. You may see a scenario-based question that describes a company and asks which edition would be the best fit for them.

Now that you have a basic understanding of vSphere and its different editions, let's take a look at how the rest of the book is structured.

CERTIFICATION OBJECTIVE 1.02

What Is Covered in This Book

This book is designed to follow the "VMware Certified Professional on vSphere 4 Blueprint" document and cover each of the listed objectives for passing the VCP exam. The Blueprint is a list of objects from VMware that will be tested on the VCP exam. My guide will give you the technical knowledge to thoroughly understand the objectives and to successfully answer the exam questions relating to each objective. This section will give you a brief overview of what each chapter will cover so that you will know what to expect.

Chapter 2: Introduction to Server Virtualization and the VMware Product Line

In this chapter I introduce you to the concept of server virtualization and discuss the advantages and disadvantages of using it. Once you know what server virtualization is, I talk about the different types of virtualization solutions and when to use each type. The chapter ends by briefly introducing VMware's virtualization products and discussing usage cases for each of them.

Chapter 3: Install, Upgrade, and Configure ESX Server

Now that you have a basic understanding of virtualization, we can move into actually installing ESX Server. VMware's ESX Server is the company's premier datacenter virtualization product and is an integral part of vSphere. Before you can perform an install, we need to discuss the minimum hardware requirements and confirm that your environment will be supported. We will then perform a number of different ESX Server installs on both local and SAN storage. Once you have ESX Server installed, we will end the chapter by implementing some basic security configurations.

Chapter 4: Install and Configure vCenter Server

In this chapter we will install and configure vCenter Server. vCenter Server is the centralized management component of vSphere. Just as we couldn't install ESX Server before reviewing the minimum hardware requirements, we will need to do the same for vCenter Server. Once you understand the minimum requirements, we will perform a step-by-step installation of vCenter Server. We will then discuss the various plug-ins that are available for vCenter Server and finally configure vCenter Server to support our vSphere environment.

Chapter 5: Understanding Networking and Virtual Switches on ESX Server

In Chapter 5 you will learn about the different networking features of ESX Server. We will start with the concept of virtual switches. Virtual switches are a critical part of ESX Server, since they allow virtual machines to connect to the company LAN. Once you understand virtual switches, we will discuss Distributed Virtual Switches, which is a new feature of vSphere that allows virtual switches to be shared across multiple ESX Servers. We will end the chapter by configuring a management network to allow you to reliably administer your ESX Server farms.

Chapter 6: Understanding and Configuring Storage on ESX Server

This chapter revolves around ESX Server Storage technologies. We will discuss and configure the various types of storage that ESX Server supports. We will discuss the advantages and disadvantages of using Fibre Channel SANs, iSCSI SANs, and NFS storage to store virtual machines. We will also discuss the VMFS file system and show how to create VMFS datastores.

Chapter 7: Create, Deploy, and Manage Virtual Machines and vApps

I'll spend this chapter discussing virtual machines. We'll have an overview of virtual machines, discuss which operating systems are supported as virtual machines, and then change the setting of an existing virtual machine. Once you understand virtual machines, we will go ahead and perform a step-by-step creation of a virtual machine. We will also discuss using a tool called VMware Converter to create virtual machines from existing physical servers. We'll finish the chapter by introducing vApps, describing virtual appliances, and discussing the Open Virtual Machine Format (OVF), a new standard for creating virtual machines.

Chapter 8: Managing vSphere Compliance

This chapter deals with meeting compliance requirements using vSphere. I'll introduce VMware vCenter Update Manager, discuss its requirements and capabilities, and perform a full step-by-step installation. Once you have Update Manager installed, we will use it to perform scans of ESX Hosts and virtual machines and to deploy updates to them. I will then introduce ESX Host Profiles and discuss how to create and use them to ensure compliance.

Chapter 9: Establishing Service Levels

VMware has taken great steps toward increasing the reliability of virtual environments. In this chapter we will discuss VMware technologies that are designed to help us maintain acceptable service levels in our virtualized datacenters. We will start with the idea of VMware Clusters and their related abilities, then move into resource pools, and finish with a discussion of different backup and restore strategies for virtual machines.

Chapter 10: Basic Troubleshooting and Alarm Management

This final chapter introduces you to basic troubleshooting and alarm management for vSphere environments. We will discuss the different types of issues you may encounter while installing and managing a virtualized datacenter and how to troubleshoot each of these issues. We will also discuss how to set up and manage the different types of alarms that are available in vSphere to keep minor issues from becoming major problems.

CERTIFICATION OBJECTIVE 1.03

What You Should Already Know

The VMware VCP exam is a demanding exam that assumes you have some understanding of servers and server technologies outside of the VMware realm. You do not need to be an expert on these technologies, but a basic understanding of computer technology will make the exam far easier to understand. You do not need to be familiar with VMware technologies, as they will be explained in this book.

Servers

You will need to have a basic understanding of computer servers and their components, such as processors, hard drives, and RAM.

Storage

You should have a basic understanding of local storage and SANs (storage area networks). We will discuss technologies like Fibre Channel and iSCSI in detail, and no prior knowledge of them is necessary.

Networking

You should have a general understanding of computer network connectivity. You should understand switches and NIC cards and the basics of how computers connect to them using TCP/IP.

CERTIFICATION SUMMARY

We started this chapter with an introduction to vSphere. We talked about what vSphere actually is and discussed many of its features. We then reviewed the different editions of vSphere that are available and the features that are included with each edition.

The next section of this chapter talked about the rest of the book. We looked at what will be covered in the remaining chapters to get a feel for how things will progress. The chapter ended with a brief description of the types of skills you should already have to be able to get the most out of the remaining chapters.

TWO-MINUTE DRILL

Introduction to vSphere

- ❏ vSMP allows a virtual machine to have more than one virtual CPU.
- ❏ Thin provisioning is used to reduce virtual machine storage requirements.
- ❏ Update Manager is a patch and update management utility.
- ❏ VMSafe provides increased security for virtual machines.
- ❏ High Availability is the ability of vSphere to restart a failed virtual machine on a different physical server.
- ❏ Data Recovery is a method of backing up and restoring virtual machines.
- ❏ Hot Add is the ability to add CPU and memory resources to a running virtual machine.
- ❏ Fault Tolerance is the ability of vSphere to eliminate virtual machine downtime by keeping a separate shadow copy of a virtual machine and activating it when the original virtual machine experiences a failure.
- ❏ vShield Zones is the ability of vSphere to enforce corporate security policies at the application level.
- ❏ VMotion is the ability of vSphere to move a running virtual machine from one physical server to another without interruption.
- ❏ Storage VMotion is the ability of vSphere to move the files that make up a running virtual machine from one SAN location to another without interruption.
- ❏ Distributed Resource Scheduling is the ability of vSphere to load-balance virtual machines across multiple physical machines.
- ❏ Distributed Power Management is the ability of vSphere to conserve energy by selectively turning off Hosts when they are not needed and turning them back on when they are needed.
- ❏ vNetwork Distributed Switch is the ability to define vSwitches at the Datacenter level instead of on each individual ESX Server.
- ❏ Host Profiles are a method for backing up the configuration information of an ESX Server and using them to quickly deploy additional ESX Servers.

What Is Covered in This Book

❑ In Chapter 2, you will learn about Server Virtualization and the VMware product line.

❑ In Chapter 3, you will learn the requirements of ESX Server and perform a number of ESX installs.

❑ In Chapter 4, you will learn to install and configure vCenter Server.

❑ In Chapter 5, you will learn about ESX Server networking and virtual switches.

❑ In Chapter 6, you will learn the types of storage that are supported under ESX Server.

❑ In Chapter 7, you will learn to create, deploy, and manage virtual machines and vApps.

❑ In Chapter 8, you will learn about vSphere's technologies for managing compliance issues.

❑ In Chapter 9, you will learn about vSphere's technologies for establishing service levels.

❑ In Chapter 10, you will learn about basic troubleshooting and alarm management in vSphere.

What You Should Already Know

❑ You will need a very basic understanding of computer technologies such as servers, storage, and networking.

SELF TEST

The following questions will help you measure your understanding of the material presented in this chapter. Read all the choices carefully and remember that there is only one best answer for each question.

Introduction to vSphere

1. Which of the following vSphere features allows a running virtual machine to be moved from one physical server to another without interruption?
   A. VMSafe
   B. Fault Tolerance
   C. VMotion
   D. Storage VMotion

2. Which of the following vSphere features provides increased security for virtual machines by allowing third-party security products to operate at the virtualization layer?
   A. VMSafe
   B. Fault Tolerance
   C. VMotion
   D. Storage VMotion

3. Which of the following vSphere features can virtually eliminate virtual machine downtime?
   A. VMSafe
   B. Fault Tolerance
   C. VMotion
   D. Storage VMotion

4. Which of the following vSphere features allow the files that make up a running virtual machine to be moved from one SAN location to another without interruption?
   A. VMSafe
   B. Fault Tolerance
   C. VMotion
   D. Storage VMotion

5. Which of the following vSphere features enable a reduction in the storage requirements for virtual machines?

   A. Hot Add

   B. Host Profiles

   C. Thin provisioning

   D. Update Manager

6. Which of the following vSphere features allow the rapid deployment of ESX Servers by using the configuration files of existing ESX Servers?

   A. Hot Add

   B. Host Profiles

   C. Thin provisioning

   D. Update Manager

7. Which of the following vSphere features allow the addition of CPU and RAM resources to running virtual machines?

   A. Hot Add

   B. Host Profiles

   C. Thin provisioning

   D. Update Manager

8. Which of the following vSphere features can be used to apply patches to virtual machines?

   A. Hot Add

   B. Host Profiles

   C. Thin provisioning

   D. Update Manager

9. What is the maximum number of cores per processor that is supported in the vSphere Essentials edition?

   A. Four

   B. Six

   C. Eight

   D. Twelve

10. What is the maximum number of cores per processor that is supported in the vSphere Advanced edition?

A. Four

B. Six

C. Eight

D. Twelve

11. Which of the following vSphere editions support Data Recovery?

A. vSphere Essentials

B. vSphere Essentials Plus

C. vSphere Standard

D. None of the above

12. Which of the following vSphere editions support Storage VMotion?

A. vSphere Standard

B. vSphere Advanced

C. vSphere Enterprise

D. None of the above

13. Which of the following vSphere editions support Host Profiles?

A. vSphere Advanced

B. vSphere Enterprise

C. vSphere Enterprise Plus

D. Both B and C

14. Which of the following vSphere editions support 256GB of memory per physical server?

A. vSphere Essentials

B. vSphere Standard

C. vSphere Advanced

D. All of the above

15. Which of the following vSphere editions support eight-way vSMP?

A. vSphere Advanced

B. vSphere Enterprise

C. vSphere Enterprise Plus

D. Both B and C

SELF TEST ANSWERS

Introduction to vSphere

1. ☑ **C.** VMotion allows a running virtual machine to be moved from one physical server to another without interruption.

   ☒ **A, B,** and **D** are incorrect. VMSafe allows third-party security vendors to operate at the virtualization layer. Fault Tolerance virtually eliminates virtual machine downtime by using a shadow virtual machine running on another physical server as a mirror. Storage VMotion allows the files that make up a running virtual machine to be moved from one SAN location to another without interruption.

2. ☑ **A.** VMSafe allows third-party security vendors to operate at the virtualization layer.

   ☒ **B, C,** and **D** are incorrect. Fault Tolerance virtually eliminates virtual machine downtime by using a shadow virtual machine running on another physical server as a mirror. VMotion allows a running virtual machine to be moved from one physical server to another without interruption. Storage VMotion allows the files that make up a running virtual machine to be moved from one SAN location to another without interruption.

3. ☑ **B.** Fault Tolerance virtually eliminates virtual machine downtime by using a shadow virtual machine running on another physical server as a mirror.

   ☒ **A, C,** and **D** are incorrect. VMSafe allows third-party security vendors to operate at the virtualization layer. VMotion allows a running virtual machine to be moved from one physical server to another without interruption. Storage VMotion allows the files that make up a running virtual machine to be moved from one SAN location to another without interruption.

4. ☑ **D.** Storage VMotion allows the files that make up a running virtual machine to be moved from one SAN location to another without interruption.

   ☒ **A, B,** and **D** are incorrect. VMSafe allows third-party security vendors to operate at the virtualization layer. Fault Tolerance virtually eliminates virtual machine downtime by using a shadow virtual machine running on another physical server as a mirror. Storage VMotion allows the files that make up a running virtual machine to be moved from one SAN location to another without interruption.

5. ☑ **C.** Thin provisioning enables a reduction in the storage requirements for virtual machines.

   ☒ **A, B,** and **D** are incorrect. Hot Add allows the addition of CPU and memory resources to a running virtual machine. Host Profiles allow configuration data to be copied from an existing ESX Server and used to rapidly deploy additional ESX Servers. Update Manager is used to deploy patches and updates to virtual machines and ESX Servers.

6. ☑ **B.** Host Profiles allow configuration data to be copied from an existing ESX Server and used to rapidly deploy additional ESX Servers.

☒ **A, C,** and **D** are incorrect. Hot Add allows the addition of CPU and memory resources to a running virtual machine. Thin provisioning enables a reduction in the storage requirements for virtual machines. Update Manager is used to deploy patches and updates to virtual machines and ESX Servers.

7. ☑ **A.** Hot Add allows the addition of CPU and memory resources to a running virtual machine.

☒ **B, C,** and **D** are incorrect. Host Profiles allow configuration data to be copied from an existing ESX Server and used to rapidly deploy additional ESX Servers. Thin provisioning enables a reduction in the storage requirements for virtual machines. Update Manager is used to deploy patches and updates to virtual machines and ESX Servers.

8. ☑ **D.** Update Manager is used to deploy patches and updates to virtual machines and ESX Servers.

☒ **A, B,** and **C** are incorrect. Hot Add allows the addition of CPU and memory resources to a running virtual machine. Host Profiles allow configuration data to be copied from an existing ESX Server and used to rapidly deploy additional ESX Servers. Thin provisioning enables a reduction in the storage requirements for virtual machines.

9. ☑ **B.** vSphere Essentials supports six cores per processor.

☒ **A, C,** and **D** are incorrect. vSphere Essentials supports as many as six cores per processor, but no more.

10. ☑ **D.** vSphere Advanced supports twelve cores per processor.

☒ **A, B,** and **C** are incorrect. vSphere Advanced does support up to twelve cores per processor.

11. ☑ **B.** vSphere Essentials Plus supports Data Recovery.

☒ **A, C,** and **D** are incorrect. vSphere Essentials does not support Data Recovery, nor does vSphere Standard.

12. ☑ **C.** vSphere Enterprise supports Storage VMotion.

☒ **A, B,** and **D** are incorrect. vSphere Standard does not support Storage VMotion, nor does vSphere Advanced.

13. ☑ **C.** vSphere Enterprise Plus supports Host Profiles.

☒ **A, B,** and **D** are incorrect. vSphere Advanced does not support Host Profiles, nor does vSphere Enterprise.

14. ☑ **D.** Every edition of vSphere supports at least 256GB of memory per physical server.

☒ **A, B,** and **C** are incorrect because none of these choices is a complete answer.

15. ☑ **C.** vSphere Enterprise Plus supports eight-way vSMP.

☒ **A, B,** and **D** are incorrect. vSphere Advanced does not support eight-way vSMP, nor does vSphere Enterprise.

2

Introduction to Server Virtualization and the VMware Product Line

I n this chapter I introduce the concept of server virtualization and discuss its advantages and disadvantages. Once you understand why you may want to use virtualization, I'll describe the different types of solutions and list the advantages and disadvantages of each. Then we'll take a look at the different product offerings from VMware to perform server virtualization and give a brief overview of each product. When we're done with this chapter, you will have a good foundation in server virtualization and a basic understanding of VMware's various offerings. Once you have this basic understanding, you will be ready to begin learning to install and run VMware's vSphere Suite.

CERTIFICATION OBJECTIVE 2.01

Introduction to Server Virtualization

Server virtualization is the act of taking a single piece of server hardware and running multiple virtual machines on it. A *virtual machine* is essentially the same as a physical machine, just without the hardware. They have the same components (i.e., CPU, memory, and storage) as a physical server, but multiple virtual machines can coexist on a single physical server at the same time. Each of these virtual machines runs a separate, independent operating system and is limited to the computing resources that are assigned to it. This can be a difficult concept to understand, but as you go through this book, it will become clear. In VMware terms virtual machines are called guests, and the physical servers they run on are called hosts. VMware has developed a number of products to enable server virtualization, and I will introduce them later in this chapter.

Advantages of Server Virtualization

There are a number of advantages to using server virtualization, and you will need to understand them for the exam. The most obvious advantage is reduced hardware costs. Most servers in datacenters rarely run at more than 20 percent utilization, and some run at far less. By enabling multiple virtual machines to run on a single piece of hardware, server virtualization allows us to run these servers at a much higher utilization rate. Since we are getting more utilization from these servers, fewer physical servers are needed to do the same number of computing tasks. Along with reduced hardware costs, we also see a reduction in datacenter costs that are associated with a large number of servers. Since there are fewer physical servers, there will be a reduction in the electrical power needed to run them and the amount of air conditioning needed to keep them cool. You also require less datacenter space, since there are fewer physical servers. This can be a significant advantage to companies whose datacenters are running out of space due to server sprawl or to companies who rent space in a datacenter and pay by physical server.

Aside from the tangible, money saving advantages of server virtualization, there are also those that are less easy to quantify. Using server virtualization, new servers can be rolled out in a fraction of the time it takes to deploy a physical server. It can typically take several weeks or more to acquire new hardware and deploy a server operating system. Using server virtualization tools from VMware, a virtual server with the same capabilities can be deployed in a matter of minutes.

VMware also provides tools (Data Recovery) that can make virtual servers easier to back up and then recover in a disaster recovery scenario.

Disadvantages of Server Virtualization

There are some disadvantages to using server virtualization. The biggest of these is the "all of your eggs in one basket" concept. Since you have multiple virtual machines running on a single piece of hardware, a failure of that hardware would impact multiple systems instead of just one. This was a very significant problem with older server virtualization solutions. Thankfully, some advances in hardware high availability and new features that were developed by VMware have gone a long way toward remediating this issue. Modern server hardware can be purchased with high availability features like RAID drive arrays, redundant memory, redundant fans, and multiple power supplies to reduce the chance of a single hardware failure causing a server to completely fail. New features in the VMware ESX product line such as High Availability (HA) allow a virtual machine to be automatically restarted on a different host server if the host it resides on experiences a hardware failure. Another potential disadvantage to server virtualization is that when using cutting-edge technologies like VMware, there's a smaller pool of highly experienced administrators available to manage your environment.

CERTIFICATION OBJECTIVE 2.02

Hosted Versus Bare-Metal Virtualization Solutions

There are two types of server virtualization solutions: hosted and bare-metal. *Hosted* solutions run as applications on top of an existing operating system. VMware's VMware Server, VMware Player, and VMware Workstation are examples of hosted virtualization solutions, also sometimes referred to as Type 2 hypervisors. *Bare-metal* solutions run directly on the hardware and install more like an operating system than as an application. VMware's ESX Server, its ESXi Server, and Citrix XenServer are examples of bare-metal solutions, also sometimes referred to as Type 1 hypervisors. Each type of server virtualization solution has advantages and disadvantages. You will need to know these to determine which solution to use in a given scenario.

Advantages of Hosted Solutions

Hosted virtualization solutions install and run like an application on an existing operating system. This gives them a number of advantages. They tend to be easier to install, since most administrators are already familiar with installing applications under Windows or Linux. They also tend to run on a wider range of supported hardware than bare-metal solutions. Since they run on top of Windows or Linux, they can usually take advantage of any hardware that is supported by the host operating system.

Disadvantages of Hosted Solutions

Because they run on top of an existing operating system, hosted virtualization solutions suffer from a number of disadvantages. The biggest disadvantage for hosted virtualization solutions is poor performance. Since they run on top of an operating system that is not specifically designed for virtualization, they suffer poor performance when compared to a bare-metal solution running on the same hardware. Another disadvantage to running as an application on a general-purpose operating system like Windows or Linux is poor reliability. Any failure of the operating system can cause the entire virtual infrastructure to fail. Bare-metal solutions have a smaller core operating system, so they are less likely to experience failures.

Usage Cases for Hosted Virtualization Solutions

There are a number of scenarios where using a hosted virtualization solution may be a good decision. A developer who needs access to a number of different operating systems for testing can use a single workstation running VMware Workstation to set up different versions of Windows or other OSs without needing additional hardware. A server administrator who wants to test a new application can run it on a virtual machine at his desk before introducing it into the production environment. A good usage case for a hosted virtualization solution applies to future VCP exam test takers who would like to practice with the components of vSphere but don't have access to a large amount of hardware. In Appendix A I will show you how to use VMware Workstation to set up a complete vSphere test lab running on a single workstation to use to study for the exam. Hosted virtualization solutions tend to work best when their guests are needed for short durations and when uptime is not critical.

Advantages of Bare-Metal Solutions

Since they install directly onto the hardware, bare-metal virtualization solutions have a number of advantages over hosted solutions. The biggest advantage is performance. Since they are written specifically to support virtualization, bare-metal solutions offer better performance than hosted solutions. Another advantage to bare-metal solutions is reliability. Since the core operating system of a bare-metal solution like VMware's ESX is only written to support virtualization, it has a much smaller core OS than other server operating systems. Because it is smaller and less general purpose, it has less of a chance of experiencing a failure that would cause the virtual environment to fail.

Disadvantages of Bare-Metal Solutions

The major disadvantage of bare-metal virtualization solutions is limited hardware compatibility. Since the core operating system is designed to be small and efficient, it has limited compatibility with hardware that would be considered out of the mainstream. VMware has made large strides with improving hardware compatibility in vSphere when compared with earlier versions of ESX. Another disadvantage of bare-metal virtualization solutions is that they tend to be more difficult to install than hosted virtualization solutions. Installing a bare-metal virtualization solution is more like installing a new operating system, while installing a hosted solution is more like installing a standard application.

Usage Cases for Bare-Metal Virtualization Solutions

Bare-metal virtualization solutions are generally found in datacenters. They are designed to support guests that are more long term and need high availability and extended uptime. A good usage case for a bare-metal virtualization solution is a datacenter that is consolidating physical servers to virtual machines or one that plans to deploy virtual machines into production.

Now that you have a basic understanding of server virtualization, let's move on and take a look at the products that VMware has to offer.

CERTIFICATION OBJECTIVE 2.03

Introduction to the VMware Product Line

VMware has created a large number of products focused on virtualization. They range from lower-end desktop products that allow you to run temporary virtual machines on a desktop PC, all the way through products that can enable you to completely virtualize your company's datacenter and manage your virtual infrastructure. We discussed vSphere in the last chapter, and in this section I will introduce VMware's other major products and give you the information you will need to know about them to pass the VCP exam.

VMware's Hosted Virtualization Solutions

VMware offers a number of hosted virtualization solutions with different capabilities to meet a variety of virtualization needs. We will talk about each of them and go over their differences and discuss usage cases for each product. You will need to know the differences between the products and should expect to see questions on the VCP exam that ask which product has a certain capability or which would be best for a given usage case.

VMware Player

VMware Player is a free product from VMware that allows a user to run virtual machines on a Windows or Linux PC. The product is designed to allow users to run virtual machines and virtual appliances, virtual machines with applications installed and configured on them, which have been created using a different virtualization product. It is capable of running virtual machines that were created using VMware Server, VMware Workstation, VMware ESX, and the Microsoft products Virtual Server and Virtual PC. It supports both 32-bit and 64-bit virtual machines. VMware Player supports two-way virtual SMP and USB 2.0 pass-through from the host system to the running virtual machines. The main thing to remember about VMware Player is that it is not capable of creating virtual machines. It is only able to run virtual machines that are created by something else. A good usage case for VMware Player is a developer who would like to share a fully installed virtual appliance, which she created using a different product, with a quality control team for testing.

VMware Workstation

VMware Workstation is a product from VMware that allows the user to run multiple guest operating systems on a single workstation. It runs as an application on Windows and Linux and supports both 32-bit and 64-bit virtual machines. VMware Workstation supports two-way virtual SMP and USB 2.0 pass-through from the host system to the running virtual machines. A major feature of VMware Workstation is the ability to use snapshots of a virtual machine. (A *snapshot* is basically a point-in-time copy of a virtual machine.) Using VMware Workstation, you can take a snapshot of a virtual machine now and easily revert to that snapshot at a later time. When you revert to a snapshot, the virtual machine will be exactly as it was when the snapshot was taken. You can have multiple snapshots of a virtual machine and revert to any of them. A good usage case for VMware Workstation is a developer who wants to test multiple changes to a virtual machine and still have the ability to revert to the original virtual machine state.

Many administrators hear that they can create virtual machines using two-way SMP and just assume that this will make their virtual machines run faster. The reality is that most applications are not written to take advantage of multiple processors and will not see any significant performance increase by using them. In some rare instances the overhead that is added by running virtual SMP can actually cause a virtual machine to suffer a performance decrease.

VMware Server

VMware Server is another free product from VMware. It allows a user to both create new virtual machines and run existing virtual machines created by others. Like Player and Workstation, it supports both 32-bit and 64-bit virtual machines as well as two-way virtual SMP and USB 2.0 pass-through from the host system to the running virtual machines. VMware Server has a number of features that make it a better choice for virtualizing production servers than VMware Workstation. It runs as a service, so it starts as soon as the host server completes booting, and it is able to auto-start guest virtual machines on host bootup. The capability to auto-start virtual guests can be very important when attempting to reduce server downtime. Another important feature of VMware Server is that it allows multiple users to access virtual guests running on the same host. A good usage case for VMware Server is a datacenter that is starting to look toward server consolidation and wants to ease into server virtualization. Virtual machines that are running on VMware Server are very easy to move to ESX or ESXi in the future.

An interesting use for VMware Server is to allow legacy applications that will not run directly on newer hardware to benefit from hardware upgrades. I was at a client that required an older DOS-based application at each of their branch offices. Due to driver issues, it would not run on their newer server standard, but it would run under VMware Server. By using VMware Server as their host, they were able to use faster and more reliable hardware without having to redesign their older applications.

INSIDE THE EXAM

Selecting an Appropriate Hosted Solution

Knowing when to use a given hosted virtualization solution is not only important in the real world but also for the VCP exam. In a production environment an administrator might use all three of VMware's hosted solutions. She may use VMware Workstation to create and run virtual machines at her desk,

VMware Server for semipermanent virtual machines in the test lab, and VMware Player to share virtual machines with end users. On the exam you should expect to be given a scenario and asked which hosted virtualization solution would be the best fit. Always remember that the test designers are not just looking for a solution that will work but for the best solution.

VMware's Datacenter Solutions

VMware offers a number of products that leverage their virtualization infrastructure to perform specific enterprise-level datacenter tasks. We will discuss the basics of each of these products next and talk about the situations where they could be used. You will not need to know these products in great detail for the exam, but you will need a basic understanding of how they are used and the types of issues they are used to address.

VMware View

VMware View is a product from VMware that allows administrators to run virtualized desktops on servers in the datacenter and present them to users on the corporate network. Running desktops in a virtualized environment provides a number of advantages. Since desktops are now centralized in the datacenter, they are easier to back up and secure. It is also easier to manage desktop images, since they will run in a standard environment instead of on disparate desktop hardware. View also allows users to access their desktop from any device on the network or even from remote devices. The main thing to remember about VMware View is that it allows desktops to be run on servers in the datacenter and gives users access to their own specific desktop. A good usage case for VMware View is an organization that wanted greater control and centralized management of their desktop environment.

vCenter Site Recovery Manager (SRM)

vCenter SRM is a disaster recovery product from VMware. vCenter SRM is designed to simplify disaster recovery by removing many of the manual steps that are required in a DR plan. It walks users through the development of their disaster recovery plans, and by leveraging an isolated virtual environment, it allows them to test these plans without disrupting the production server environment. The main thing to remember about SRM is that it uses a virtual environment to improve disaster recovery planning and testing. A good usage case for vCenter SRM is any datacenter that is concerned about reducing server downtime and ensuring successful disaster recovery operations.

vCenter Lab Manager

vCenter Lab Manager is a product from VMware which allows server administrators to create complex libraries of virtual machines that can be deployed as needed easily and quickly. Lab Manager allows you to set up complete test environments that can be easily provisioned when needed and do not use valuable storage space and server resources when they are not. It includes a web-based interface that allows users to deploy these environments without the need for administrator intervention. The main thing to remember for vCenter Lab Manager is that it can be used to easily and quickly deploy entire test lab environments. A good usage case for vCenter Lab Manager is an environment where multiple test lab configurations are required but each is required for only a limited time.

CERTIFICATION SUMMARY

In this chapter we started by discussing the concept of server virtualization. We talked about the advantages, like improved hardware utilization. We then discussed some of the disadvantages of server virtualization, like the concern of putting all of your eggs in one basket.

Next we reviewed the two types of server virtualization: hosted and bare-metal. We talked about the advantages and disadvantages of each solution and gave usage cases where each solution would be a good choice.

Finally, we looked at some of the packages in the VMware virtualization product line. We discussed both desktop and datacenter products and gave good usage cases for each of them.

✓ TWO-MINUTE DRILL

Introduction to Server Virtualization

❑ Server virtualization is the act of running multiple virtual servers on a single piece of hardware.

❑ The tangible advantages of server virtualization include reduced hardware costs, reduced datacenter costs, and reduced space requirements.

❑ The intangible benefits of server virtualization include faster server deployments and simplified disaster recovery requirements.

❑ The main disadvantage of server virtualization is that with multiple virtual servers running on a single piece of hardware, a failure of that hardware will be more significant.

Hosted Versus Bare-Metal Virtualization Solutions

❑ Hosted virtualization solutions run as an application on top of an existing operating system.

❑ Bare-metal virtualization solutions run as their own separate operating system.

❑ The advantage of hosted virtualization solutions is that they tend to be easier to install than bare-metal solutions. Their main disadvantages are reduced performance and reliability when compared to bare-metal virtualization solutions.

❑ The advantages of bare-metal virtualization solutions are increased performance and reliability when compared to hosted solutions. Their main disadvantage is reduced hardware compatibility and being relatively difficult to install.

Introduction to the VMware Product Line

❑ VMware Player is a hosted virtualization solution that allows users to run virtual machines that were created with another virtualization solution.

❑ VMware Server is a hosted virtualization solution that supports the creation of virtual machines and has the ability to auto-start virtual guests at system boot.

❑ VMware Workstation is a hosted virtualization solution that supports the creation of virtual machines and supports multiple virtual machine snapshots.

❑ VMware Player, Server, and Workstation all support both 32-bit and 64-bit virtual machines as well as two-way virtual SMP and USB 2.0 pass-through.

❑ VMware View is designed to allow user desktops to be virtualized, stored on ESX servers in the datacenter, and presented to users when needed.

❑ vCenter Site Recovery Manager is a VMware product designed to ease disaster recovery planning and execution.

❑ vCenter Lab Manager is a VMware product designed to allow administrators to quickly provision virtual testing environments.

SELF TEST

The following questions will help you measure your understanding of the material presented in this chapter. Read all the choices carefully because there might be more than one correct answer. Choose all correct answers for each question.

Introduction to Server Virtualization

1. How does VMware refer to virtual machines?
    A. Hosts
    B. Partitions
    C. Guests
    D. Frames

2. How does VMware refer to the physical server that virtual machines run on?
    A. Hosts
    B. Partitions
    C. Guests
    D. Frames

3. Which of the following is an advantage of server virtualization?
    A. Reduced hardware costs
    B. Reduced datacenter costs
    C. Reduced server deployment times
    D. All of the above

Hosted Versus Bare-Metal Virtualization Solutions

4. Which of the following is an example of a hosted virtualization solution?
    A. VMware ESX
    B. VMware Workstation
    C. VMware ESXi
    D. All of the above

5. Which of the following is an example of a bare-metal virtualization solution?
   A. VMware ESX
   B. VMware Workstation
   C. VMware Player

6. Which of the following is an advantage of using a bare-metal virtualization solution?
   A. Ease of installation
   B. Extensive hardware compatibility
   C. Improved performance
   D. None of the above

7. Which of the following would be a good usage case for a hosted virtualization solution?
   A. A production datacenter
   B. A developer's test lab
   C. A critical server that requires 100 percent uptime
   D. None of the above

Introduction to the VMware Product Line

8. Which of the following VMware products allows the use of multiple snapshots for a virtual guest?
   A. VMware Player
   B. VMware Server
   C. VMware Workstation
   D. None of the above

9. Which of the following VMware products is able to auto-start guest virtual machines on host bootup?
   A. VMware Player
   B. VMware Server
   C. VMware Workstation
   D. None of the above

10. Which of the following VMware products supports both 32-bit and 64-bit guest operating systems?
   A. VMware Player
   B. VMware Server
   C. VMware Workstation
   D. All of the above

11. Which of the following VMware products would be a best choice for a user who only wants to be able to run virtual appliances that were created by someone else?
   A. VMware Player
   B. VMware Server
   C. VMware Workstation
   D. All of the above

12. Which of the following VMware products is designed to simplify disaster recovery planning and testing?
   A. vCenter Site Recovery Manager
   B. VMware View
   C. vCenter Lab Manager
   D. None of the above

13. Which of the following VMware products is designed to allow administrators to quickly provision virtual testing environments?
   A. vCenter Site Recovery Manager
   B. VMware View
   C. vCenter Lab Manager
   D. VMotion

SELF TEST ANSWERS

Introduction to Server Virtualization

1. ☑ **C.** VMware refers to virtual machines as guests.
☒ **A, B,** and **C** are incorrect. Hosts are the physical servers that contain virtual machines. Partitions is a mainframe virtualization term. Frames is a mainframe virtualization term.

2. ☑ **A.** VMware refers to physical servers that host guest virtual machines as hosts.
☒ **B, C,** and **D** are incorrect. Partitions is a mainframe virtualization term. VMware refers to virtual machines as guests. Frames is a mainframe virtualization term.

3. ☑ **D.** All of the above.
☒ **A, B,** and **C** are incorrect. Reduced hardware costs, reduced datacenter costs, and reduced server deployment times are all advantages of server virtualization, so no one of these is the correct answer.

Hosted Versus Bare-Metal Virtualization Solutions

4. ☑ **B.** VMware Workstation is a hosted virtualization solution.
☒ **A, C,** and **D** are incorrect. VMware ESX is a bare-metal solution, as is VMware ESXi.

5. ☑ **A.** VMware ESX is a bare-metal virtualization solution.
☒ **B, C,** and **D** are incorrect. VMware Workstation is a hosted solution, as is VMware Player.

6. ☑ **C.** Bare-metal virtualization solutions have better performance than hosted.
☒ **A, B,** and **D** are incorrect. Ease of installation is an advantage of hosted virtualization solutions, as is extensive hardware compatibility.

7. ☑ **B.** A test lab is a good usage case for a hosted virtualization solution.
☒ **A, C,** and **D** are incorrect. A production datacenter would be a good usage case for a bare-metal solution. Reliability is an advantage of bare-metal solutions.

Introduction to the VMware Product Line

8. ☑ **C.** VMware Workstation allows the use of multiple snapshots.
☒ **A, B,** and **D** are incorrect. VMware Player does not allow the use of multiple snapshots, nor does VMware Server.

9. ☑ **B.** Since VMware Server starts as a service, it is able to auto-start guest virtual machines at host bootup.

   ☒ **A, C,** and **D** are incorrect. VMware Player is not able to auto-start guest virtual machines, nor is VMware Workstation.

10. ☑ **D.** All of the above.

   ☒ **A, B,** and **C** are incorrect. All of these products support 32-bit and 64-bit guest operating systems; therefore, no one of them is correct.

11. ☑ **A.** VMware Player is designed to run virtual machines and virtual appliances that were created by someone else.

   ☒ **B, C,** and **D** are incorrect. VMware Server and VMware Workstation will run virtual appliances that were created by someone else, but they also have additional features that are not desired by the user.

12. ☑ **A.** vCenter Site Recovery Manager is designed to simplify disaster recovery planning and testing.

   ☒ **B, C,** and **D** are incorrect. VMware View is designed to simplify centralized desktop management. vCenter Lab Manager is designed to allow users and administrators to quickly provision test lab environments.

13. ☑ **C.** vCenter Lab Manager is designed to allow administrators to quickly provision virtual testing environments.

   ☒ **A, B,** and **D** are incorrect. vCenter Site Recovery Manager is designed to simplify disaster recovery planning and testing. VMware View is designed to simplify centralized desktop management. VMotion is a feature of vSphere that allows a running virtual machine to be moved from one physical server to another without interruption.

3

Install, Upgrade, and Configure ESX Server

I n this chapter I will introduce VMware ESX Server 4.0 and ESXi Server 4.0. We'll talk about the installation requirements for running ESX Server and about its basic architecture. Once you understand the installation requirements, we will perform a number of step-by-step installations and then do a step-by-step upgrade of an existing ESX 3.5 Server. Once we have all of these ESX 4.0 Servers, we will set up some basic security for them.

CERTIFICATION OBJECTIVE 3.01

Introduction to ESX Server

ESX Server 4.0 and ESXi Server 4.0 are the latest versions of VMware's highly successful bare-metal enterprise-level virtualization platforms. They are the workhorse components in the vSphere Suite of products. They allow administrators to virtualize large numbers of servers in their datacenters in a secure and highly reliable architecture. You will come to understand ESX Server more as we discuss its architecture and then perform a number of installs and upgrades.

ESX and ESXi Server Architecture

VMware ESX Server and VMware ESXi Server have very similar architectures. They are both hypervisors that create a virtualization layer between the existing physical hardware and some number of virtual machines that run on top of the virtualization layer. This virtualization layer, known as the vmkernel, allows the virtual machines to run on the same hardware at the same time but appear to be completely separate, self-contained servers. The primary difference between ESX Server and ESXi Server is the addition of the Service Console as shown in Figures 3-1 and 3-2. This Service Console runs as a separate virtual machine and is the first virtual machine to be brought online during the ESX Server boot process. It

For the exam remember that the primary difference between ESX Server and ESXi Server is the lack of a Service Console on ESXi. You may be asked questions to determine if you understand this fundamental difference.

is used to help manage the ESX Host boot process and as a management interface to the vmkernel virtualization layer. VMware has said that their stated direction is to move forward with the ESXi platform and do away with the inclusion of the Service Console. Figures 3-1 and 3-2 show the ESX and ESXi architectures. Notice the lack of a Service Console in the ESXi Architecture.

FIGURE 3-1

The ESX architecture. Notice the Service Console.

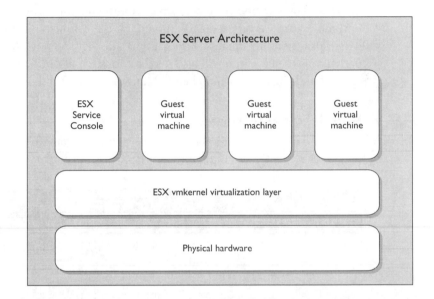

FIGURE 3-2

The ESXi architecture. Notice the absence of a Service Console.

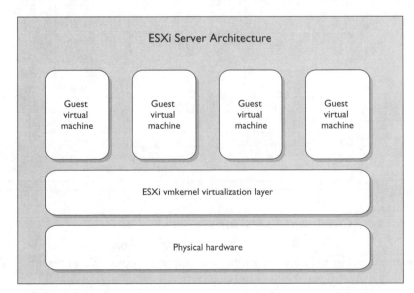

ESX Server 4.0 Disk Partitions

Disk partitioning is a method of breaking up a server's storage into several different areas called partitions. Each of these partitions contains different types of files that have different uses to the operating system. An example would be the boot partition. The *boot* partition holds files that are used during the boot process. VMware ESX Server 4.0 uses a very specific disk partitioning scheme. There are both required and optional partitions on each ESX Server. For the exam you will need to understand which partitions are created during an install, their default sizes, and what each partition is used for. You will also need to know what optional partitions can be created and what they would be used for.

Required Partitions

The following table shows the partitions that are created by default during an install of ESX Server 4.0 and are required for ESX Server to operate correctly.

Mount Point	Partition Type	Default Size	Description
/boot	ext3	1.25GB shared with the vmkcore partition	This default partition is used to store boot information for the ESX Host.
NA	swap	600MB minimum	This default partition is used to allow an ESX Host to swap memory to disk space when additional memory is needed.
/	ext3	5GB	This default partition is the root of the ESX operating system. It contains files needed to maintain the Service Console as well as third-party applications.
NA	VMFS3	1200MB	This default partition is used to store virtual machines.
NA	vmkcore	1.25GB shared with the /boot partition	This default partition is used to store core dumps and debugging information.

Optional Partitions

The following table shows the optional partitions that can be created on an ESX Host. These partitions are completely optional, and the ESX Host can run correctly without them.

Mount Point	Partition Type	Recommended Size	Description
/usr	ext3	NA	This optional partition is used to store user-specific data.
/var/log	ext3	2000MB	This optional partition is used to store system log files.
/tmp	ext3	1GB	This optional partition is used to story temporary files.
/home	ext3	512MB	This optional partition is used to store data for a single user.

INSIDE THE EXAM

Server Disk Partitioning

You will need to understand the default partitions for the exam. You should have a good understanding of which partitions are created by default and which are optional. You should also understand the default sizes for these partitions and how each partition is used. In previous versions of the exam drive partitioning was covered extensively. To prepare for the exam, you will need to memorize the information in the Required Partitions and Optional Partitions tables.

CERTIFICATION OBJECTIVE 3.02

ESX Server Installations

In this section we will discuss the hardware requirements for ESX Server and introduce the VMware Hardware Compatibility Guide. Once you are sure your hardware meets the minimum requirements, we will perform a step-by-step installation of ESX Server on local storage. We will finish up by installing the Network Time Protocol on our newly created ESX Server, since our virtual environment relies on keeping accurate time to perform many of its advanced functions.

ESX Server Minimum Requirements

There are a number of hardware requirements for installing and running ESX Server 4.0. If you are familiar with the 3.x versions of ESX Server you will notice that the hardware requirements for ESX 4.0 are significantly more demanding, requiring additional RAM and a 64-bit processor.

ESX Server 4.0 has the following hardware requirements:

- **CPU**   ESX Server 4.0 requires a 64-bit x86-based CPU to run.
- **RAM**   A minimum of 2GB of RAM is required.
- **Network Adapters**   One or more supported NICs are required.
- **Disk Storage**   ESX Server 4.0 supports the following forms of disk storage for the Host installation:
    - SCSI Disks
    - Fibre Channel LUN
    - RAID LUN
    - Hardware iSCSI
    - SATA Disks

on the
ⓘob
Remember that the hardware requirements listed in this section are minimum requirements for an ESX Server to install and run. In a production datacenter an ESX Server with only 2GB of RAM would have very limited uses, since the Host itself wants 2GB and each virtual machine requires some additional RAM.

e x a m
ⓦatch
For the exam you will need to remember the minimum hardware requirements to install an ESX Host. You should expect to see a question that details a system and asks which components do not meet the minimum hardware specification for ESX.

VMware Compatibility Guide

The VMware Compatibility Guide is a web site maintained by VMware that allows you to confirm that each component of your hardware solution has been tested and is certified to be compatible with the VMware product you are setting up. Before proceeding with any hardware purchases, you should check them against the VMware Compatibility Guide to make sure they will work properly. If a hardware component is not on the VMware Compatibility Guide, that does not mean that it will not work properly with VMware, just that it has not been tested and certified. The Guide can be found at www.vmware.com/go/hcl.

on the
Job

On a number of occasions, reviewing hardware orders against the VMware Compatibility Guide has kept me from ordering hardware that would not be guaranteed to work correctly with VMware products. Many clients will use a standard hardware platform for their servers and will want to use it for the VMware environment as well. Unfortunately, sometimes their standard is not compatible with VMware.

ESX Server Installation on Local Storage

Now that you understand the basics of ESX Server and you have confirmed that your hardware meets the minimal hardware requirements, let's go ahead and discuss the installation of ESX Server 4.0. To keep this first install simple, you will select the default values for most of the screens. When you set up your lab in Appendix A, you should perform a large number of ESX Server installs so that you can become familiar with the different installation options. I have performed a step-by-step installation of ESX Server and will show screenshots for the most interesting screens so that we can talk about them further. To get the most from this section, you should perform an actual installation of ESX Server, either on physical hardware if you have it available or on the virtual lab that is described in Appendix A.

During the install, you will need to enter the following information:

- The serial number you received from VMware (This will be blank if you are using an evaluation version of ESX Server.)
- Networking information like IP Address, Subnet Mask, and DNS Servers
- The time zone where the server is located
- The password you want to use for the root account

Once you have gathered the information, you need to perform the following steps to complete your first installation of ESX Server:

1. Ensure that your hardware meets the minimum requirements for ESX Server.

2. Insert the ESX Server DVD into your server and power it on.

3. The Virtual Infrastructure For The Enterprise window will pop up. Highlight Install ESX In Graphical Mode and press ENTER to begin the installation.

4. A Welcome screen will pop up. Click Next to continue the installation.

5. You will be prompted to read and agree to the license agreement. Check the radio box for "I agree to the terms of the license agreement" and click Next to continue the installation.

6. You will be prompted to select the type of keyboard you are using on your server. Select U.S. English and click Next to continue the installation.

7. The Custom Drivers window will pop up. Since you are using supported hardware, you should not need any custom drivers. Click Next to continue the installation.

8. You will be prompted to "Enter a serial number now" or "Enter a serial number later." Check the radio box for "Enter a serial number later" and click Next to continue the installation.

9. The Network Configuration window will pop up. Your network card should be discovered automatically. Click Next to continue the installation.

10. A second Network Configuration window will pop up. On this window you can select to manually enter IP information for the server or select DHCP if you have a DHCP server available. Make your selection and click Next to continue the installation.

11. You will be prompted to perform a Standard Setup or Advanced Setup. The Advanced Setup option will allow you to view the default disk partitions. Check the radio box for Advanced Setup and click Next to continue the installation.

12. The ESX Storage Device window will pop up. Select the drive where you want to install ESX Server and click Next to continue the installation.

13. You will be warned that the drive you selected will be erased. Click Next to continue the installation.

14. You will be prompted to either create a new datastore or select an existing datastore to store virtual machines. By default a new datastore will be created. Click Next to create a new datastore and continue the installation.

15. The Service Console Virtual Disk Image window will pop up. This window shows you the default partitions that are created for the Service Console and allows you to add additional partitions. The default partitions are sufficient, so click Next to continue the installation.

16. You will be prompted to enter the Time Zone where your server resides. Enter the time zone and click Next to continue the installation.

17. You will be prompted to enter the Date and Time for the server. You can enter a NTP server here, but since we will do that later, manually enter the date and time. Click Next to continue the installation.

18. You will be prompted to enter a password for the root user account. You should make this password sufficiently difficult that it can't be easily guessed. Click Next to continue the installation.

19. You will be presented with a summary screen of the installation settings. This screen shows things like your network settings and default disk partitions. This summary screen is shown in Figure 3-3. Click Next to continue the installation.

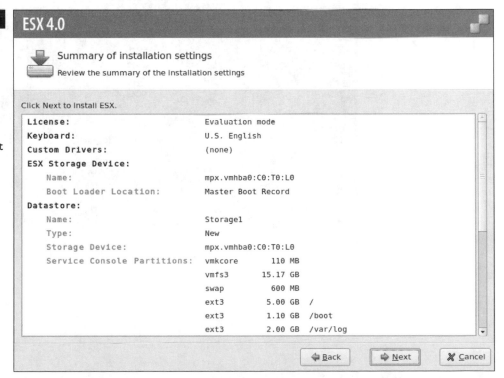

FIGURE 3-3

The ESX 4.0 Summary of Installation Settings screen. Review this screen and notice the default partitions that are configured with an ESX 4.0 installation.

20. Now that you have entered all of the required installation information, the installation process will take over and install all of the required packages for ESX Server. This process can take some time, and you should expect to wait between 10 and 30 minutes, depending on your hardware.

21. Once the installation packages have been installed, you will be presented with an Installation Successful screen. Click Finish to reboot the server and complete the installation.

22. Once the server reboots, you will see the console screen of the newly installed ESX 4.0 Server as shown in Figure 3-4.

xYou have now gone through your first install of ESX Server 4.0. In the next section we will perform an install of ESXi Server 4.0.

The console screen of our newly installed ESX 4.0 Server

```
VMware ESX 4.0.0 build-171294

VMware, Inc. VMware Virtual Platform

AMD Phenom(tm) 9550 Quad-Core Processor
2 GB Memory

Download tools to manage this host from:

    http://192.168.1.40/

To open the ESX console, press Alt-F1.
To return to this screen, press Alt-F11.
```

ESXi Server Installation on Local Storage

Now that you have installed an ESX 4.0 Host, let's go ahead and install an ESXi 4.0 Host. One feature of ESXi that is different than ESX is that it can be purchased as an embedded OS on some newer hardware. Because of this feature, it may not be necessary for you to actually perform any installs of ESXi to have it running in your datacenter. To allow administrators to install ESXi on existing hardware, it is also available as an installable OS. We will perform our install using a DVD from VMware. The installation for ESXi is significantly less complicated than the installation for ESX and has fewer steps. There is very little configuration that can be done during the installation of ESXi, so for this installation, we will accept the default values for all of the installation screens.

Perform the following steps to complete your first installation of ESXi Server:

1. Ensure that your hardware meets the minimum requirements for ESXi Server.

2. Insert the ESXi Server DVD into your server and power it on.

3. You will be prompted to run the ESXi Installer or boot from a local disk. Click ESXi Installer to begin the installation.

4. You will be presented with a Welcome screen. Press ENTER to continue the install.

5. You will be presented with the End User License Agreement screen. Press F11 to accept the license agreement and continue the install.

6. The Select A Disk window will pop up. Select the drive where you want to install ESXi Server and press ENTER to continue the installation.

7. The Confirm Install window will pop up. Press ENTER to continue the installation.

8. Now that you have entered all of the required installation information, the installation process will take over and install all of the required packages for ESXi Server. This process can take some time but is generally faster than the install of ESX Server.

9. You will be presented with the Installation Complete window. Press ENTER to reboot the server and complete the installation.

10. Once the server has rebooted, you will be presented with the ESXi 4.0 console screen as shown in Figure 3-5.

The console screen of our newly installed ESXi 4.0 Server

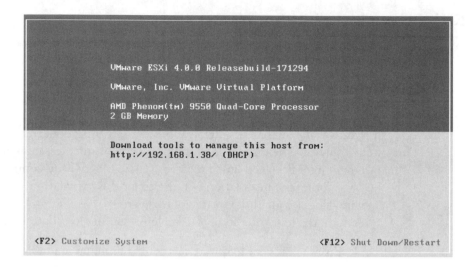

```
        VMware ESXi 4.0.0 Releasebuild-171294

        VMware, Inc. VMware Virtual Platform

        AMD Phenom(tm) 9550 Quad-Core Processor
        2 GB Memory


        Download tools to manage this host from:
        http://192.168.1.38/ (DHCP)




<F2> Customize System                        <F12> Shut Down/Restart
```

You have now gone through your first install of ESXi Server 4.0. In the next section we will look at the first tool you will use to manage this new ESXi Host: the vSphere Client.

CERTIFICATION OBJECTIVE 3.03

The vSphere Client

The vSphere Client is a utility provided by VMware that allows you to manage your ESX and ESXi Host servers. It is included with the installs of both ESX and ESXi. In the next section we will perform a complete install of the vSphere Client; in the remainder of the chapter and in Chapters 4 and 5 we will explore its ability to manage your vSphere environment.

exam
watch

For the exam you will need to be familiar with the vSphere Client. You will need to know which tab you need to go to in order to perform specific tasks. We will cover these tabs in this chapter and in Chapters 4 and 5.

Installing the vSphere Client and vSphere Host Update Utility

Now that you understand a little about the vSphere Client, I will demonstrate a step-by-step install. I will also install the vSphere Host Update Utility at the same time. We will talk about the vSphere Host Update Utility in the next section and use it to upgrade an ESX 3.5 Host to ESX 4.0.

Perform the following steps to install the vSphere Client:

1. Use a browser to connect to the IP address of an existing ESX 4.0 Host. You may see an SSL warning. This is normal, since the Host uses a generic SSL certificate.

2. You will be presented with a Welcome screen. Click Download vSphere Client to begin the download.

3. You will be asked if you want to Run or Save the file you are downloading. Select Run to begin the installation.

4. You will be presented with a warning that "The publisher could not be verified." This is normal warning and can be ignored. Click Run to continue the installation.

5. You will be prompted to "Select the Language for the Installation." Select English and click Next to continue the installation.

6. You will be presented with another Welcome screen. Click Next to continue the installation.

7. You will be prompted to read and agree to the license agreement. Check the radio box for "I agree to the terms of the license agreement" and click Next to continue the installation.

8. You will be prompted to enter your name and the name of your organization. Enter this information and click Next to continue the installation.

9. You will be presented with a Custom Installation screen. On this screen make sure you check the radio button next to Install vSphere Host Update Utility 4.0 to install the Host Update Utility, since we will use this utility later. Click Next to continue the installation.

10. You will be prompted to select a destination folder to install the vSphere Client. Click Next to accept the default location and continue the installation.

11. You will be presented with a Ready To Install window. Click Install to complete the installation.

12. Now that you have entered all of the necessary information, the installation will begin. The installation should take less than a minute.

13. You will be presented with an Installation Completed window. Click Finish to close the window.

You have now successfully installed the vSphere Client and the vSphere Host Update Utility.

Configure Network Time Protocol

Since vSphere must synchronize activities across multiple ESX Host Servers, keeping accurate system time is very important. ESX Server and ESXi Server use the Network Time Protocol, or NTP, to keep accurate system time. Since you have installed an ESX Server, we will now configure it to use the Network Time Protocol.

Perform the following steps to configure the Network Time Protocol using the vSphere Client:

1. Launch the vSphere Client and enter the IP Address of your ESX Host, the User Name of **root**, and the password you configured for root during the ESX Host install as shown in Figure 3-6. Click Login to connect to the ESX Host.

FIGURE 3-6

The vSphere
Client login
screen

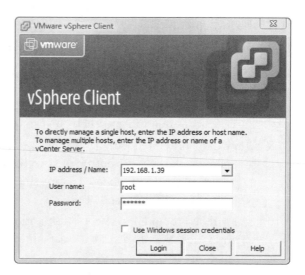

2. Once you are connected to the ESX Host, select the Configuration tab.

3. You will be presented with the Configuration tab as shown in Figure 3-7. On the left hand side under Software, click Time Configuration.

4. You will be presented with the Time Configuration window as shown in Figure 3-8. On this window click the Options button to open the NTP Daemon Options window.

5. You will be presented with the NTP Daemon Options window. Click NTP Settings to show the current NTP settings for the ESX Host.

FIGURE 3-7   The ESX Host Time Configuration tab

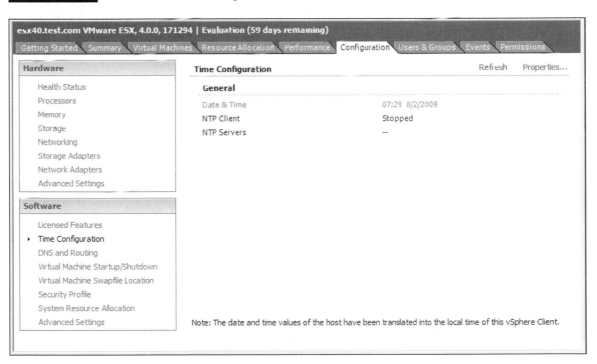

FIGURE 3-8

The ESX
Host Time
Configuration
window

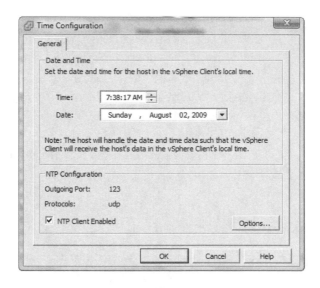

6. Under NTP Servers click Add to add a new NTP Server.
7. You will be presented with the Add NTP Server window. Add the address of an existing NTP Server and click OK to add the new NTP Server. Figure 3-9 shows the newly added NTP Server.

You have now successfully configured the Network Time Protocol for this Host.

FIGURE 3-9

The newly added
NTP Server

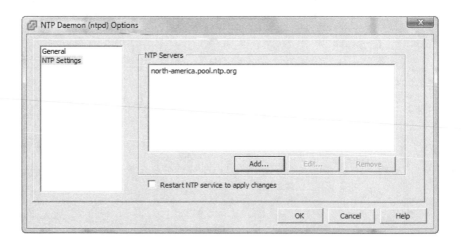

CERTIFICATION OBJECTIVE 3.04

Upgrade to ESX Server 4.0

For the exam you will need to be able to understand the process of upgrading from ESX Server 3.x to ESX Server 4.0. In this section we will discuss the prerequisites for upgrading an ESX 3.x Host and introduce the vSphere Host Update Utility. We will then use the vSphere Host Update Utility to perform a step-by-step upgrade of an ESX 3.5 Host into an ESX 4.0 Host.

Planning an ESX Server Upgrade

Before you can upgrade an ESX 3.x Host to ESX 4.0 or an ESXi 3.x Host to ESXi 4.0, you will need to perform the following steps:

- Confirm that the ESX 3.x Host is in maintenance mode.
- Ensure that the ESX 3.x Host meets the minimum hardware requirements for ESX Server 4.0.
- Ensure that all of the components of the ESX 3.x Host are supported using the VMware Compatibility Guide.

Once you have confirmed that your ESX 3.x Host meets these requirements, you are ready to perform the upgrade. The tool we will use for this is the vSphere Host Update Utility.

vSphere Host Update Utility

The vSphere Host Update Utility is a Windows program that allows you to upgrade ESX Server 3.x and ESXi Server 3.x Hosts to ESX Server 4.0 or ESXi Server 4.0. ESX 3.x Hosts are upgraded to ESX 4.0, and ESXi 3.x Hosts are upgraded to ESXi 4.0. These upgrades can be performed remotely and do not require an update CD to be placed into the remote Host. This utility is designed for sites that have a relatively small number of Hosts. Sites with a larger number of Hosts would benefit from using Update Manager to perform their updates, since it has additional features that simplify performing multiple updates. We will discuss Update Manager in Chapter 8.

Step-by-Step Upgrade

Now that you have a basic understanding of the vSphere Host Update Utility and have confirmed that your current ESX 3.5 Host meets the minimum hardware requirements for an ESX 4.0 Host, I will demonstrate a step-by-step upgrade from ESX 3.5 to ESX 4.0.

Perform the following steps to upgrade an ESX 3.5 Host to ESX 4.0 using the vSphere Host Update Utility:

1. Launch the vSphere Host Update Utility that we installed in the last section and select the Host you want to upgrade. Figure 3-10 shows the vSphere Host Update Utility and an available ESX 3.5 Host. This utility will show the version and build for each available ESX or ESXi Host. If your Host is not shown, you can use the Add Host link on the upper right of the window to add it to the list. Click Upgrade Host to begin the upgrade process.

FIGURE 3-10

The vSphere
Host Update
Utility

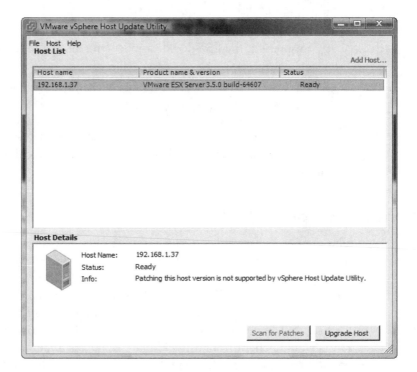

2. You will be presented with a Welcome screen. On this screen you need to specify the path to either an installable ESX 4.0/ESXi 4.0 DVD or ISO image. This DVD does not need to be local to the ESX Host you are upgrading. This allows you to perform remote upgrades of your ESX and ESXi Hosts. Click Next to continue the upgrade.

3. You will be prompted to read and agree to the license agreement. Check the radio box for "I agree to the terms of the license agreement" and click Next to continue the upgrade.

4. You will be prompted to enter a User Name and Password combination that has the authority to manage the Host you wish to upgrade. Enter the User Name and Password and press Next to continue the upgrade.

5. You are then prompted to select a datastore where the new console OS will be located. Click Next to select the default datastore and continue the upgrade. It is recommended that you use a local VMFS datastore rather than one located on a SAN volume.

6. You will be prompted to specify Post-Upgrade options for failback. Click Next to select the default options and continue the upgrade.

7. You are presented with the Ready To Complete screen. Click Next to begin the upgrade.

8. The status on the vSphere Host Update Utility screen will change to "Upgrading to ESX 4.0" and the upgrade will run. This upgrade can take a great deal of time and may appear to hang. The first upgrade I performed took nearly 40 minutes.

9. When the upgrade is complete, the status on the vSphere Host Update Utility screen will change to "Successfully upgraded" and will show the new version and build number of the upgraded Host.

10. A quick look at the console of the ESX Server as shown in Figure 3-11 will show that the upgrade completed successfully. Notice that the version number is now 4.0.0.

The console screen of the newly upgraded ESX Host showing a version number of 4.0.0

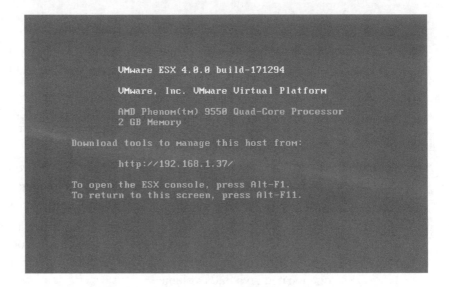

```
VMware ESX 4.0.0 build-171294

VMware, Inc. VMware Virtual Platform

AMD Phenom(tm) 9550 Quad-Core Processor
2 GB Memory

Download tools to manage this host from:

    http://192.168.1.37/

To open the ESX console, press Alt-F1.
To return to this screen, press Alt-F11.
```

Congratulations, you now know how to successfully upgrade a Host from ESX 3.5 to ESX 4.0.

Rollback Options for ESX/ESXi Upgrades

In some instances the upgrade process will fail and a rollback to the previous version is required. In the case of ESX the vSphere Host Update Utility will roll back to the previous version if the upgrade fails to complete. In the case of ESXi, the vSphere Host Update Utility does not support rollback.

CERTIFICATION OBJECTIVE 3.05

Configure Basic ESX Server Security

In this section we will discuss some basic security configurations for ESX and ESXi Hosts. We will talk about the Service Console Firewall that is configured for ESX Hosts. We will then discuss the main security settings that are preconfigured for our Host servers, and finally we will go over creating users and groups using the vSphere Client.

Service Console Firewall

By default a firewall exists between the ESX Service Console and the rest of the network. You can administer this firewall through the vSphere Client.

Perform the following steps to access the Service Console Firewall:

1. Launch the vSphere Client and enter the IP Address of your ESX Host, the User Name of **root**, and the password you configured for root during the ESX Host install. Click Login to connect to the ESX Host.

2. Once you are connected to the ESX Host, select the Configuration tab.

3. You will be presented with the Configuration window. On the left-hand side under Software click Security Profile.

4. You will be presented with the Security Profile screen as shown in Figure 3-12.

FIGURE 3-12 The ESX Host Security Profile screen

5. To open and close ports in the firewall, click the Properties button on the Security Profile window.

6. You will be presented with the Firewall Properties window as shown in Figure 3-13. By putting a check in the box next to a service, you enable its ports, and by removing a check from a service, you disable its ports.

The ESX
Host Firewall
Properties
window

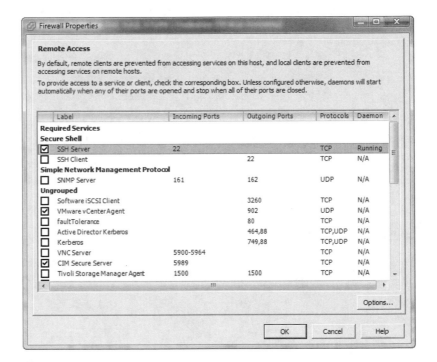

<hr>

INSIDE THE EXAM

ESXi and the Service Console Firewall

To test your knowledge of the differences between ESX and ESXi Hosts, you may see a question on the exam about configuring the Service Console Firewall for an ESXi Host. This would be a trick question. Remember that since an ESXi Host does not have a Service Console, it does not have a Service Console Firewall.

Service Console Security Levels

There are three Service Console security levels on an ESX Server. They depend on the condition of the incoming and outgoing ports. If the incoming ports are blocked and the outgoing ports are blocked, the Service Console security level is set to High. If the incoming ports are blocked and the outgoing ports are not blocked, the Service Console security level is set to Medium. If the incoming ports are not blocked and the outgoing ports are not blocked the Service Console security level is set to Low. The following table shows this:

Service Console Security Level	Incoming Ports	Outgoing Ports
High	Blocked	Blocked
Medium	Blocked	Not blocked
Low	Not blocked	Not blocked

Default Roles

Roles are used in conjunction with user and group accounts to control access to objects on ESX and ESXi Hosts. Three default roles are created during the installation of an ESX Host: No Access, Read-Only, and Administrator. By default the root account is assigned to the Administrator role. The No Access role means that a user has no access to the given object. The user is not able to administer the object or even to view its properties. The Read-Only role allows a user to look at the properties of an object but not to change them. The Administrator role gives a user the ability to both view the properties of an object and make changes to them.

exam

ⓦ a t c h   *The default roles for an ESX Server using the vSphere Client are not the same as the default roles in vCenter Server. For the exam you will need to keep these roles separated. We will discuss vCenter Server later, in Chapter 6.*

Users and Groups

User accounts and groups are used by ESX and ESXi Hosts in conjunction with roles to grant access to objects like virtual machines. Users and groups are created using the vSphere Client. Let's go ahead and create a new user account on our test ESX Host.

Perform the following steps to access the Service Console Firewall:

1. Launch the vSphere Client and enter the IP Address of your ESX Host, the User Name of **root**, and the password you configured for root during the ESX Host install. Click Login to connect to the ESX Host.

2. Once you are connected to the ESX Host select the Users & Groups tab.

3. You will be presented with the Users & Groups window as shown in Figure 3-14. Right-click one of the users and select New to create a new user.

4. You will be presented with the Add New User window as shown in Figure 3-15. On this window you can enter a Login ID, User Name, and password for the new user as well as grant him shell access and add him to groups. When you have entered the Login ID, User Name, and Password, click OK to create the new user.

FIGURE 3-14   The ESX Host Users and Groups window

esx40.test.com VMware ESX, 4.0.0, 171294 | Evaluation (59 days remaining)

Getting Started   Summary   Virtual Machines   Resource Allocation   Performance   Configuration   Users & Groups   Events   Permissions

View: Users Groups   Refresh

UID	User	Name
3	adm	adm
1	bin	bin
2	daemon	daemon
14	ftp	FTP User
13	gopher	gopher
7	halt	halt
4	lp	lp
8	mail	mail
9	news	news
429496...	nfsnobody	Anonymous NFS User
99	nobody	Nobody
28	nscd	NSCD Daemon
38	ntp	
11	operator	operator
77	pcap	
0	root	root
32	rpc	Portmapper RPC user
29	rpcuser	RPC Service User
37	rpm	
6	shutdown	shutdown

The ESX Host
Add New User
window

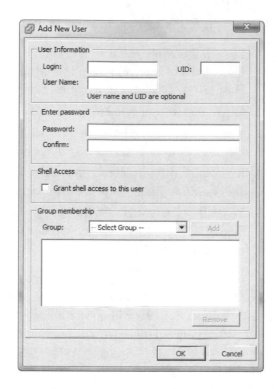

You have now created a new ESX Host user.

Make sure you create user accounts for your administrators and do not just use the root account. I have worked at a number of companies who regularly use the root account and are no longer able to track which administrator is performing actions because the logs only show root.

Assigning Rights to a Virtual Machine

Now that you have a basic understanding of roles and have created a new user, let's assign the new user rights to an existing virtual machine. For this example I have downloaded a virtual machine named "Nostalgia" from VMware to our test Host.

Perform the following steps to assign rights to an existing virtual machine:

1. Launch the vSphere Client and enter the IP Address of your ESX Host, the User Name of **root**, and the password you configured for root during the ESX Host install. Click Login to connect to the ESX Host.

2. Once you are connected to the ESX Host, select the Virtual Machines tab.

3. You will be presented with the Virtual Machines window as shown in Figure 3-16. You will see a virtual machine named Nostalgia.

4. Right-click this virtual machine and select Add Permission to begin giving your new user rights to this virtual machine.

5. You will be presented with the Assign Permissions window as shown in Figure 3-17. Under Users And Group click Add and select the new user you created from the list. Under Assigned Role use the drop-down box to select Administrator. Click OK to grant this user the new right.

We have now given the new user access to the virtual machine Nostalgia with a role of Administrator. She will now be able to fully administer the virtual machine.

Using this system of users, groups, and roles, you can be very granular with the amount of access you give to any user or group. You are able to assign a single user different roles for each object or assign an entire group of users the same role for each object.

FIGURE 3-16   The ESX Host Virtual Machines window

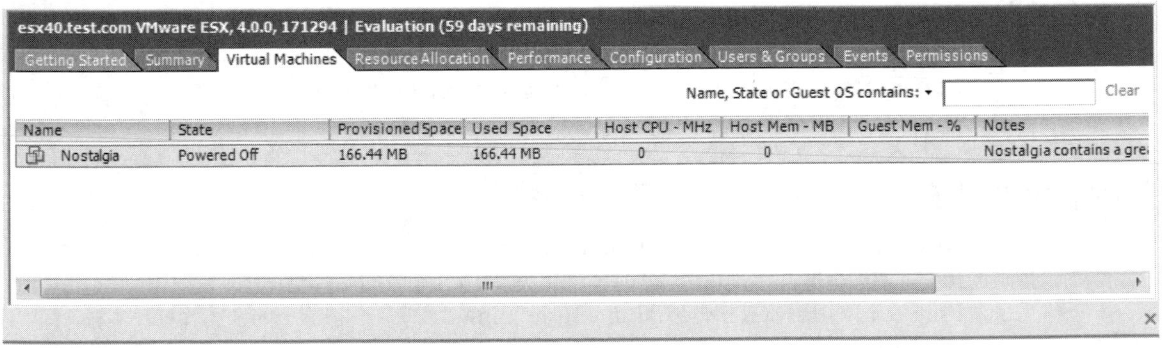

FIGURE 3-17

The ESX
Host Assign
Permissions
window

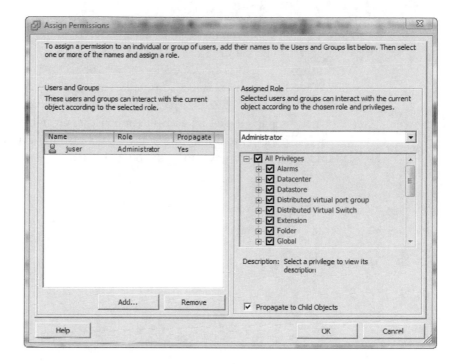

CERTIFICATION SUMMARY

We started this chapter with an introduction to ESX Server and ESXi Server. We discussed their architectures and reviewed the disk partitions that make up an ESX Server.

Next we planned an install of ESX Server and of ESXi Server. We reviewed the minimum hardware requirements and introduced the VMware Compatibility Guide. Once we were sure our hardware met the minimum requirements and was on the VMware Compatibility Guide, we performed a step-by-step installation of ESX and of ESXi.

After installing the Hosts, we talked about the vSphere Client and performed a step-by-step installation. We then used the vSphere Client to configure the Network

Time Protocol on our new ESX Server. As we were installing the vSphere Client, we also installed the vSphere Host Update Utility. We then used the utility to upgrade a ESX 3.5 Server to ESX 4.0.

We finished the chapter by discussing some basic security configurations for ESX Servers. We looked at the Service Console Firewall and then reviewed how Users, Groups, and Roles are used to control access to Objects on ESX Servers. We then created a new user and gave him access to an existing virtual machine.

We covered a lot of ground in this chapter and hopefully you now have a good base of understanding to move on to the next chapter.

✓ TWO-MINUTE DRILL

Introduction to ESX Server

❏ The vmkernel is a virtualization layer that allows virtual machines to run on the same hardware at the same time and appear to be running on separate servers.

❏ ESX Servers have a Service Console. ESXi Servers do not.

❏ The /boot partition is a required partition of type ext3 that is used to store boot information for an ESX Host.

❏ The swap partition is a required partition of type swap that is used to allow the Service Console in ESX to swap memory to disk.

❏ The / partition is a required partition of type ext3 that is the root of the ESX Service Console operating system.

❏ VMFS3 partitions are used to store virtual machines.

❏ You use vmkcore partitions to store core dumps and debugging information.

ESX Server Installations

❏ ESX Server requires a 64-bit x86-based CPU.

❏ ESX Server requires a minimum of 2GB of RAM.

❏ ESX Server requires one or more supported NICs.

❏ The VMware Compatibility Guide is an excellent resource to determine if a given server solution has been tested to be compatible with VMware products.

The vSphere Client

❏ The vSphere Client can be used to administer ESX and ESXi Hosts and to connect and administer VMware vCenter Servers.

❏ The Network Time Protocol is important for ESX Hosts and can be configured using the vSphere Client.

Upgrade to ESX Server 4.0

❏ The vSphere Host Update Utility can be used to upgrade ESX and ESXi Hosts to 4.0.

❏ The vSphere Host Update Utility supports rollback for ESX Hosts.

❏ The vSphere Host Update Utility does not support rollback for ESXi Hosts.

Configure Basic ESX Server Security

❏ There is a firewall between the Service Console on ESX Hosts and the rest of the network.

❏ The Service Console security level is set to High if both incoming and outgoing ports are blocked.

❏ The Service Console security level is set to Medium if incoming ports are blocked and outgoing ports are not blocked.

❏ The Service Console security level is set to Low if neither incoming nor outgoing ports are blocked.

❏ There are three default roles for an ESX(i) Server: No Access, Read-Only, and Administrator.

SELF TEST

The following questions will help you measure your understanding of the material presented in this chapter. Read all the choices carefully and remember that there is only one best answer for each question.

Introduction to ESX Server

1. Which of the following is not a required partition for ESX Server 4.0?
   A. /usr
   B. /
   C. /boot
   D. swap

2. Which of the following partitions is used to store core dumps?
   A. swap
   B. vmfs3
   C. vmkcore
   D. /boot

3. Which of the following partitions is used to store virtual machines?
   A. swap
   B. vmfs3
   C. vmkcore
   D. /boot

ESX Server Installations

4. What is the minimum amount of RAM required to install ESX 4.0?
   A. 1GB
   B. 2GB
   C. 3GB
   D. 4GB

5. Given a server with the following specifications, which component will cause ESX 4.0 to not be able to be installed: x86 32-bit processor, 2GB RAM, SCSI hard disk?

    A. x86 32-bit processor

    B. 2GB RAM

    C. SCSI hard disk

    D. ESX 4.0 will install correctly

The vSphere Client

6. What is the first step for installing the vSphere Client?

    A. Insert the ESX Server Installation DVD.

    B. Download the installer from vmware.com.

    C. Use a browser to attach to the IP address of your ESX 4.0 Server.

    D. Insert the vSphere Client Installation CD.

7. Which other VMware software package can be loaded at the same time as the vSphere Client?

    A. VMware Workstation

    B. vSphere Host Update Utility

    C. vCenter Server

    D. VMware View

Upgrade to ESX Server 4.0

8. Which of the following is not a true statement when upgrading an ESX 3.x Host to ESX 4.0 using the vSphere Host Update Utility?

    A. The ESX 3.x Host must be in maintenance mode.

    B. The ESX 3.x Host must meet the minimum hardware requirements for ESX 4.0.

    C. The components of the ESX 3.5 Host should be supported under the VMware Compatibility Guide.

    D. The ESX 3.x Host must have all of the available security patches installed.

Configure Basic ESX Server Security

9. What VMware tool is used to manage the Service Console Firewall on an ESXi 4.0 Host?
   A. vSphere Host Update Utility
   B. vSphere Client
   C. vCenter Server
   D. None of the above

10. If incoming firewall ports are blocked and outgoing firewall ports are blocked, what is the Service Console security level?
   A. Strong
   B. High
   C. Medium
   D. Low

11. If incoming firewall ports are blocked and outgoing firewall ports are not blocked, what is the Service Console security level?
   A. High
   B. Medium
   C. Low
   D. Weak

12. Which of the following is not a default role on an ESX 4.0 Server?
   A. No Access
   B. Guest
   C. Read-Only
   D. Administrator

SELF TEST ANSWERS

Introduction to ESX Server

1. ☑ **A.** The /usr partition is an optional partition.
   ☒ **B, C,** and **D** are incorrect: /, /boot, and swap are all required partitions.

2. ☑ **C.** The vmkcore partition is used to store core dumps.
   ☒ **A, B,** and **D** are incorrect. The swap partition is used for memory swapping. vmfs volumes are used to store virtual machines. The /boot partition is used to store boot information.

3. ☑ **B.** The vmfs partitions are used to store virtual machines.
   ☒ **A, C,** and **D** are incorrect. The swap partition is used for memory swapping. The vmkcore partition is used to store core dumps. The /boot partition is used to store boot information.

ESX Server Installations

4. ☑ **B.** Two gigabytes of RAM is the minimum required to install ESX 4.0.
   ☒ **A, C,** and **D** are incorrect: 2GB of RAM is the minimum required to install ESX 4.0.

5. ☑ **A.** ESX 4.0 requires a 64-bit processor.
   ☒ **B, C,** and **D** are incorrect. ESX 4.0 requires at least 2GB of RAM. SCSI disks are supported.

The vSphere Client

6. ☑ **C.** The vSphere Client is installed by using a browser to connect to an existing ESX 4.0 Server.
   ☒ **A, B,** and **D** are incorrect. The vSphere Client is not available on the ESX Server Installation DVD. The vSphere Client cannot be downloaded from vmware.com. There is no separate vSphere Client Installation CD.

7. ☑ **B.** The vSphere Host Update Utility can be installed at the same time as the vSphere Client.
   ☒ **A, C,** and **D** are incorrect. VMware Workstation, vCenter Server, and VMware View are separate programs that need to be installed separately from the vSphere Client.

Upgrade to ESX Server 4.0

8. ☑ **D.** There is no requirement for security patches to be installed on the 3.x Host.
☒ **A, B,** and **C** are incorrect. When upgrading an ESX 3.x Host to ESX 4.0 the host must be in maintenance mode. It must meet the minimum hardware requirements for ESX 4.0. All of the 3.x Hosts systems should be confirmed to be compatible by using the VMware Compatibility Guide.

Configure Basic ESX Server Security

9. ☑ **D.** This is a trick question. Since ESXi does not have a Service Console, it docs not have a Service Console Firewall.
☒ **A, B,** and **C** are incorrect. The vSphere Host Update Utility is used to update ESX 3.x and ESXi 3.x Hosts to ESX 4.0 or ESXi 4.0. The vSphere Client can be used to manage the Service Console Firewall on ESX 4.0 Hosts. vCenter is an advanced management tool that we will discuss in Chapter 6.

10. ☑ **B.** If both incoming and outgoing ports are blocked, the Service Console security level is set to High.
☒ **A, C,** and **D** are incorrect. Strong is not a Service Console security level. A Medium Service Console security level is when incoming ports are blocked and outgoing ports are not blocked. A Low Service Console security level is when neither incoming nor outgoing ports are blocked.

11. ☑ **B.** If incoming ports are blocked and outgoing ports are not blocked, the Service Console security level is set to Medium.
☒ **A, C,** and **D** are incorrect. A High Service Console security level is when both incoming and outgoing ports are blocked. A Low Service Console security level is when neither incoming nor outgoing ports are blocked. Weak is not a Service Console security level.

12. ☑ **B.** Guest is not a default role on ESX 4.0 Servers.
☒ **A, C,** and **D** are incorrect. No Access, Read-Only, and Administrator are default roles on ESX 4.0 Servers.

4

Install and Configure vCenter Server

W elcome to Chapter 4. In this chapter you will learn about vCenter Server. I will explain what vCenter Server is and the different versions that are available. We will then discuss the requirements to install vCenter Server and some of the additional modules that are available. Once you know how to install vCenter Server, we will end the chapter by configuring our vCenter Server and discussing access control. By the end of this chapter, you will be ready to install vCenter Server in your environment and pass this section of the VCP exam.

CERTIFICATION OBJECTIVE 4.01

Introduction to vCenter Server

vCenter Server is the high-end management module for vSphere. The vSphere Client allows the management of individual ESX Hosts and the virtual machines running on them. vCenter Server takes that management functionality to the next level and allows centralized management of the entire datacenter from a single management console. This tool allows the administrator to see and manage all of her ESX and ESXi Hosts from a single window. It also allows many of the advanced features of vSphere such as VMotion and DRS that are not available without vCenter Server.

We will discuss these advanced features in later chapters, and the importance of vCenter Server will become readily apparent. Now that you have a rough idea of what vCenter Server is, let's take a look at the different editions that are available.

on the

Job

While on the job you may hear people refer to vCenter Server as Virtual Center. In earlier versions of the VMware product line Virtual Center was the primary centralized management component.

vCenter Server Editions

vCenter Server is available in three different editions that are designed for organizations of different sizes. The first of these editions, vCenter Server for Essentials, is designed for small office deployments and is included with the vSphere

Essentials and vSphere Essentials Plus packages. It allows support for up to three Hosts.

The second edition, vCenter Server Foundation, is limited to managing only three ESX or ESXI Hosts. The final edition, vCenter Server Standard, is a full-featured version and is able to manage up to 300 Hosts.

All of the editions of vCenter Server include the following features:

- **The vSphere Client**   The vSphere Client is the basic interface to manage both individual ESX Hosts and vCenter Servers.
- **The vCenter Server Management Server**   The vCenter Server Management Server is the vCenter Server Console.
- **The vCenter Server Database Server**   The vCenter Server Database Server is a database that contains information about the configuration and performance of every object that is managed by the vCenter Server.
- **The vCenter Server Search Engine**   The vCenter Server Search Engine is a search engine that allows administrators to search for individual objects that are managed by their vCenter Servers.
- **The VMware vCenter Web Access Portal**   The VMware vCenter Web Access Portal is a web-based interface to the vCenter Server that allows administrators to access their vCenter Servers from anywhere using a standard web browser.
- **The VMware vCenter APIs and .NET Extension**   The VMware vCenter APIs and .NET Extension are programming extensions that allow third-party developers to develop software that can interact directly with vCenter Server.

The following features are only available in the vCenter Server Standard edition:

- **VMware vCenter Orchestrator**   The VMware vCenter Orchestrator is an automation tool that allows administrators to simplify the administration of their datacenters by automating repetitive tasks.
- **vCenter Server Linked Mode Groups**   vCenter Server Linked Mode Groups allow multiple vCenter Servers to see each other's inventories, providing a degree of redundancy that was missing in earlier versions of Virtual Center.

vCenter Server Linked Mode Groups

vCenter Server Linked Mode Groups is a feature of vCenter Server Standard edition that allows multiple vCenter Servers to be joined together into a group. Each of the vCenter Server members of this group can see the inventories of the other members. An Administrator can access any of the member vCenter Servers and have access to all of the resources controlled by all of the member servers from a single console. Linked Mode Groups can be particularly useful in large environments, since they allow a larger number of Hosts and virtual machines to be managed from a single location. They can also be useful for companies that have a number of datacenters that are in different geographical locations. A vCenter Server can be located in each datacenter, and by using Linked Mode Groups, they can all be managed from a centralized location.

vCenter Server Maximums

All of the editions of vCenter Server are subject to a number of maximums. Unfortunately, for the exam these maximums will simply need to be memorized. The following table lists the maximums you need to know for vCenter Server:

Description	(32-bit vCenter Server)	(64-bit vCenter Server)	Linked Mode Groups
Hosts	200	300	1000
Powered-on virtual machines	2000	3000	10,000
Registered virtual machines	3000	4500	15,000
Linked vCenter Server systems	NA	NA	10
Concurrent vSphere Client connections	15	30	NA
Hosts per datacenter	1000	1000	1000

Now that you have a basic understanding of vCenter Server and its strengths and limitations, let's move ahead and talk about installing a vCenter Server.

CERTIFICATION OBJECTIVE 4.02

Install vCenter Server and Additional vCenter Modules

In this section we will discuss the installation of a vCenter Server. We will review the hardware and software requirements that must be met before performing the install and go through the process of performing an actual installation. Once we have completed the installation of the vCenter Server, we will look at some additional modules that can be added to the vCenter Server Console.

vCenter Server Installation

In this section we will review the hardware and database requirements to install vCenter Server. We will then walk through the steps of performing the installation. Before we can begin the install process, we need to look at the hardware requirements.

Hardware Requirements

Before you can install vCenter Server, you need to make sure that your hardware meets the minimum hardware requirements. The minimum hardware requirements for vCenter Server are

- 2 CPUs
- 2.0 GHz Intel or AMD processor
- 3GB RAM
- 2GB of disk storage in addition to the OS
- 1 NIC: A Gigabit NIC is recommended but not required

Once you have ensured that your hardware meets these basic requirements, you can move on to the next stage of the installation.

e x a m

For the exam you may see a question that gives the hardware specs of a server and asks which specification *would not meet the minimum hardware requirements for vCenter Server.*

INSIDE THE EXAM

vCenter Server and Microsoft Access

To test your knowledge of the differences between vCenter Server and older versions of Virtual Center, you may see a question asking if Microsoft Access is a supported database for vCenter Server. Some older versions of Virtual Center would use Microsoft Access as its database. vCenter Server supports Microsoft SQL Server 2005 Express instead of Access.

vCenter Server Database Requirements

In the same way that vCenter Server has specific hardware requirements it also has specific database requirements. vCenter Server needs a database to keep configuration and performance information about the objects that it manages. vCenter Server is supported on the following databases:

- Microsoft SQL Server 2005 Express
- Microsoft SQL Server 2005
- Microsoft SQL Server 2008
- Oracle 10g
- Oracle 11g

If you do not have a database server available for your vCenter Server, you can install Microsoft SQL Server 2005 Express on the vCenter Server as a part of the vCenter Server installation. For our installation we will use Microsoft SQL Server 2005 Express as our database server. Once you have confirmed that your hardware meets the minimum requirements and that you have a supported database, you are ready to begin the install of vCenter Server.

Install vCenter Server

In this section we will review the steps for installing vCenter Server. vCenter Server installs like any application, and the installation is relatively straightforward.

Perform the following steps to complete your first installation of vCenter Server:

1. Ensure that your hardware meets the minimum requirements for vCenter Server.
2. Ensure that you have access to a supported database server or determine how to use Microsoft SQL Server 2005 Express.
3. Insert the vCenter Server DVD into your server.
4. The VMware vCenter Installer window will appear as shown in Figure 4-1. Click vCenter Server to begin the installation.

FIGURE 4-1

The VMware vCenter Installer window

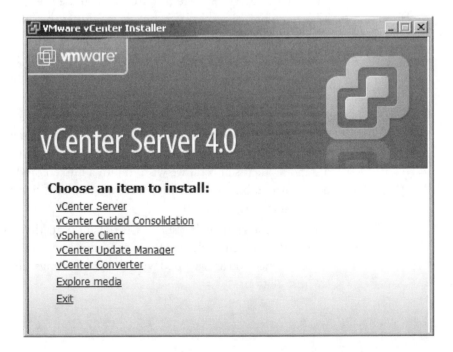

5. You will be prompted to Choose The Setup Language. Select English from the drop-down menu and click OK to continue the installation.

6. A Welcome screen will pop up. Click Next to continue the installation.

7. You will be prompted to read and agree to the license agreement. Check the radio box for "I agree to the terms of the license agreement" and click Next to continue the installation.

8. You will be prompted to enter your Name, Organization, and License Key. Enter your Name and Organization. If you have a license key from VMware, enter it. If you do not have a license key, do not enter anything and vCenter Server will install in evaluation mode. You can enter a license key later without needing to reinstall. Click Next to continue the installation.

9. You will be prompted to enter your database information. If you have an existing database that you wish to use, enter the Data Source Name. If you want to install Microsoft SQL Server 2005 Express, check the radio box next to Install A Microsoft SQL Server 2005 Instance. Click Next to continue the installation.

10. You will be prompted to enter the account information that will be used by the vCenter Server Service to start. You can use the system account or specify a local or domain account for the service. Enter the information and click Next to continue the installation.

11. You will be prompted to enter a Destination Folder for the install of vCenter Server. The default installation path is "C:\Program Files\VMware\Infrastructure." If you wish to change this path, do so and then click Next to continue the installation.

12. You will then be prompted to install a stand-alone instance of vCenter Server or to join a Linked Mode Group. Since this is our first install, we will select a stand-alone instance. If we wish to join a Linked Mode Group later, we can do so without having to reinstall vCenter Server. Click Next to continue the installation.

13. You will see a window that shows the default ports that are used by vCenter Server. If you need to change these ports due to firewall settings, you can do so here. Once you are satisfied with the port settings, click Next to continue the installation.

14. The next screen confirms that the installation is ready to begin. Click Install to continue the installation.

15. You will then be shown a screen that shows the progress of the installation components. On my test system this step took approximately ten minutes.

16. Once the installation is complete, you will see an Installation Successful screen. Click Finish to complete the installation.

Install Additional vCenter Modules

Now that you have an instance of vCenter Server installed, we will look at some additional modules that can be added to vCenter Server to give it additional functionality. In this section we will look at the following modules: vCenter Guided Consolidation, vCenter Update Manager, and vCenter Converter. Let's look at vCenter Guided Consolidation first.

vCenter Guided Consolidation

vCenter Guided Consolidation is an additional module for vCenter Server that allows an administrator to virtualize an existing physical datacenter. It can create an inventory of existing physical servers that would be good candidates for virtualization by gathering performance statistics from the physical servers. vCenter Guided Consolidation can then be used to perform the actual physical-to-virtual conversions of the servers by initiating VMware vCenter Converter. And finally it can help decide which ESX or ESXi host the newly converted virtual machines should be placed on, depending on available resources.

The installation of vCenter Guided Consolidation is relatively straightforward. It installs like an application and can be installed on the same server as vCenter Server. Perform the following steps to install vCenter Guided Consolidation:

1. Insert the vCenter Server DVD into your server.

2. The VMware vCenter Installer window will appear. Click vCenter Guided Consolidation to begin the installation.

3. You will be prompted to Choose The Setup Language. Select English from the drop-down menu and click OK to continue the installation.

4. A Welcome screen will pop up. Click Next to continue the installation.

5. You will be prompted to read and agree to the license agreement. Check the radio box for "I agree to the terms of the license agreement" and click Next to continue the installation.

6. You will be prompted to enter a Destination Folder for the install of vCenter Guided Consolidation. The default installation path is "C:\Program Files\VMware\Infrastructure." If you wish to change this path, do so, and then click Next to continue the installation.

7. You will be prompted to enter the account information that will be used by the vCenter Collector Service to start. You can use the system account or specify a local or domain account for the service. Enter the information and click Next to continue the installation. It is recommended that the chosen account be a member of the Domain Admins group if you are using Active Directory, since this account will be used to query the physical servers.

8. The next screen shows the default ports that are used by vCenter Collector Service. If you need to change these ports due to firewall settings, you can do so here. Once you are satisfied with the port settings, click Next to continue the installation.

9. You will be prompted to enter the IP Address of your vCenter Server as well as a user account and password that has access to the vCenter Server. Enter this information and click Next to continue the installation.

10. You will be prompted to enter the Server Identity. Select the server identity from the drop-down list and click Next to continue the installation.

11. The next screen confirms that the installation is ready to begin. Click Install to continue the installation.

12. Once the installation is complete, you will see an Installation Successful screen. Click Finish to complete the installation.

vCenter Update Manager

vCenter Update Manager is an additional module for vCenter Server that can be used by administrators to simplify the process of patch management for ESX Hosts as well as Windows and Linux virtual machines. In previous versions of ESX Server patch management had to be performed on individual machines and did not scale well to large environments. With the addition of vCenter Update Manager, patch management has been greatly simplified.

The installation of vCenter Update Manager is relatively straightforward. It installs like an application and can be installed on the same server as vCenter Server. Perform the following steps to install vCenter Update Manager:

1. Insert the vCenter Server DVD into your server.

2. The VMware vCenter Installer window will appear. Click vCenter Update Manager to begin the installation.

3. You will be prompted to Choose The Setup Language. Select English from the drop-down menu and click OK to continue the installation.

4. A Welcome screen will pop up. Click Next to continue the installation.

5. You will be prompted to read and agree to the license agreement. Check the radio box for "I agree to the terms of the license agreement" and click Next to continue the installation.

6. You will be prompted to enter the IP Address of your vCenter Server as well as a user account and password that has access to the vCenter Server. Enter this information and click Next to continue the installation.

7. You will be prompted to configure Database options. If you are installing vCenter Update Manager on a separate server from your vCenter Server, you can select to install a new instance of Microsoft SQL Server 2005 Express or to connect to an existing supported database. If you are installing vCenter Update Manager on the same server as your VCenter Server, you can select to use the existing vCenter Server database or to connect to an existing supported database. Select a database and click Next to continue the installation.

8. You will be prompted to enter a username and password that has access to the database you selected in the last step. Enter this information and click Next to continue the installation.

9. You will be prompted for the fully qualified domain name or IP address to identify this instance of vCenter Update Manager. Enter this information and click Next to continue.

10. You will be prompted to enter port numbers for your connection. Click Next to continue and accept the default ports.

11. You will be prompted to enter an installation location for the installation. Click Next to continue the installation and accept the default installation location.

12. You will be prompted to enter a location for patch downloads. Click Next to continue the installation and accept the default installation location.

13. The next screen confirms that the installation is ready to begin. Click Install to continue the installation.

14. Once the installation is complete, you will see an Installation Successful screen. Click Finish to complete the installation.

vCenter Converter

vCenter Converter is an additional module for vCenter Server that helps to simplify the migration of physical machines into virtual machines. Whereas vCenter Guided Consolidation is designed to help migrate entire physical datacenters into virtual machines, vCenter Converter is designed to convert individual physical machines into virtual machines. It can also be used to convert virtual machines from one format to another. This can be useful when converting virtual machines that were created with other VMware products or those that are created using other third-party virtualization products.

The installation of vCenter Converter is relatively straightforward. It installs like an application and can be installed on the same server as vCenter Server. Perform the following steps to install vCenter Converter:

1. Insert the vCenter Server DVD into your server.

2. The VMware vCenter Installer window will appear. Click vCenter Converter to begin the installation.

3. You will be prompted to Choose The Setup Language. Select English from the drop-down menu and click OK to continue the installation.

4. A Welcome screen will pop up. Click Next to continue the installation.

5. You will be prompted to read and agree to the license agreement. Check the radio box for "I agree to the terms of the license agreement" and click Next to continue the installation.

6. You will be prompted to enter a Destination Folder for the install of vCenter Converter. The default installation path is "C:\Program Files\VMware\Infrastructure." If you wish to change this path, do so, and then click Next to continue the installation.

7. You will be prompted to perform either a Typical or Custom installation. For most users, the Typical installation will be sufficient. When you have set up your test lab in Appendix A, you should attempt to perform a Custom installation of vCenter Converter. For this example, select Typical and click Next to continue the installation.

8. You will be prompted to enter the IP Address of your vCenter Server as well as a user account and password that has access to the vCenter Server. Enter this information and click Next to continue the installation.

9. The next screen shows the default ports that are used by vCenter Converter. If you need to change these ports due to firewall settings, you can do so here. Once you are satisfied with the port settings, click Next to continue the installation.

10. You will be prompted to enter the Server Identity. Select the server identity from the drop-down list and click Next to continue the installation.

11. The next screen confirms that the installation is ready to begin. Click Install to continue the installation.

12. Once the installation is complete, you will see an Installation Successful screen. Click Finish to complete the installation.

CERTIFICATION OBJECTIVE 4.03

Configure and Manage vCenter Server

Now that we have gone through the install of a vCenter Server and some of its add-on modules, we can start to configure and use the vCenter Server. The first step you will need to take before you can configure a vCenter Server is to connect to it. You connect to a vCenter Server using the vSphere Client the same way we connected to individual Hosts in Chapter 3. Follow these steps to connect to your vCenter Server:

1. Launch the vSphere Client.

2. Enter the Server Name or IP Address of your vCenter Server into the client.

3. Enter a username and password into the client and click Login to connect to the vCenter Server. You will now be connected to the vCenter Server as shown in Figure 4-2.

FIGURE 4-2 The vSphere Client view of a vCenter Server

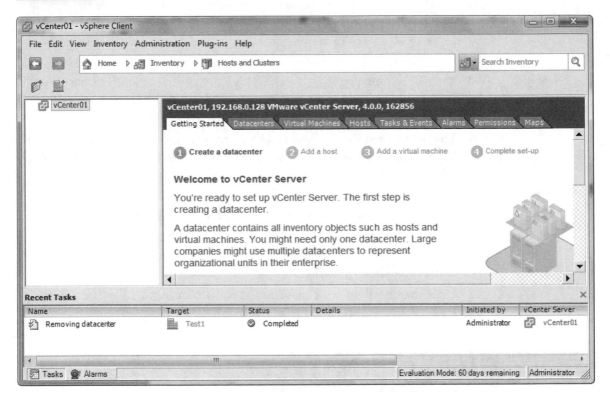

Work with Datacenters and Folders

One of the first things you will need to do once you have your vCenter Server installed is to add a new Datacenter. Datacenters and folders are logical containers in vCenter Server that contain Host objects. They help to organize your objects into a more understandable structure. In general a Datacenter will represent your physical datacenter and will contain all of the Hosts that are in your physical datacenter. To create your first Datacenter, follow these steps:

1. Launch the vSphere Client and connect to your vCenter Server.
2. Select the vCenter Server in the leftmost frame.

3. From the File menu select New and then Datacenter.
4. A new Datacenter object will be created under the vCenter Server. Give it a meaningful name. Your naming standard should have some meaning to you. I tend to use location names for Datacenter objects. For this example I will use Cleveland01 to mean the first Datacenter in the Cleveland office.

You should now be able to see the new Datacenter as shown in Figure 4-3.

At first you may not think you will need to use folders to organize your environment, but as you add additional Hosts, your environment can become very sloppy. Folders and Datacenters can help you to keep it more organized and help to create a security structure for role-based access controls.

FIGURE 4-3   You can now see the newly created Datacenter.

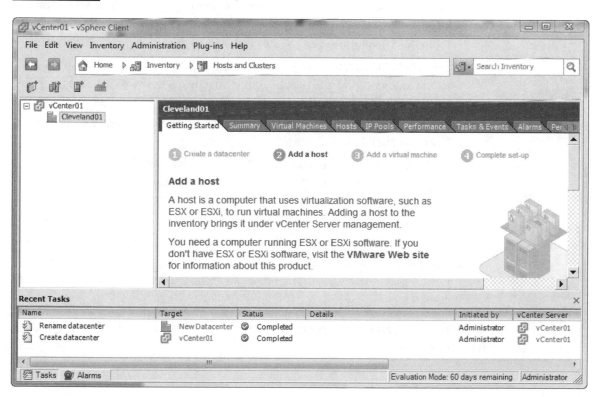

on the **!** o b *When I am on a client site they will often have what they consider special projects that require a number of virtual servers. I will usually create a folder for each of the projects and put all of the virtual servers that are created for the project into its folder. I can then easily give project team members access to their virtual servers and keep them separated from the rest of my virtual environment.*

Join an ESX Host to vCenter Server

Once you have a Datacenter configured, you will need to start adding Hosts to it. To add a host to your newly created Datacenter, follow these steps:

1. Launch the vSphere Client and connect to your vCenter Server.
2. Select the Datacenter in the leftmost frame that you wish to add the Host into.
3. From the File menu select New and then Add Host.
4. You will be prompted to enter the Name or IP Address of the Host you wish to add and a user ID and password that has the authority to manage the Host. Enter this information and click Next to continue.
5. A Host Information window will pop up. Confirm you are adding the correct Host and click Next to continue.
6. You will be prompted to add a new license key to your Host or continue to use the existing key. Select to use the existing license key and click Next to continue.
7. You will be prompted to select a location for the virtual machines from the Host. To keep the virtual machines where they are, click Next to continue.
8. You will be shown a window that says the operation is ready to be performed. Click Finish to continue. The process will start and can take a few minutes to complete.

Once the process has completed, you will be able to see the new Host, as shown in Figure 4-4.

FIGURE 4-4   You can now see the newly added Host.

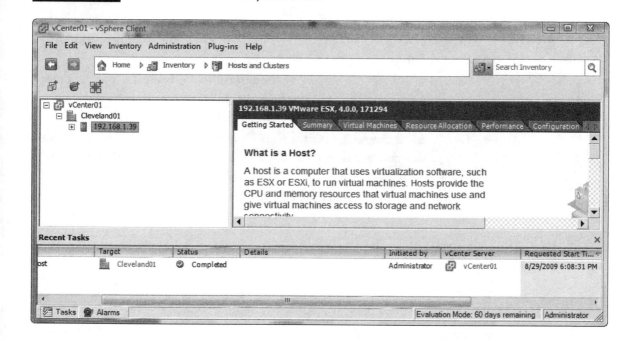

Configure vCenter Server Settings

There are a large number of configurable settings for vCenter Server. The settings control everything from how vCenter Server is licensed, to how long it keeps statistics, and how it does logging. You can review and change these settings by following these steps:

1. Launch the vSphere Client and connect to your vCenter Server.
2. From the Administration menu select vCenter Server Settings.
3. You will now see the vCenter Server Settings window.
4. In this window you will see a list of vCenter Server Settings classes in the left-hand pane. By clicking these classes, you will see the settings that are available in each class.

The following classes of settings can be changed in vCenter Server:

- **Licensing**   Under the Licensing class of settings you can add additional licenses to your vCenter Server and select whether or not to use a VMware License Server.

- **Statistics**   Under the Statistics class of settings you can configure the time durations that statistics are kept. You can also compute a rough estimate of the space your vCenter Server database will require.

- **Run Time Settings**   Under the Run Time Settings class of settings you can change the managed IP Address of your vCenter Server or change the name of the vCenter Server.

- **Active Directory**   Under the Active Directory class of settings you can specify the timeout values that vCenter Server uses when dealing with Active Directory.

- **Mail**   Under the Mail class of settings you can configure the SMTP Server and Mail Send accounts that are used by vCenter Server.

- **SNMP**   Under the SNMP class of settings you can configure up to four SNMP Receiver URLs, Ports, and Community Strings.

- **Ports**   Under the Ports class of settings you can configure the HTTP and HTTPS ports that will be used by vCenter Server.

- **Timeout Settings**   Under the Timeout Settings class of settings you can configure the Client Connection timeouts for both Normal and Long operations.

- **Logging Options**   Under the Logging Options class of settings you can configure the detail level of vCenter Server logging.

- **Database**   Under the Database class of settings you can configure the maximum number of database connections that will be used by vCenter Server.

- **Database Retention Policy**   Under the Database Retention Policy class of settings you can configure how long tasks and events are retained in the vCenter Server database.

- **SSL Settings** Under the SSL Settings class of settings you can configure your vCenter Server to require verified Host SSL certificates when communicating with ESX and ESXi Hosts.
- **Advanced Settings** It is recommended that you not make any changes in this section unless you are directed by VMware Support to do so.

Now that you know how to configure setting for your vCenter Servers, let's take a look at the types of tasks you can use vCenter Server to perform.

For the exam you may see a question that asks which class of settings you would go to in order to change a specific setting. For example, to change SMTP Settings, you need to go to the Mail class of settings.

Configure Scheduled Tasks

Many of the tasks that you will be required to perform as a system administrator need to take place outside of business hours or even in the middle of the night. In an attempt to make your life a little easier, VMware has included the ability to schedule some tasks to occur at a later time in vSphere. In this section we will look at the Scheduled Tasks window and will discuss the types of tasks that can be scheduled.

To access the Scheduled Tasks window, perform the following steps:

1. Launch the vSphere Client and connect to your vCenter Server.
2. In the right-hand frame select Tasks & Events.
3. In the right-hand frame click Scheduled Tasks and you will see the Scheduled Tasks window as shown in Figure 4-5.
4. To add a new Scheduled Task, just click New on the left side of the window.

FIGURE 4-5   The Scheduled Tasks window

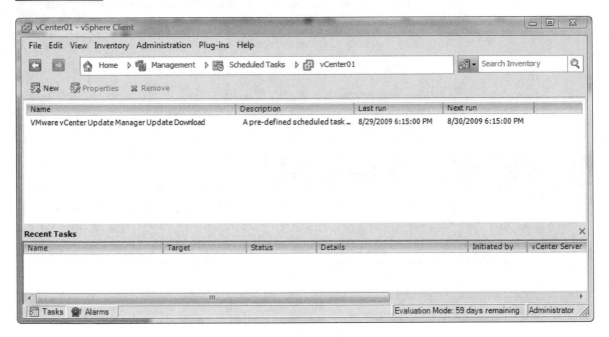

There are a large number of tasks in vCenter Server that can be scheduled. The following list shows the tasks that can be scheduled and briefly describes what each task can do:

- **Change the power state of a virtual machine**   Using this scheduled task, you can power a virtual machine on or off.

- **Clone a virtual machine**   Using this scheduled task, you can create a clone of a virtual machine and place it on a new Host.

- **Deploy a virtual machine**   Using this scheduled task, you can deploy a new virtual machine from a virtual machine template.

- **Migrate a virtual machine**   Using this scheduled task, you can migrate a virtual machine to run on a different host, to move its storage to a different datastore, or both.

- **Create a virtual machine**   Using this scheduled task, you can create a new virtual machine and assign it to a given Host.

- **Make a snapshot of a virtual machine**   Using this scheduled task, you can create a snapshot of a virtual machine. We will discuss snapshots in Chapter 7.

- **Add a host**   Using this scheduled task, you can add a Host to a Datacenter.

- **Change resource settings of resource pool or virtual machine**   Using this scheduled task, you can change the resource settings that are assigned to a resource pool or virtual machine. We will discuss resource pools in Chapter 9.

- **Check compliance for a profile**   Using this scheduled task, you can compare the configuration of a Host against an established Host Profile. We will discuss Host Profiles in Chapter 8.

View and Manage Tasks and Events

One of the major responsibilities of a system administrator is to monitor her systems for abnormal events. An *event* is basically any action that occurs to an object that is in the vCenter Server's inventory. In vCenter Server you can monitor events from the Tasks & Events window.

To view this window, follow these steps:

1. Launch the vSphere Client and connect to your vCenter Server.

2. Select your vCenter Server in the left-hand frame and select the Tasks & Events tab in the right-hand frame. You should now see the Tasks & Events window as shown in Figure 4-6.

3. Click the Events button to display all of the events or Tasks to display all of the ongoing tasks.

In the Tasks window you can perform the following actions:

- You can review all of the ongoing and recently completed tasks for your entire vCenter Server.

- You can review an individual task to determine who initiated a task, its start time and completion time, and its status.

- You can get more details about a task by double-clicking the individual task.

FIGURE 4-6   The Tasks & Events window

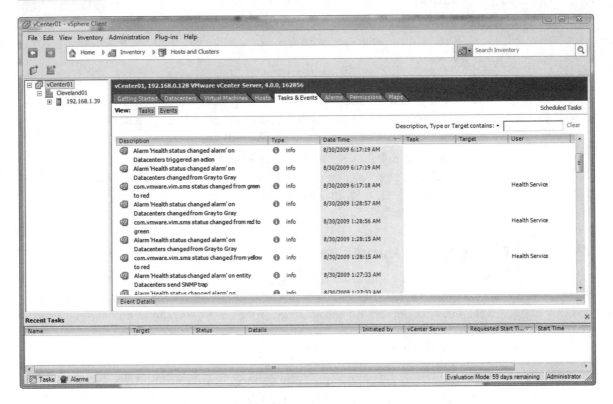

In the Events window you can perform the following actions:

■ You can review all of the events that have occurred for your entire vCenter Server.

■ You can review events that occur to any container object in your vCenter Server by selecting the container in the left-hand frame.

■ You can get more details about an event by double-clicking the event.

■ You can filter the events by entering search terms into the search box at the top right of the Tasks & Events window.

■ You can export the events list by going to the File menu, selecting Export, and then selecting Export Events.

The Tasks & Events window will often be your first stop when troubleshooting issues in your virtual environment. From this window you can get a good idea of everything that is happening in your Datacenters and across your vSphere environment.

At this point you should have a basic understanding of some of the things you can do with vCenter Server. As we go through the remaining chapters, you will continue to add additional functionality and round out your knowledge of vCenter Server and vSphere. In the next section we will talk about restricting access to your vCenter Servers.

CERTIFICATION OBJECTIVE 4.04

Configure Access Control Through vCenter Server

Configuring access control is a very important part of configuring your vCenter Servers. In almost any environment many different users will need to have access to the virtual machines running in the Datacenter. Sometimes these users will have greatly different levels of experience and ability. If some of these less experienced users are given full control of the virtual environment, they could unintentionally cause system outages and other potential problems. To help to avoid this situation, vCenter Server has a built-in access control mechanism that allows the system administrators to assign different users different levels of access. Using a combination of user IDs and roles, administrators can assign users very specific rights to the vCenter Server objects that they need to access and restrict them from having rights to other objects.

In this section we discuss the predefined roles that are included with vCenter Server. We will learn how to edit these predefined roles to better fit our needs and how to create our own custom roles. We will then use these roles to allow and restrict access to objects in our vCenter Server inventory. We will finish the section and this chapter by discussing how privileges propagate down the inventory tree structure. Let's get started by looking at the predefined roles.

Review vCenter Predefined Roles and Privileges

Just like on our ESX Hosts, vCenter includes a number of predefined roles that can be used to assign access to objects in the vCenter Server's inventory. Each of these roles contains a set of privileges. The following roles are predefined in vCenter Server:

- **No Access** The holder of the No Access role has no privileges on the assigned object. He or she cannot view or change anything on the assigned object.

- **Read-Only** The holder of the Read-Only role has the ability to read the properties of the assigned object. He or she can view but cannot change anything on the assigned object.

- **Administrator** The holder of the Administrator role has full privileges to the properties of the assigned object. He or she can view, change, delete, and assign access rights to the properties of the assigned object.

- **Virtual Machine Power User** The holder of the Virtual Machine Power User role has the ability to make hardware changes to the virtual machine that the role is assigned to as well as to create snapshots of the virtual machine.

- **Virtual Machine User** The holder of the Virtual Machine User role has the ability to power virtual machines on and off and access the virtual machine through the console. He or she cannot create snapshots or make hardware changes to the virtual machine.

- **Resource Pool Administrator** The holder of the Resource Pool Administrator role has the ability to create child resource pools under the assigned resource pool. He or she also has the ability to assign virtual machines to the assigned resource pool. We will discuss resource pools in Chapter 9.

- **VMware Consolidated Backup User** This role is used by VMware Consolidated Backup and should not be altered.

- **Datastore Consumer** The holder of the Datastore Consumer role is able to utilize space from a datastore. This role would be used in conjunction with other roles that would require the holder to create addition disk drives or snapshots.

■ **Network Consumer**   The holder of the Network Consumer role is able to assign virtual machines to the virtual networks that the role is assigned to. The holder would also need rights to the virtual machines he or she wishes to assign the network to.

Using these predefined roles, you should be able to assign access control on your vCenter Server to a very granular level. You can allow users to have full control on some virtual machines using the Administrator role, limited access on other virtual machines using the Virtual Machine User role, and absolutely no access on other virtual machines using the No Access role.

e x a m

ⓦ**a t c h**   *For the exam you may see a question that gives you a list of what appear to be roles and asks which is or is not a predefined role in vCenter Server.*

Create, Clone, and Edit vCenter Roles

vCenter Server comes with a decent set of predefined roles, but you may find that you need more customized roles to better fit your environment. There are three ways that you can change the roles that are available in vCenter Server. You can edit an existing role to add or remove privileges. You can create a new role from scratch and assign it the privileges you want it to have. The last way to create a new role is to clone an existing role that is close to the role you would like to have and edit its assigned privileges. We will look at each of these methods in this section.

Edit an Existing Role

While configuring access control on your vCenter Server, you may find that none of the existing roles is exactly what you need but that one of them is very close. You can edit the privileges that are assigned to an existing role to make it a better fit. To edit an existing role, follow these steps:

1. Launch the vSphere Client and connect to your vCenter Server.
2. From the View menu select Administration and then select Roles. You should now see the Roles window as shown in Figure 4-7.

FIGURE 4-7   The Roles window

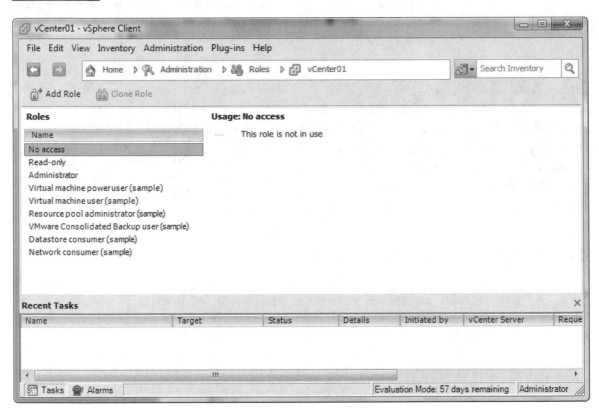

3. Right-click the role that you wish to edit and select Edit Role to enter the Edit Role window as shown in Figure 4-8.
4. From this window check the privileges you wish the role to have and uncheck the privileges you do not want it to have.
5. Click OK to save your changes.

FIGURE 4-8

The Edit Role
window

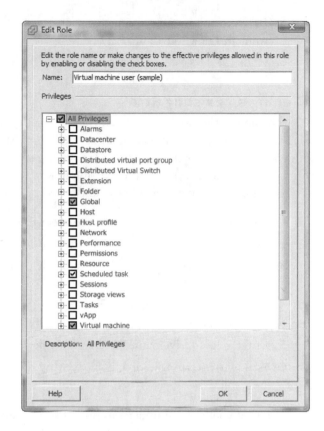

Creating a New Role

While configuring access control on your vCenter Server, you may find that
none of the existing roles is exactly what you need and you want to create a new
role. You can create a new role and assign it privileges that will be unique to your
environment.

To create a new role, follow these steps:

1. Launch the vSphere Client and connect to your vCenter Server.
2. From the View menu select Administration and then select Roles.
3. Click the Add Role button to begin creating a new role.
4. You will be presented with the Add New Role window.

5. In this window enter a name for your new role and check the privileges you want this new role to have.

6. Click OK to save your new role.

Cloning an Existing Role

Cloning an existing role and then editing its privileges is probably the most common way to create a new role in vCenter Server. This method has the advantages of allowing you to customize a role without having to start from scratch and not fundamentally altering any of the existing roles.

To clone an existing role, follow these steps:

1. Launch the vSphere Client and connect to your vCenter Server.

2. From the View menu select Administration and then select Roles.

3. Right-click the role on the left-hand side that you wish to clone and select Clone.

4. A new role will appear named "Clone of . . . ." Right-click this new role and select Rename.

5. Enter a descriptive name for this new role.

6. Follow the steps for editing an existing role to set the privileges for this new role.

Now that you have an understanding of the default roles and know how to create and edit your own roles, let's take a look at how to use these roles to assign rights to users.

on the job

When I am on a client site, I will never edit the settings of an existing predefined role. I always clone an existing role and make my changes to the clone. If I make changes to a predefined role, it could cause issues for the client down the road when they try to use that role and it doesn't do exactly what they expect because I changed it.

Assign Access to vCenter Inventory Objects

In the last few sections we looked at the preconfigured roles in vCenter Server and learned how to create our own custom roles. In this section we will see how to apply these roles to give users access to objects in the vCenter Server inventory. The first step to assigning a user privileges to an object in the vCenter Server inventory is determining which role will give him the privileges he needs without giving him any that he doesn't need. You can do this by looking at the preconfigured roles to see if any are a match. If none of them is a good match, you can create a new role. Once you know the role that you want to assign, follow these steps to give the user privileges to an object:

1. Launch the vSphere Client and connect to your vCenter Server.
2. In the left-hand frame locate the object for which you wish to assign privileges to the user.
3. Right-click the object and select Add Permission. You should now see the Assign Permissions window as shown in Figure 4-9.
4. In the left-hand frame add the user you want to give permissions and in the right-hand frame select the role that you want to assign to the user.
5. Click OK and the user will now have the assigned role to the object.

FIGURE 4-9

The Assign Permissions window

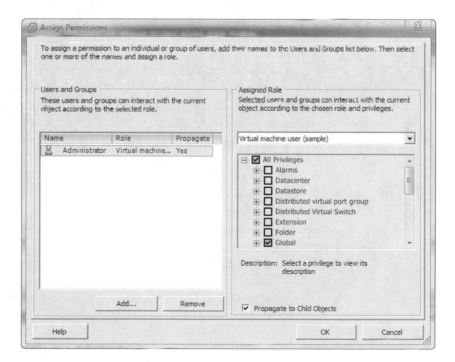

If you have a large number of users that will need the same access to inventory objects you can create a group and include all of the users as members. Roles can be assigned to groups the same way they can be assigned to individual users.

Understanding Privilege Propagation

When you look at the structure of a vCenter Server inventory, it is basically a number of containers (such as Datacenters, Folders, Clusters) that contain other containers and end objects (such as virtual machines). If you are familiar with Active Directory, note that the structure of the vCenter Server inventory is very similar to the Active Directory Organization Unit structure. This containers-inside-of-containers structure can help you to organize your virtual environment and can be used to simplify the assignment of privileges.

In vCenter Server privileges that are assigned to a container can be set to flow down to the objects that are located within the container. This includes other containers that are located within the original container. To set privileges to flow down, make sure to select "Propagate to Child Objects" when adding a privilege. This flow-down method of assigning privileges can be very useful by reducing the number of explicit privileges you need to assign. If you have an administrator that you wish to have full control of your virtual environment, you can simply assign her the Administrator role at the top of the vCenter Server inventory and it will flow down to all of the objects in the inventory. If this flow-down method did not exist, you would need to assign her the Administrator role at each individual object.

When assigning privileges to objects in the vCenter Server inventory, note that assignments to child objects always take precedence to assignments that flow down from above. If a user is assigned the Administrator privilege to a container and the No Access privilege to an object in the container, that user will have No Access to the object. By assigning reduced privileges or No Access to a container, you can stop flow-down privileges from flowing into the container.

At this point you should have a good understanding of how to install and configure a vCenter Server. You should know how to create Datacenters and add Hosts to them. You should also have a basic understanding of how access control is managed in vCenter Server. In the following chapters we will continue to add to your understanding of vCenter Server and vSphere by configuring networking, storage, and virtual machines.

CERTIFICATION SUMMARY

We started this chapter with an introduction to vCenter Server. We looked at the different editions of vCenter Server that are available and the features of each edition. We then talked about Linked Mode Groups and ended the section by looking at the vCenter Server maximums that will need to be memorized for the exam.

In the next section we discussed the installation of vCenter Server and some of its additional modules. We discussed the hardware and database requirements that need to be met before we can install vCenter Server. We then went through the steps of the actual install. Once we had vCenter Server installed, we went ahead and installed vCenter Guided Consolidation, vCenter Update Manager, and vCenter Converter.

In the next section we performed some basic configuration for our vCenter Server. We created a Datacenter and joined an ESX Host to our vCenter Server. We then discussed the various settings that are available on vCenter Server and we looked at the available scheduled tasks.

In the last section we discussed access control on vCenter Server. We looked at the predefined roles that are included with vCenter Server, and we learned how to create our own roles. We then used these roles to give a user permissions to an object in the vCenter Server inventory. We finished the chapter by briefly discussing privilege propagation.

TWO-MINUTE DRILL

Introduction to vCenter Server

❑ vCenter Server provides centralized management for vSphere environments.

❑ vCenter Server for Essentials is included with vSphere Essentials and vSphere Essentials Plus and is designed for small office deployments.

❑ vCenter Server Foundation is limited to managing only three ESX or ESXi Hosts.

❑ vCenter Server Standard has no licensed limit to the number of ESX and ESXi Hosts it can manage.

❑ vCenter Server Standard includes VMware vCenter Orchestrator, which is an automation tool for virtual environments.

❑ vCenter Server Standard includes vCenter Server Linked Mode Groups, which allow multiple vCenter Servers to share their item inventories.

❑ vCenter Server has a maximum number of Hosts of 200 on a 32-bit OS, 300 on a 64-bit OS, and 1000 when using Linked Mode Groups.

❑ vCenter Server has a maximum number of powered-on virtual machines of 2000 on a 32-bit OS, 3000 on a 64-bit OS, and 10,000 when using Linked Mode Groups.

❑ vCenter Server has a maximum number of registered virtual machines of 3000 on a 32-bit OS, 4500 on a 64-bit OS, and 15,000 when using Linked Mode Groups.

❑ vCenter Server Linked Mode Groups have a maximum of 10 vCenter Servers as members.

❑ vCenter Server has a maximum number of concurrent vSphere Client connections of 15 on a 32-bit OS and 30 on a 64-bit OS.

Install vCenter Server and Additional vCenter Modules

❑ vCenter Server has a minimum requirement of 2 CPUs.

❑ vCenter Server has a minimum requirement of a 2.0 GHz Intel or AMD processor.

❏ vCenter Server has a minimum requirement of 3GB of RAM.

❏ vCenter Server has a minimum requirement of 2GB of disk space.

❏ vCenter Server has a minimum requirement of 1 NIC.

❏ vCenter Guided Consolidation is an additional module for vCenter Server that allows an administrator to virtualize an existing physical datacenter.

❏ vCenter Update Manager is an additional module for vCenter Server that can be used by administrators to simplify the process of patch management for ESX Hosts as well as Windows and Linux virtual machines.

❏ vCenter Converter is an additional module for vCenter Server that helps to simplify the migration of physical machines into virtual machines.

Configure and Manage vCenter Server

❏ A Datacenter object in vCenter Server represents your physical datacenter.

❏ "Change the power state of a virtual machine" is a task that can be scheduled in vCenter Server.

❏ "Clone a virtual machine" is a task that can be scheduled in vCenter Server.

❏ "Deploy a virtual machine" is a task that can be scheduled in vCenter Server.

❏ "Migrate a virtual machine" is a task that can be scheduled in vCenter Server.

❏ "Create a virtual machine" is a task that can be scheduled in vCenter Server.

❏ "Make a snapshot of a virtual machine" is a task that can be scheduled in vCenter Server.

❏ "Add a host" is a task that can be scheduled in vCenter Server.

❏ "Change resource settings of resource pool or virtual machine" is a task that can be scheduled in vCenter Server.

❏ "Check compliance for a profile" is a task that can be scheduled in vCenter Server.

❏ Tasks and events can be viewed in the Tasks & Events window using the vSphere Client.

Configure Access Control Through vCenter Server

❑ Access Control in vCenter Server is achieved by matching a user ID to a role.

❑ No Access is a predefined role in vCenter Server.

❑ Read-Only is a predefined role in vCenter Server.

❑ Administrator is a predefined role in vCenter Server.

❑ Virtual Machine Power User is a predefined role in vCenter Server.

❑ Virtual Machine User is a predefined role in vCenter Server.

❑ Resource Pool Administrator is a predefined role in vCenter Server.

❑ VMware Consolidated Backup User is a predefined role in vCenter Server.

❑ Datastore Consumer is a predefined role in vCenter Server.

❑ Network Consumer is a predefined Role in vCenter Server.

❑ Roles can be edited, created from scratch, or cloned.

❑ Privileges can be configured to propagate, or flow down, to child objects.

SELF TEST

The following questions will help you measure your understanding of the material presented in this chapter. Read all the choices carefully and remember that there is only one best answer for each question.

Introduction to vCenter Server

1. Which feature of vCenter Server allows third-party developers to access the vCenter Server?
   A. The vCenter Server Search Engine
   B. The VMware vCenter Web Access Portal
   C. The VMware vCenter APIs and .NET Extension
   D. The vCenter Server Management Server

2. Which feature of vCenter Server allows administrators to search for individual objects that are managed by their vCenter Servers?
   A. The vCenter Server Search Engine
   B. The VMware vCenter Web Access Portal
   C. The VMware vCenter APIs and .NET Extension
   D. The vCenter Server Management Server

3. Which edition of vCenter Server includes VMware vCenter Orchestrator?
   A. vCenter Server for Essentials
   B. vCenter Server Foundation
   C. vCenter Server Standard
   D. vCenter Server Premium

4. What is the maximum number of Hosts that is supported on a 32-bit vCenter Server?
   A. 100
   B. 200
   C. 300
   D. 1000

5. What is the maximum number of vCenter Servers that can be a member of a Linked Mode Group?
   A. 10
   B. 20
   C. 50
   D. 100

Install vCenter Server and Additional vCenter Modules

6. What is the minimum number of CPUs that are required for vCenter Server?
   A. 1
   B. 2
   C. 3
   D. 4

7. What is the minimum amount of RAM that is required for vCenter Server?
   A. 1GB
   B. 2GB
   C. 3GB
   D. 4GB

8. What is the minimum amount of disk storage that is required exclusively for vCenter Server?
   A. 1GB
   B. 2GB
   C. 3GB
   D. 4GB

9. Which of the following database servers is not supported by vCenter Server?
   A. Microsoft SQL Server 2000
   B. Microsoft SQL Server 2005
   C. Microsoft SQL Server 2008
   D. Oracle 11g

10. Which of the following vCenter Server modules can be used to simplify Host patch management?
   A. vCenter Guided Consolidation
   B. vCenter Update Manager
   C. vCenter Converter
   D. vSphere Client

Configure and Manage vCenter Server

11. Under which class of vCenter Server settings can you configure the SMTP Server that is used by vCenter Server?

A. Mail

B. SNMP

C. Ports

D. Timeout Settings

12. Under which class of vCenter Server settings can you configure Community Strings?

A. Mail

B. SNMP

C. Ports

D. Timeout Settings

13. Which of the following is not a scheduled task that is available in vCenter Server?

A. Deploy a virtual machine.

B. Clone a virtual machine.

C. Delete a virtual machine.

D. Create a virtual machine.

14. Which of the following is a scheduled task that is available in vCenter Server?

A. Deploy a host.

B. Add a host.

C. Delete a host.

D. Create a host.

Configure Access Control Through vCenter Server

15. Which of the following is not a predefined role in vCenter Server?

A. Virtual Machine Power User

B. VMware Consolidated Backup User

C. Host Power User

D. Network Consumer

SELF TEST ANSWERS

Introduction to vCenter Server

1. ☑ **C.** The VMware vCenter APIs and .NET Extension are programming extensions that allow third-party developers to develop software that can interact directly with vCenter Server.

☒ **A, B,** and **D** are incorrect. The vCenter Server Search Engine is a search engine that allows administrators to search for individual objects that are managed by their vCenter Servers. The VMware vCenter Web Access Portal is a web-based interface to the vCenter Server that allows administrators to access their vCenter Servers from anywhere using a standard web browser. The vCenter Server Management Server is the vCenter Server Console.

2. ☑ **A.** The vCenter Server Search Engine is a search engine that allows administrators to search for individual objects that are managed by their vCenter Servers.

☒ **B, C,** and **D** are incorrect. The VMware vCenter Web Access Portal is a web-based interface to the vCenter Server that allows administrators to access their vCenter Servers from anywhere using a standard web browser. The VMware vCenter APIs and .NET Extension are programming extensions that allow third-party developers to develop software that can interact directly with vCenter Server. The vCenter Server Management Server is the vCenter Server Console.

3. ☑ **C.** vCenter Server Standard includes VMware vCenter Orchestrator.

☒ **A, B,** and **D** are incorrect. vCenter Server for Essentials and vCenter Server Foundation do not include VMware vCenter Orchestrator. vCenter Server Premium is not a real edition of vCenter Server.

4. ☑ **B.** 200 Hosts are supported on a 32-bit vCenter Server.

☒ **A, C,** and **D** are incorrect. 300 Hosts are supported on a 64-bit vCenter Server. 1000 Hosts are supported in a Linked Mode Group.

5. ☑ **A.** A Linked Mode Group can have a maximum of ten members.

☒ **A, B,** and **D** are incorrect. Ten members is the only possible answer.

Install vCenter Server and Additional vCenter Modules

6. ☑ **B.** vCenter Server requires a minimum of 2 CPUs.

☒ **A, C,** and **D** are incorrect. vCenter Server requires two CPUs and no more.

7. ☑ **C.** vCenter Server requires a minimum of 3GB of RAM.

☒ **A, B,** and **D** are incorrect. vCenter Server requires 3GB of RAM; more may be helpful.

8. ☑ **B.** vCenter Server requires a minimum of 2GB of disk storage.

☒ **A, C,** and **D** are incorrect. vCenter Server requires 2GB of disk storage in addition to the OS.

9. ☑ **A.** Microsoft SQL Server 2000 is not supported by vCenter Server.

   ☒ **B, C,** and **D** are incorrect. Microsoft SQL Server 2005 and 2008 are supported by vCenter Server. Oracle 11g is also supported by vCenter Server.

10. ☑ **B.** vCenter Update Manager is used to simplify Host patch management.

    ☒ **A, C,** and **D** are incorrect. vCenter Guided Consolidation is used to help virtualize existing physical environments. vCenter Converter is used to convert individual physical servers into virtual machines. The vSphere Client is used to connect to ESX Hosts and vCenter Servers.

Configure and Manage vCenter Server

11. ☑ **A.** Under the Mail class of settings you can configure the SMTP Server and Mail Send accounts that are used by vCenter Server.

    ☒ **B, C,** and **D** are incorrect. Under the SNMP class of settings you can configure SNMP Receiver URLs, Ports, and Community Strings. Under the Ports class of settings you can configure the HTTP and HTTPS ports that will be used by vCenter Server. Under the Timeout Settings class of settings you can configure the Client Connection timeouts for both Normal and Long operations.

12. ☑ **B.** Under the SNMP class of settings you can configure SNMP Receiver URLs, Ports, and Community Strings.

    ☒ **A, C,** and **D** are incorrect. Under the Mail class of settings you can configure the SMTP Server and Mail Send accounts that are used by vCenter Server. Under the Ports class of settings you can configure the HTTP and HTTPS ports that will be used by vCenter Server. Under the Timeout Settings class of settings you can configure the Client Connection timeouts for both Normal and Long operations.

13. ☑ **C.** Delete a virtual machine is not a scheduled task that is available in vCenter Server.

    ☒ **A, B,** and **D** are incorrect. Deploy a virtual machine, clone a virtual machine, and create a virtual machine are all scheduled tasks that are available in vCenter Server.

14. ☑ **B.** Add a host is a scheduled task that is available in vCenter Server.

    ☒ **A, C,** and **D** are incorrect. Deploy a host, delete a host, and create a host are not scheduled tasks that are available in vCenter Server.

Configure Access Control Through vCenter Server

15. ☑ **C.** Host Power User is not a predefined role in vCenter Server.

    ☒ **A, B,** and **D** are incorrect. Virtual Machine Power User, VMware Consolidated Backup User, and Network Consumer are all predefined roles in vCenter Server.

5

Understanding Networking and Virtual Switches on ESX and ESXi Servers

Welcome to Chapter 5. In this chapter we will look at how networking is implemented in a vSphere environment. We will start the chapter by creating and configuring virtual switches and port groups. We will then review the NIC teaming and security policies that can be applied to virtual switches. Once we understand virtual switches, we will look at a vSphere feature called vNetwork Distributed Switches, which allows you to create switches at the vCenter level and attach Hosts to them. We will then end the chapter by discussing ESX Host networking and how to configure the ESX/ESXi management network. Let's start the chapter by taking a look at virtual switches.

CERTIFICATION OBJECTIVE 5.01

Understand and Configure Virtual Switches

Virtual switches perform the same function for virtual machines that physical switches perform for physical servers. They are used to route virtual machine traffic between virtual machines and to other physical machines on the network. In this section we will discuss the capabilities and limitations of virtual switches. We will look at the different NIC teaming and security policies that can be applied to a virtual switch, and then we will create and delete a virtual switch. We will end the section by adding physical NICs to a virtual switch to allow it to communicate with the outside network.

Virtual Switch, NIC, and Port Maximums

Before we can begin creating and working with virtual switches and port groups, we will need to understand their limitations under vSphere. VMware refers to these limitations as Virtual Switch and Port Group maximums. The following table lists the maximums for virtual switches, NICs, and port groups. You will need to memorize these for the exam.

Device	Maximum
Broadcom bnx2 1GB Ethernet port	16
Broadcom bnx2x 10GB Ethernet port	4

Device	Maximum
Broadcom tg3 1GB Ethernet port	32
Intel e1000 NIC Ethernet port	32
Intel e1000e NIC Ethernet port	32
Intel igb 1GB Ethernet port	16
Intel ixgbe Oplin 10GB Ethernet port	4
Neterion s2io 10GB Ethernet port	4
NetXen nx_nic 10GB Ethernet port	4
Nvidia forcedeth 1GB Ethernet port	2
Virtual Switch ports per Host	4096
Virtual Switch ports per switch	4088
Port groups per switch	512
Switches per Host	248

on the
Öob

It is very common to use NIC cards that have multiple network connections in ESX Hosts to increase the number of connections the server can support. Be very careful when using these types of NICs in conjunction with NIC teaming to make sure that the loss of a single NIC card would not bring down an entire virtual switch.

Now that you understand the networking maximums for vSphere, let's go ahead and look at some other networking features.

INSIDE THE EXAM

Hardware Maximums

To test your knowledge of vSphere Networking, you should expect to see at least one or two questions that ask about networking maximums. These values will need to be memorized to give you the best chance of passing the exam.

NIC Teaming Policies

NIC teaming is the ability to use more than one network adapter to increase the bandwidth or availability of your network connection for a virtual switch. A virtual switch on a ESX Host can increase network throughput by allowing load balancing across a NIC team. The following load-balancing policies are available for a virtual switch:

- **Route based on the originating virtual port ID**   Using this method, the route is based on the port ID of the virtual machine that is sending the packet. This can be a useful setting because it works for all protocols, but it can be inefficient if the virtual machines on a Host have very different throughput requirements.

- **Route based on IP hash**   Using this method, the route is based on the IP hash of the packet that is being sent. This can be useful if the virtual machines are communicating with TCP/IP, but if they are using a different protocol, the routing will default to round-robin assignments of the network connections, which can be inefficient.

- **Route based on source MAC hash**   Using this method, the route is based on the MAC address of the virtual machine that is sending the packet.

- **Use explicit failover order**   This method is not so much load balancing as it is failover. Under this method you assign a specific order in which the NICs should be used if the current NIC fails. This can be useful to increase reliability for the virtual switch, but it does not increase bandwidth.

vSwitch Security Policies

Just as you can set security settings on the ports of a physical switch, you can do the same with a virtual switch. The following security policies are available for a virtual switch:

- **Promiscuous Mode**   If this setting is set to Reject and the NIC of the guest is set to promiscuous mode, the guest will still receive only the packets that are intended for it. If it is set to Accept and the NIC of the guest is set to promiscuous mode, the guest will receive all packets that are transmitted through the switch.

- **MAC Address Changes**   If this setting is set to Reject and the guest has a different MAC address than what is specified in its .vmx file, the packet will be dropped. If it is set to Accept and the guest has a different MAC address than what is specified in its .vmx file, the packet will be accepted.
- **Forged Transmits**   If this setting is set to Reject, any outbound packet with a different MAC address than what is set on the adapter will be dropped. If it is set to Accept, then all packets will be forwarded without any inspection.

vSwitch Traffic Shaping Policies

In addition to NIC teaming and security policies, virtual switches also can be configured to provide a limited degree of outbound network traffic shaping. The following traffic shaping policies are available for a virtual switch:

- **Average Bandwidth**   The Average Bandwidth setting determines the number of bits per second that will be allowed through a port averaged over time.
- **Burst Size**   The Burst Size setting determines the maximum number of bytes that a port can transmit in a single burst.
- **Peak Bandwidth**   The Peak Bandwidth setting determines the maximum number of bits per second a port can transmit when it is sending a burst of traffic.

Now that you understand the NIC teaming, security, and traffic shaping policies for virtual switches, let's go ahead and create a new virtual switch.

Create and Delete Virtual Switches

The next step toward understanding virtual switches is to go ahead and create one. To create a new virtual switch, follow these steps:

1. Launch the vSphere Client and connect to your ESX Host.
2. In the navigation bar select Home | Inventory.

3. Select the Host in the left frame and click the Configuration tab in the right.

4. Select Networking from the Hardware box on the left.

5. Click Add Networking to launch the Add Network Wizard.

6. You will be prompted to select a Connection Type. Select the radio button next to Virtual Machine to create a vSwitch to handle virtual machine network traffic. We will look at the other options—VMkernel and Service Console—later in the chapter. Click Next to continue.

7. On the next screen select the radio button next to Create A Virtual Switch and click Next to continue.

8. You are prompted to enter a Network Label and a VLAN ID for the new switch. The Network Label is a name for the virtual switch, and the VLAN ID is optional and depends on your physical switch network. For this example enter a Network Label and click Next to continue.

9. You are presented with a summary screen. Click Finish to continue and create the new virtual switch. You can see vSwitch1 in Figure 5-1.

Now that you know how to create virtual switches, let's look at how to delete a virtual switch.

To delete an existing virtual switch, follow these steps:

1. Launch the vSphere Client and connect to your ESX Host.

2. In the navigation bar select Home | Inventory.

3. Select the Host in the left frame and click the Configuration tab in the right.

4. Select Networking from the Hardware box on the left.

5. Click Remove to the right of the virtual switch you wish to delete.

6. You will be prompted to confirm the deletion. Click Yes to continue and delete the virtual switch. Be careful when deleting a vSwitch that contains the port group that is being used for the Service Console of the management network, since this can cause you to lose connectivity to your Host.

FIGURE 5-1

The newly
created vSwitch1

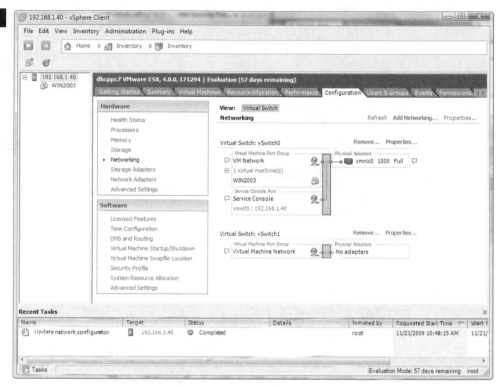

Create Ports and Port Groups

Virtual ports are nearly identical to physical ports on a switch. They are the logical connections for a virtual machine to access the network. *Port groups* are collections of ports that can be configured as a single entity. Each vSwitch can have a maximum of 512 port groups.

To create a new virtual machine port group to a virtual switch, follow these steps:

1. Launch the vSphere Client and connect to your ESX Host.
2. In the navigation bar select Home | Inventory.
3. Select the Host in the left frame and click the Configuration tab in the right.
4. Select Networking from the Hardware box on the left.

5. Click Add Networking to launch the Add Network Wizard.

6. You will be prompted to select a Connection Type. Click the radio button for Virtual Machine to create a virtual switch for virtual machines. Click Next to continue.

7. On the next screen select the radio button next to the virtual switch on which you want to create the port group and click Next to continue.

8. You are prompted to enter a Network Label and a VLAN ID for the new switch. The Network Label is a name for the virtual switch, and the VLAN ID is optional and depends on your physical switch network. For this example enter a Network Label and click Next to continue.

9. You are presented with a summary screen. Click Finish to continue and create the new virtual switch. Figure 5-2 shows the newly created port group Virtual Machine Network.

FIGURE 5-2	

The newly created Virtual Machine Network port group

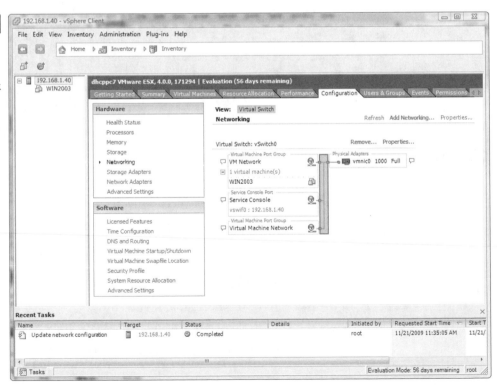

Assign Physical NICs to a Virtual Switch

A virtual switch can be used without any physical NICs assigned to it, allowing virtual machines on that same virtual switch to communicate with each other, but the real power of virtual switches is when they can communicate with other networks. The first step to allowing them to communicate with other networks is to assign one or more physical NICs to the virtual switch.

To assign a physical NIC to a virtual switch, follow these steps:

1. Launch the vSphere Client and connect to your ESX Host.
2. In the navigation bar select Home | Inventory.
3. Select the Host in the left frame and click the Configuration tab in the right.
4. Select Networking from the Hardware box on the left.
5. Click Properties to the right of the virtual switch you wish to configure.
6. You will be presented with the Properties window for the virtual switch. Click the Network Adapters tab and click Add.
7. You will be presented with a list of the available NICs on the ESX Host. Add a check next to the NICs you want to assign to the virtual switch and click Next to continue.

Modify vSwitch NIC Teaming and Failover Policies

Now that you understand how to create new virtual switches, let's take a look at how to modify the NIC teaming and failover policies that were introduced earlier in the chapter.

To modify NIC teaming and failover policies for a virtual switch, follow these steps:

1. Launch the vSphere Client and connect to your ESX Host.
2. In the navigation bar select Home | Inventory.
3. Select the Host in the left frame and click the Configuration tab in the right.
4. Select Networking from the Hardware box on the left.

5. Click Properties to the right of the virtual switch you wish to configure.

6. You will be presented with the Properties window for the virtual switch. Select the virtual switch and click Edit.

7. You will be presented with another Properties window for the virtual switch. Select the NIC Teaming tab.

8. You will be presented with the NIC Teaming tab as shown in Figure 5-3.

9. Under Load Balancing, select the NIC teaming method you wish to use. The options are "Route based on the originating virtual port ID," "Route based on IP hash," "Route based on source MAC hash," and "Use explicit failover order." These were discussed earlier in the chapter.

10. Under Network Failover Detection, select the method that the virtual switch will use to detect a network failure. The options are Link Status Only, which only uses the status of the links to determine if they have failed, or Beacon Probing, which uses active probing to determine if a link has failed.

11. Under Notify Switches, select Yes or No. Some switches will isolate a failed port if they are notified that it has failed.

12. Under Failback, select Yes or No. If you select Yes, the system will try to fail back to a network adapter once it has determined that it is no longer in a failed state. If you select No the system will continue to use the new network adapter and will not attempt to fail back.

13. Under Failover Order, select the explicit order in which network adapters will be used in the event of a failure.

14. Once you have set the NIC teaming and failover policies you want, click OK to continue.

15. You will be presented with the Properties windows. Click Close to exit.

on the *Job*

It is a best practice to set Failback to No if the port group is being used for IP-based storage. Servers can occasionally suffer a condition known as NIC flapping, where a NIC repeatedly fails and then recovers. If Failback is set to Yes, this condition can cause very undesirable results.

FIGURE 5-3

The virtual switch
NIC Teaming
settings tab

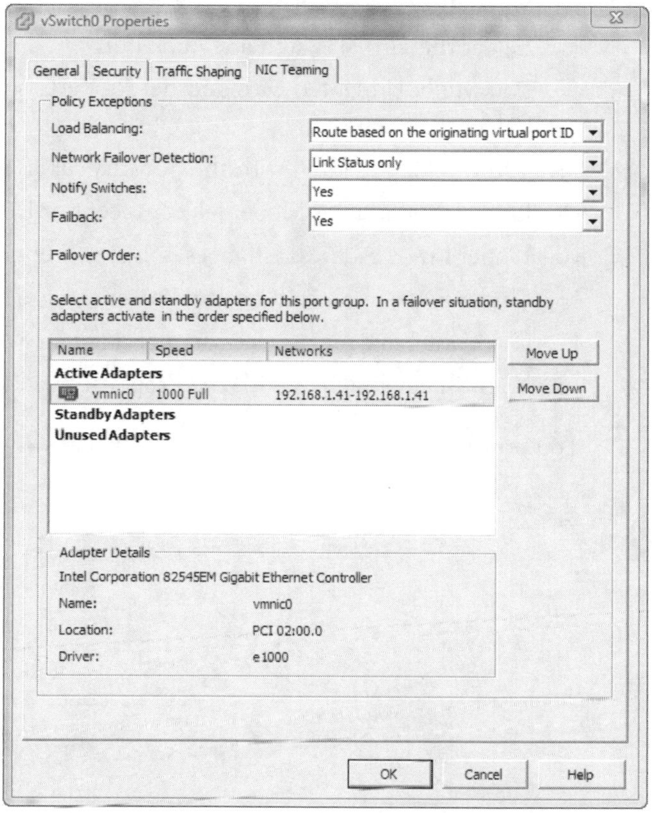

Modify vSwitch Security Policies

Now that we have modified the NIC teaming and failover policies, let's modify the security policies for a virtual switch that we introduced earlier in the chapter.

To modify security policies and VLAN settings for a virtual switch, follow these steps:

1. Launch the vSphere Client and connect to your ESX Host.
2. In the navigation bar select Home | Inventory.
3. Select the Host in the left frame and click the Configuration tab in the right.
4. Select Networking from the Hardware box on the left.
5. Click Properties to the right of the virtual switch you wish to configure.

6. You will be presented with the Properties window for the virtual switch. Select the virtual switch and click Edit.

7. You will be presented with another Properties window for the virtual switch. Select the Security tab.

8. You will be presented with the Security tab as shown in Figure 5-4.

9. Under Promiscuous Mode, select Accept or Reject.

10. Under MAC Address Changes, select Accept or Reject.

11. Under Forged Transmits, select Accept or Reject.

12. Once you have set the Security policies you want, click OK to continue.

13. You will be presented with the Properties windows. Click Close to exit.

You now have a good understanding of virtual switches on ESX Hosts.

FIGURE 5-4

The virtual switch Security settings tab

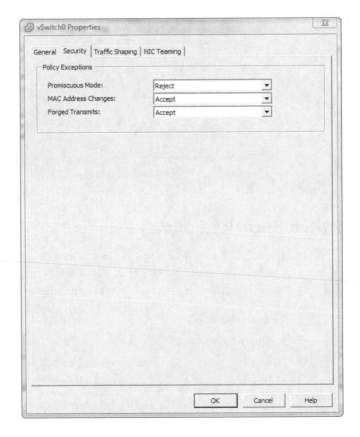

CERTIFICATION OBJECTIVE 5.02

Understand and Configure vNetwork Distributed Switches

A vNetwork Distributed Switch is a virtual device that exists at the vCenter level. It allows a single point of administration for the virtual networking for all of the Hosts in a Datacenter. By using vNetwork Distributed Switches, administrators will no longer need to manage networking on individual ESX Hosts and can reduce the deployment time for new ESX Hosts.

vNetwork Distributed Switch Maximums

Before we can begin creating and working with vNetwork Distributed Switches, we will need to understand their limitations under vSphere. VMware refers to these limitations as vNetwork Distributed Switch maximums. The following table lists the maximums for vNetwork Distributed Switches. You will need to memorize these for the exam.

Device	Maximum
Distributed vNetwork Switch Ports per vCenter	6000
Distributed Port Groups per vCenter	512
Distributed Switches per vCenter	16
Hosts per Distributed Switch	64

Now that you understand the networking maximums for vNetwork Distributed Switches, let's go ahead and create a new vNetwork Distributed Switch.

Create and Modify a vNetwork Distributed Switch

The next step toward understanding vNetwork Distributed Switches is to go ahead and create one.

To create a new vNetwork Distributed Switch, follow these steps:

1. Launch the vSphere Client and connect to your vCenter Server.

2. In the navigation bar select Home | Inventory | Networking.

3. Right-click the Datacenter where you want to create the new vNetwork Distributed Switch in the left frame and select New vNetwork Distributed Switch.

4. You will be presented with the Create vNetwork Distributed Switch Wizard. On this screen enter a name for the new vNetwork Distributed Switch and select the number of dvUplink ports that will be allowed. dvUplink ports specify the maximum number of network connections any single Host can have to the vNetwork Distributed Switch. Leave this at the default and click Next to continue.

5. You are prompted to decide if you want to add Hosts now or later. We will add Hosts later, so select Add Later and click Next to continue.

6. You are prompted to decide if you want a default port group to be created on the new vNetwork Distributed Switch. The default is to automatically create the default port group. Accept the default and click Finish to exit and create the new vNetwork Distributed Switch. Two vNetwork Distributed Switches, dvSwitch and dvSwitch2, are shown in Figure 5-5.

Create and Modify Uplink Group and dvPort Group Settings

A large number of settings can be configured for uplink and dvPort groups. vNetwork Distributed Switches have the same NIC teaming and security policies as standard virtual switches. They also have the same traffic shaping policies, except that vNetwork Distributed Switches are able to perform traffic shaping on both incoming and outgoing traffic. Incoming network traffic is referred to as *ingress traffic*, and outgoing network traffic is referred to as *egress traffic*.

FIGURE 5-5 The vNetwork Distributed Switches dvSwitch and dvSwitch2

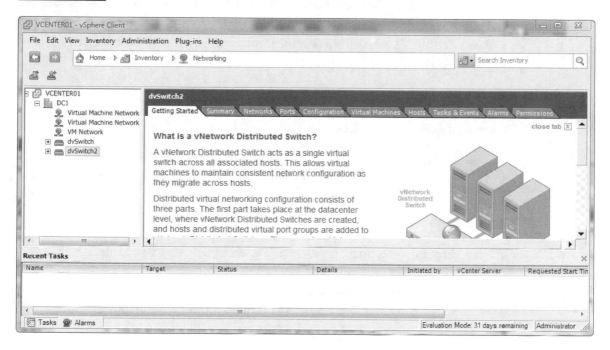

In addition to the policies that they share with standard virtual switches, vNetwork Distributed Switches also have a few unique policies. One of these is the VLAN policy. This policy controls how the vNetwork Distributed Switch handles VLANs; it can have the following settings:

- **None** If this setting is selected, the vNetwork Distributed Switch will not use a VLAN.
- **VLAN** If this setting is selected, you will be prompted to enter a VLAN number and the vNetwork Distributed Switch will use the VLAN.

- **VLAN Trunking** If this setting is selected, you will be prompted to enter a VLAN trunk range and the vNetwork Distributed Switch will use the VLANs from the range.
- **Private VLAN** If this setting is selected, you will be prompted to select a private VLAN and the vNetwork Distributed Switch will use the private VLAN.

Another unique set of policies is found under Advanced. Under Advanced you can configure the following settings:

- **Override port policies** If this setting is selected, dvPort group settings can be configured to be overridden on a per-port level. You will be presented with a list of port group policies that you can individually allow to be overridden. These settings are: Block Port, Traffic Shaping, Vendor Configuration, VLAN, DVUplink Teaming, and Security Policy.
- **Live Port Moving** If this setting is selected, ports will be able to be moved even if they are being used.
- **Configure reset at disconnect** If this setting is selected, a dvPort will return to the configuration of the dvPort Group when it is disconnected from a virtual machine and any per-port overrides will be lost.

To modify Uplink Group and dvPort Group Settings, follow these steps:

1. Launch the vSphere Client and connect to your vCenter Server.
2. In the navigation bar select Home | Inventory | Networking.
3. Expand the vNetwork Distributed Switch that contains the Uplink Group or dvPort group that you want to edit.
4. Right-click the Uplink Group or dvPort group that you want to edit and select Edit Settings from the pop-up menu.
5. You will be presented with the dvSwitch Settings window as shown in Figure 5-6. Make any policy changes that you wish on this window and click OK to save the changes and exit.

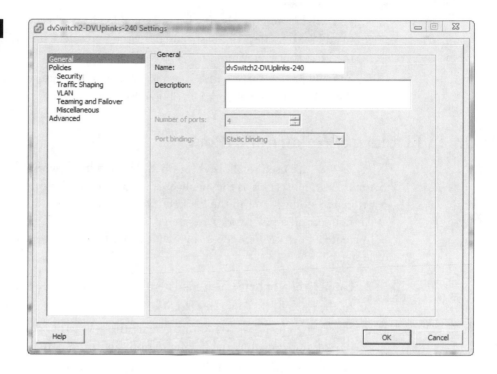

FIGURE 5-6

The dvSwitch
Settings window

Add an ESX Host to a vNetwork Distributed Switch

Now that we have a fully configured vNetwork Distributed Switch, the next step is to add an ESX Host to it. This will allow us to manage networking for the ESX Host at the Datacenter level.

To create a new vNetwork Distributed Switch, follow these steps:

1. Launch the vSphere Client and connect to your vCenter Server.

2. In the navigation bar select Home | Inventory | Networking.

3. Right-click the vNetwork Distributed Switch that you want to add a Host to and select Add Host.

4. You will be presented with a list of available Hosts. Select the Host you wish to add to the vNetwork Distributed Switch and select the NIC or NICs on the Host that you want to use. Click Next to continue.

5. You will be presented with a summary screen. Click Finish to exit and add the Host to the vNetwork Distributed Switch.

Add and Delete a VMkernel dvPort

VMkernel ports are used to allow vMotion and to attach network-based storage to ESX and ESXi Hosts and as the management port for ESXi Hosts. We will cover vMotion and storage later in the book, but for now you should know how to create a VMkernel port on a vNetwork Distributed Switch.

To create a new VMkernel port on a vNetwork Distributed Switch, follow these steps:

1. Launch the vSphere Client and connect to your vCenter Server.

2. In the navigation bar select Home | Inventory | Hosts And Clusters.

3. Select the Host that you want to create the VMkernel port for in the left-hand frame and click the Configuration tab in the right-hand frame.

4. Select Networking from the Hardware box, click the Distributed Virtual Switch from the view menu, and click Manage Virtual Adapters.

5. You will be presented with the Manage Virtual Adapters window. Click Add to begin adding a new VMkernel port.

6. You will be presented with the Creation Type window. Select New Virtual Adapter and click Next to continue.

7. You will be presented with the Virtual Adapter Type window. Select VMkernel and click Next to continue.

8. You will be presented with the Connection Settings window. Select a port group on the dvSwitch where you want to create the new VMkernel port and click Next to continue.

9. You will be presented with the VMkernel | IP Connection Settings window. In this window either enter the IP information for the VMkernel port or select Obtain IP Settings Automatically and click Next to continue.

10. You will be presented with a summary screen. Click Finish to exit and create the new VMkernel port.

Migrate a Virtual Machine to a vNetwork Distributed Switch

Now that we have created a new vNetwork Distributed Switch, we may want to move some of our existing virtual machines to it.

To migrate an existing virtual machine to a vNetwork Distributed Switch, follow these steps:

1. Launch the vSphere Client and connect to your vCenter Server.
2. In the navigation bar select Home | Inventory | Networking.
3. From the Inventory drop-down menu select Distributed Virtual Switch and then Migrate Virtual Switch Networking. You will be presented with the Migrate Virtual Machine Networking window.
4. From the Source Network drop-down select the virtual machine network that contains the virtual machine you wish to migrate.
5. From the Destination Network drop-down select the vNetwork Distributed Switch that you wish to migrate to.
6. Click Show Virtual Machines to display a list of the virtual machines that are available on the source network.
7. Put a check in the check box next to each virtual machine that you wish to migrate and click OK to exit and migrate the virtual machines.

CERTIFICATION OBJECTIVE 5.03

Understand and Configure the ESX/ESXi Management Network

In this section we will discuss the IP configuration of an ESX Host and the ESX/ESXi management network. We will also look at ways to increase the availability of the Service Console by adding multiple connections to it. Just like any other server that uses TCP/IP as its communication protocol, an ESX Host must have a properly configured IP address, subnet mask, default gateway, and DNS server. Many companies elect to put the management interface for their ESX Hosts on a different subnet than they use for virtual machines. This network, called the

ESX/ESXi management network, can help to isolate the ESX and ESXi Hosts from the rest of the network and increase security for the Hosts.

Modify the Service Console's IP Settings

Sometimes it is necessary to change the IP settings of the Service Console. This can happen if you need to move the ESX Host from one subnet to another.

To change the IP Settings of the Service Console, follow these steps:

1. Disconnect and remove the Host from vCenter.
2. Log in to the ESX Host console as root.
3. Stop the network service by issuing the following command: **service network stop**.
4. Change the IP address of the Host by issuing the following command: **esxcfg-vswif -i IP_Address -n Net_Mask vswif0**, where *IP_Address* is the new IP address and *Net_Mask* is the new subnet mask.
5. If the Host is moving to a new subnet, you will need to edit the file /etc/sysconfig/network and change the default gateway.
6. Restart the network service by issuing the following command: **service network start**.
7. Re-add the Host to vCenter.

Configure Service Console Availability

In many instances you may be required to manage ESX Hosts that are physically located at a remote location. In these instances it is very important that you have guaranteed IP connectivity to the Service Console of these Hosts. One way to increase the availability of the Service Console is to create a second Service Console port group on a different virtual switch than the first. This will give you two points of access to the Service Console.

To add a Service Console Port Group for an ESX Host, follow these steps:

1. Launch the vSphere Client and connect to your ESX Host.
2. In the navigation bar select Home | Inventory.
3. Select the Host in the left frame and click the Configuration tab in the right.

4. Select Networking from the Hardware box on the left.

5. Click Add Networking to launch the Add Network Wizard.

6. You will be prompted to select a Connection Type. Click the radio button for Service Console to create a port group for Host Management.

7. You will be prompted to select the virtual switch you want to create the port group on. Select a virtual switch and click Next to continue.

8. You will be prompted to enter a Network Label for the port group. Enter a label and click Next to continue.

9. You will be prompted to enter an IP Address for the Service Console connection. Enter an IP Address or use DHCP to assign an address automatically. Click Next to continue.

10. You will be presented with a summary screen. Click Finish to create the new Service Console connection and exit.

on the *Job*

Since many administrators are required to manage virtual infrastructures that are physically located in remote datacenters, it is very important that they be able to reach these servers over the network. Having multiple Service Console port connections increases their ability to reach the Hosts even if there is a single network failure. These connections are also used for VMware HA, and redundancy in this network is considered a best practice.

Configure the DNS and Routing Settings for an ESX Host

Changes to your network may require you to change the DNS Servers or Default Gateway for your ESX Hosts. You can edit these settings for an ESX Host either by connecting to it with the vSphere Client or by connecting to the vCenter Server with the vSphere Client.

To configure the DNS settings of an ESX Host, follow these steps:

1. Launch the vSphere Client and connect to your vCenter Server or to the ESX Host.

2. In the navigation bar select Home | Inventory | Hosts and Clusters if you connected to the VCenter Server and Home | Inventory if you connected to the ESX Host.

3. Select the Host that you want to modify in the left-hand frame and click the Configuration tab in the right-hand frame.

4. Select DNS and Routing from the Software box and click Properties. You will be presented with the DNS And Routing Configuration window.

5. Select the DNS Configuration tab and you will see the DNS Configuration window as shown in Figure 5-7.

6. In this window you can configure a preferred and alternate DNS server or you can elect to have your DHCP server automatically assign DNS servers for the Host. Once you have made these settings, click OK to save your changes.

To configure Routing settings of an ESX Host, follow these steps:

1. Launch the vSphere Client and connect to your vCenter Server or to the ESX Host.

2. In the navigation bar select Home | Inventory | Hosts And Clusters if you connected to the VCenter Server and Home | Inventory if you connected to the ESX Host.

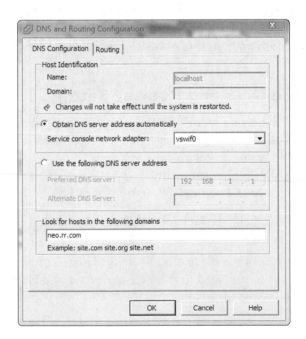

FIGURE 5-7

The DNS Configuration window for an ESX Host

FIGURE 5-8

The Routing
window for an
ESX Host

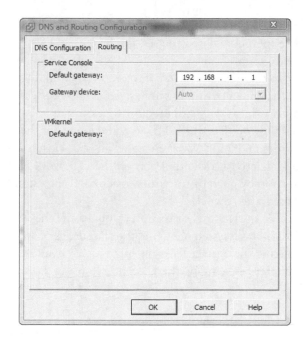

3. Select the Host that you want to modify in the left-hand frame and click the Configuration tab in the right-hand frame.

4. Select DNS And Routing from the Software box and click Properties. You will be presented with the DNS And Routing Configuration window.

5. Select the Routing tab and you will see the Routing window as shown in Figure 5-8.

6. In this window you can configure the default Gateway for the Service Console and for the VMkernel. Once you have made these settings, click OK to save your changes.

CERTIFICATION SUMMARY

We started this chapter with an introduction to standard virtual switches and port groups and discussed the maximums that are associated with them. Once you understood the maximums, we looked at the different NIC teaming, security, and traffic shaping policies that are associated with virtual switches and port groups. We then completed the section by creating and configuring a virtual switch and a port group.

In the next section we discussed vNetwork Distributed Switches. Just as we did with standard virtual switches, we discussed the maximums that are associated with vNetwork Distributed Switches and distributed port groups. We then created a vNetwork Distributed Switch and looked at the various policies that can be configured for it. We then added an ESX Host to the Distributed Switch and created and deleted a VMkernel port on the vNetwork Distributed Switch. We ended the section by migrating a virtual machine from a standard virtual switch to a vNetwork Distributed Switch.

We started the last section by discussing the ESX/ESXi management network. We then discussed changing the IP settings of an ESX Host's Service Console and making the Service Console more highly available. We ended the section and the chapter by changing the DNS and Routing settings for an ESX Host.

TWO-MINUTE DRILL

Understand and Configure Virtual Switches

❑ A virtual switch performs the same functions for virtual machines that a physical switch performs for physical servers.

❑ An ESX Host can have a maximum of 16 Broadcom bnx2 1GB NICs.

❑ An ESX Host can have a maximum of 4 Broadcom bnx2x 10GB NICs.

❑ An ESX Host can have a maximum of 32 Broadcom tg3 1GB NICs.

❑ An ESX Host can have a maximum of 32 Intel e1000 NICs.

❑ An ESX Host can have a maximum of 32 Intel e1000e NICs.

❑ An ESX Host can have a maximum of 16 Intel igb 1GB NICs.

❑ An ESX Host can have a maximum of 4 Intel ixgbe Oplin 10GB NICs.

❑ An ESX Host can have a maximum of 4 Neterion s2io 10GB NICs.

❑ An ESX Host can have a maximum of 4 NetXen nx_nic 10GB NICs.

❑ An ESX Host can have a maximum of 2 Nvidia forcedeth 1GB NICs.

❑ An ESX Host can have a maximum of 4096 virtual switch ports.

❑ A virtual switch can have a maximum of 4088 virtual switch ports.

❑ A virtual switch can have a maximum of 512 port groups.

❑ An ESX Host can have a maximum of 248 virtual switches.

❑ Under the NIC teaming policy "Route based on the originating virtual port ID," the route is based on the port ID of the virtual machine that is sending the packet.

❑ Under the NIC teaming policy "Route based on IP hash," the route is based on the IP hash of the packet that is being sent.

❑ Under the NIC teaming policy "Route based on source MAC hash," the route is based on the MAC address of the virtual machine that is sending the packet.

❑ Under the NIC teaming policy "Use explicit failover order," you assign a specific order in which the NICs should be used if the current NIC fails.

❏ If the security policy Promiscuous Mode is set to Accept and the Guest NIC is set to promiscuous mode, the Guest will see all of the traffic on the network switch.

❏ If the security policy MAC Address Changes is set to Reject and the guest has a different MAC address than what is specified in its .vmx file, the packet will be dropped.

❏ If the security policy Forged Transmits is set to Reject, any outbound packet with a different MAC address than what is set on the adapter will be dropped.

❏ The following traffic shaping policies can be configured for outbound traffic on a virtual switch: Average Bandwidth, Burst Size, and Peak Bandwidth.

Understand and Configure vNetwork Distributed Switches

❏ A vNetwork Distributed Switch is a virtual device that exists at the vCenter level.

❏ There can be a maximum of 6000 Distributed vNetwork Switch ports per vCenter.

❏ There can be a maximum of 512 Distributed Port groups per vCenter.

❏ There can be a maximum of 16 Distributed Switches per vCenter.

❏ There can be a maximum of 64 Hosts per Distributed Virtual Switch.

❏ A Distributed Virtual Switch can perform traffic shaping on both inbound and outbound network traffic.

❏ A Distributed Virtual Switch and Distributed port group can have the following VLAN settings: None, VLAN, VLAN Trunking, Private VLAN.

Understand and Configure the ESX/ESXi Management Network

❏ The ESX/ESXi management network is a separate network for managing ESX and ESXi Hosts.

❏ The Service Console's IP address is modified from the Host's console.

❏ Add additional Service Console ports to increase the availability of the Service Console.

SELF TEST

The following questions will help you measure your understanding of the material presented in this chapter. Read all the choices carefully and remember that there is only one best answer for each question.

Understand and Configure Virtual Switches

1. What is the maximum number of Intel e1000 NICs per ESX Host?
   A. 4
   B. 16
   C. 32
   D. 64

2. What is the maximum number of virtual switches per ESX Host?
   A. 24
   B. 248
   C. 512
   D. 1024

3. What is the maximum number of port groups per virtual switch?
   A. 64
   B. 128
   C. 256
   D. 512

4. Which virtual switch NIC teaming policy allows you to select the order in which NICs will be used?
   A. Route based on the originating port ID
   B. Route based on IP hash
   C. Route based on source MAC hash
   D. Use explicit failover order

5. Which of the following is not a configurable security policy on a virtual switch?
   A. Promiscuous Mode
   B. MAC Address Changes
   C. Host Name Conflict
   D. Forged Transmits

Understand and Configure vNetwork Distributed Switches

6. What is the maximum number of distributed switches per vCenter?

A. 4

B. 16

C. 32

D. 64

7. What is the maximum number of distributed port groups per vCenter?

A. 64

B. 256

C. 512

D. 1024

8. What is the maximum number of Hosts that can be connected to a distributed switch?

A. 32

B. 64

C. 128

D. 256

9. Which Distributed Virtual Switch VLAN policy requires you to enter a range of VLAN IDs?

A. None

B. VLAN

C. VLAN Trunking

D. Private VLAN

10. Which of the following virtual switch port types can be used to attach network-based storage to an ESX Host?

A. VMkernel port

B. Virtual Machine port

C. Service Console port

D. None of the above

Understand and Configure the ESX/ESXi Management Network

11. Which of the following commands is used to stop the network service on an ESX Host?

   A. net stop

   B. service network stop

   C. network stop

   D. network service stop

12. In which configuration file on an ESX Host can you configure the default gateway?

   A. /etc/sysconfig/network

   B. /etc/network/tcp

   C. /system32/network

   D. /system32/network

SELF TEST ANSWERS

Understand and Configure Virtual Switches

1. ☑ **C.** An ESX Host can have a maximum of 32 Intel e1000 NICs.
   ☒ **A, B,** and **D** are incorrect. None of these choices represents the maximum number of Intel e1000 NICs for an ESX Host.

2. ☑ **B.** An ESX Host can have a maximum of 248 virtual switches.
   ☒ **A, C,** and **D** are incorrect. None of these choices represents the maximum number of virtual switches for an ESX Host.

3. ☑ **D.** A virtual switch can have a maximum of 512 port groups.
   ☒ **A, B,** and **C** are incorrect. None of these choices represent the maximum number of port groups.

4. ☑ **D.** The "Use explicit failover order" NIC teaming policy allows you to specify the explicit failover order that NICs will be used in.
   ☒ **A, B,** and **C** are incorrect. The "Route based on the originating virtual port ID," "Route based on IP hash," and "Route based on source MAC hash" NIC teaming policies do not allow you to specify the order in which NICs will be used.

5. ☑ **C.** Host Name Conflict is not a configurable security policy on a virtual switch.
   ☒ **A, B,** and **C** are incorrect. Promiscuous Mode, MAC Address Changes, and Forged Transmits are all configurable security policies on a virtual switch.

Understand and Configure vNetwork Distributed Switches

6. ☑ **B.** There can be a maximum of 16 distributed switches per vCenter.
   ☒ **A, C,** and **D** are incorrect. None of these are the maximum number of distributed switches per vCenter.

7. ☑ **C.** There can be a maximum of 512 distributed port groups per vCenter.
   ☒ **A, B,** and **D** are incorrect. None of these are the maximum number of distributed port groups per vCenter.

8. ☑ **B.** There can be a maximum of 64 Hosts connected to a distributed switch.
   ☒ **A, C,** and **D** are incorrect. None of these are the maximum number of Hosts connected to a distributed switch.

9. ☑ **C.** The VLAN Trunking VLAN policy requires you to enter a VLAN Trunk range.
☒ **A, B,** and **D** are incorrect. The None, VLAN, and Private VLAN policies do not require you to enter a range of VLAN IDs.

10. ☑ **A.** VMkernel ports can be used to connect network-based storage to an ESX Host.
☒ **B, C,** and **D** are incorrect. Virtual Machine ports and Service Console ports are not used to connect network-based storage.

Understand and Configure the ESX/ESXi Management Network

11. ☑ **B.** The command to stop the network service on an ESX Host is service network stop.
☒ **A, C,** and **D** are incorrect. The only command to stop the network service on an ESX Host is service network stop.

12. ☑ **A.** The default gateway for an ESX Host is configured in the /etc/sysconfig/network file.
☒ **B, C,** and **D** are incorrect. None of these choices is where the default gateway for an ESX Host is configured.

6

Understanding and Configuring Storage on ESX/ESXi Servers

Welcome to Chapter 6. In this chapter we will look at how storage is implemented in a vSphere environment. We will start the chapter by working with Fibre Channel SAN storage. We will talk about what FC SAN storage is and how it is implemented. We will then review iSCSI SAN storage—what it is and how it is implemented. We will then look at NFS datastores and how they can be used by vSphere. We end the chapter by discussing how to configure and manage VMFS datastores.

CERTIFICATION OBJECTIVE 6.01

Configure FC SAN Storage

In this section we will discuss Fibre Channel SANs. We will look at the types of hardware that make up FC SANs and how SAN storage is presented to our ESX/ESXi Servers. We will then discuss the concepts of zoning and LUN masking. We will end the section by discussing multipathing policies and how they are implemented in vSphere.

Identify FC SAN Hardware Components

A Fibre Channel SAN comprises a number of hardware components that work together to present storage to a single ESX/ESXi Server or shared storage to a number of ESX/ESXi Servers at the same time. These hardware components include

- **Host bus adapters** Host bus adapters are similar to NIC cards that are installed in the ESX/ESXi Server that allows them to connect via a Fibre Optic cable to an FC SAN switch.

- **FC SAN switches** SAN switches are physical switches that are very similar to network switches except that they connect FC networks. An FC SAN switch connects the Hosts to the FC SAN controllers. Most FC SANs will contain multiple FC SAN switches to help keep the SAN from having a single point of failure.

■ **FC SAN controller**   The FC SAN controller is a device that controls how FC storage is allocated into LUNs (logical units) and how it is presented to the Hosts. Most FC SANs will contain multiple SAN controllers to help keep the SAN from having a single point of failure.

Identify How ESX Server Connections Are Made to FC SAN Storage

In a vSphere environment using FC SAN storage each Host would have one or more FC HBAs installed and configured. These HBAs would be connected via Fibre cables to FC SAN switches. Each FC SAN switch is connected to an FC SAN controller. The FC SAN controllers manage the actual SAN storage and separate it into LUNs. The LUNs are allocated to an individual Host or group of Hosts by the SAN controllers. Once a LUN is connected to a Host, the Host sees it as if it is local storage, and in many instances it will have better performance than local storage.

Describe ESX Server FC SAN Storage Addressing

Now that you have a basic understanding of the hardware components that make up an FC SAN, let's look at how LUNs are addresses by a Host. FC SAN storage is presented to an ESX/ESXi Host as a LUN, or logical unit. Each of these LUNs is presented with a unique four-part identifier of the form Adapter:Channel:Target:LUN. An example would be vmhba0:1:2:3. In this example,

■ Adapter = vmhba0
■ Channel = 1
■ Target = 2
■ LUN = 3

Describe Zoning and LUN Masking

Zoning and LUN masking are two different ways to hide FC LUNs from ESX/ESXi Hosts. You can use zoning and LUN masking to restrict which Hosts can see any given LUN. Each HBA in a Host has a unique identifier known as a World Wide Name, or WWN.

- **Zoning** Zoning can be used to hide FC LUNs from ESX/ESXi Hosts as well as from non-VMware systems. Each HBA in a server has a unique identifier known as a World Wide Name, or WWN. The FC switches can use these WWNs to restrict access to FC LUNs.
- **LUN Masking** LUN masking is used on an ESX/ESXi Host to hide a LUN or range of LUNs from the Host.

Configure LUN Masking

Now that you know what LUN masking is, let's talk about why you would want to use it and how it is implemented. By default any LUN that is presented to a Host is visible. If you are working in a large environment, you may have many LUNs presented to your Hosts that you are not actively using. To avoid the possibility of accidentally damaging the data on these LUNs, you may want to use LUN masking to hide them from your Host. To configure LUN masking, we will use claim rules to mask each path to the LUN.

Example: To mask LUN 5 on targets T1 and T2 on HBAs vmhba0 and vmhba1, follow these steps:

1. Use the following command to determine the next available claim rule: **esxcli corestorage claimrule list**.
2. Issue the following commands:

```
#esxcli corestorage claimrule add -P MASK_PATH -r 103 -t location -A vmhba0 -C 0
-T 1 -L 5
#esxcli corestorage claimrule add -P MASK_PATH -r 104 -t location -A vmhba1 -C 0
-T 1 -L 5
#esxcli corestorage claimrule add -P MASK_PATH -r 105 -t location -A vmhba0 -C 0
-T 2 -L 5
#esxcli corestorage claimrule add -P MASK_PATH -r 106 -t location -A vmhba1 -C 0
-T 2 -L 5

#esxcli corestorage claimrule load
#esxcli corestorage claimrule list
#esxcli corestorage claiming unclaim -t location -A vmhba0
#esxcli corestorage claiming unclaim -t location -A vmhba1
#esxcli corestorage claimrule run
```

In many companies separate teams administer the SANs and the servers. Because of this, you may find that you have limited control of how zoning is configured on the SAN controllers, and in some instances all of the LUNs are made available to all of the ESX Hosts to make the SAN administrator's job easier. LUN masking gives you a way as the server administrator to limit the LUNs that are seen by each Host.

Scan for NEW LUNs

When a new LUN is presented to an ESX/ESXi Host, it will not automatically be available to the Host. Before these new LUNs are available, the Host will need to perform a rescan of the HBA where the new LUNs have been presented.

To rescan an HBA, follow these steps:

1. Launch the vSphere Client and connect to your ESX Host.
2. In the navigation bar select Home | Inventory.
3. Select the Host in the left frame and click the Configuration tab in the right.
4. Select Storage Adapters from the Hardware box on the left.
5. Select the HBA that you wish to scan.
6. Click Rescan.
7. You will be presented with the Rescan window as shown in Figure 6-1. Click OK to scan for new storage devices and new VMFS volumes.
8. When the rescan is finished, you will now be able to see any new LUNs that were presented to the Host.

FIGURE 6-1

The Rescan window

Determine and Configure the Appropriate Multipathing Policy

Multipathing is a technique to ensure that there are multiple paths to any given LUN. Multipathing can help to reduce the possibility of a single failure causing a SAN LUN to become unavailable. ESX Servers can use the following multipathing policies:

- **Fixed**   Fixed is the default multipathing policy for LUNs presented by an active/active storage array. This policy uses the first path that it finds and continues to use it. If this path becomes unavailable, a new path is used. If the original path becomes available again, the Fixed policy reverts to it.

- **Most Recently Used (MRU)**   MRU is the default multipathing policy for LUNs presented by an active/passive storage array. This policy uses the first path that it finds and continues to use it. If this path becomes unavailable, a new path is used. If the original path becomes available again, the MRU policy does not revert to it.

- **Round Robin**   Round Robin is a multipathing policy that uses all of the active paths that are available for a LUN. It rotates through all of the available paths to achieve load balancing across all of the paths.

Differentiate Between NMP and Third-Party MPP

The VMware Native Multipathing Plugin (NMP) is a plugin provided by VMware to manage multipathing plugins. Storage Array Type Plugins (SATPs) and Selection Plugins (PSPs) can be provided by VMware or by third parties and are used to manage multipathing for storage devices. An MPP, or Multipathing Plugin, is a special plugin that is used to control a single type of storage array and is generally provided by the manufacturer of the storage array. Since an MPP is specially designed for a given storage array, it can usually provide better performance for that array than the NMP plugins can.

CERTIFICATION OBJECTIVE 6.02

Configure iSCSI SAN Storage

In this section we will discuss iSCSI SANs. We will look at the types of hardware that make up iSCSI SANs and how SAN storage is presented to our ESX/ESXi

Servers. We will then discuss the concepts of the iSCSI software initiator and dynamic and static discovery of iSCSI storage. We will end the section by discussing how iSCSI addressing is configured on our ESX/ESXi Hosts.

Identify iSCSI SAN Hardware Components

An iSCSI SAN comprises a number of hardware components that work together to present storage to a single ESX/ESXi Server or shared storage to a number of ESX/ESXi Servers at the same time. These hardware components include

- **iSCSI initiator**   The iSCSI initiator is the system that is requesting storage from the iSCSI SAN. For a vSphere environment, the iSCSI Initiator is a Host. The Host can use either a software or hardware initiator.
- **iSCSI software initiator**   The iSCSI software initiator is a standard NIC connection on the Host.
- **iSCSI hardware initiator**   The iSCSI hardware initiator is an additional piece of hardware that is installed into the Host and acts as an iSCSI NIC.
- **iSCSI target**   The iSCSI target is the disk controller that manages the storage array.
- **Network switch**   iSCSI uses standard network switches to provide storage over IP. It is recommended that separate switches be used for network and IP storage traffic.

Determine Usage Cases for Hardware vs. Software iSCSI Initiators

ESX and ESXi Hosts support both hardware and software iSCSI initiators. Both of these types of initiators have their advantages and disadvantages.

- *Software iSCSI initiators* have the advantage of using a standard NIC port, so they are cheap and are already installed on most servers. They have the disadvantage of requiring more overhead from the vmkernel, since they rely on it for functionality. They should be used when no hardware initiators are available but when vmkernel resources are available. Software iSCSI initiators have come a long way with modern servers and can come very close to the performance of hardware iSCSI initiators without the additional cost.

■ *Hardware iSCSI initiators* have the advantage of being able to offload some of the storage processing requirements from the vmkernel to the hardware initiator. They have the disadvantage of being more expensive than software initiators. They should be used when the additional cost of the hardware is less of a concern than the gain in performance that can be achieved.

on the
Üob

Because it uses a company's existing network infrastructure, iSCSI can be a very cost-effective way to introduce SAN connectivity to your ESX Hosts without the costs and infrastructure changes that are associated with an FC SAN.

Configure the iSCSI Software Initiator

Now that you have a basic understanding of the hardware components of an iSCSI SAN, let's go ahead and configure the iSCSI software initiator.

To configure an iSCSI software initiator, follow these steps:

1. Launch the vSphere Client and connect to your ESX Host.
2. In the navigation bar select Home | Inventory.
3. Select the Host in the left frame and click the Configuration tab in the right.
4. Select Networking from the Hardware box on the left.
5. Select Add Networking.

INSIDE THE EXAM

iSCSI Hardware Initiator

In previous versions of ESX the iSCSI hardware initiator was not supported. To test your knowledge of the new features of vSphere versus older versions, you may see a question asking if the iSCSI hardware initiator is supported.

6. You will be presented with the Connection Type window. Check the radio box next to VMkernel and click Next to continue.

7. You will be presented with the VMkernel – Network Access window. Check the radio box next to Create A Virtual Switch to create a new switch or check the radio box to Use An Existing vSwitch and click Next to continue.

8. You will be presented with the VMkernel – Connection Settings window. Enter a meaningful Network Label and click Next to continue.

9. You will be presented with the VMkernel – IP Connection Settings window. Enter an IP Address and Subnet Mask for the new network connection.

10. You will be presented with the Ready To Complete window. Click Finish to create the new port group and exit.

11. You will be presented with the Configuration window. Select Storage Adapters from the Hardware box on the left.

12. Select the iSCSI Software Adapter from the device list and click Properties.

13. You will be presented with the iSCSI Initiator Properties window. Click Configure.

14. You will be presented with the iSCSI General Properties window. Check the box next to Enabled and click OK to continue and then Close to exit.

You have now configured the iSCSI software initiator.

Configure Dynamic/Static Discovery

ESX/ESXi Hosts can use either static or dynamic discovery for iSCSI LUNs. When using static discovery, you must manually enter connection information for each LUN. When using dynamic discovery, each time the Host contacts an iSCSI server, it sends a Send Targets request to the iSCSI server asking it to supply a list of available iSCSI targets.

To configure dynamic discovery, follow these steps:

1. Launch the vSphere Client and connect to your ESX Host.

2. In the navigation bar select Home | Inventory.

3. Select the Host in the left frame and click the Configuration tab in the right.

4. Select Storage Adapters from the Hardware box on the left.

5. Select the iSCSI Adapter you wish to configure and click Properties.

6. You will be presented with the iSCSI Initiator Properties window. Click the Dynamic Discovery tab.

7. You will be presented with the Dynamic Discovery tab for the iSCSI initiator as shown in Figure 6-2. Click Add to add a new iSCSI server.

8. You will be presented with the Add Send Target Server window. Enter the DNS Name or IP Address of the iSCSI server you want to add and click OK to continue.

9. Confirm that your iSCSI server has been added and click Close to exit.

FIGURE 6-2

The iSCSI Dynamic Discovery tab

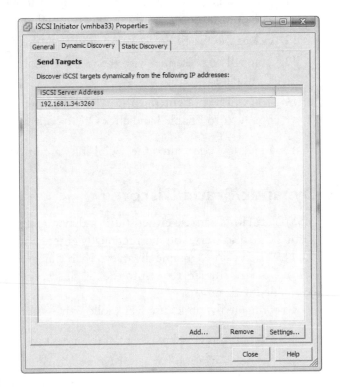

To configure Static Discovery, follow these steps:

1. Launch the vSphere Client and connect to your ESX Host.
2. In the navigation bar select Home | Inventory.
3. Select the Host in the left frame and click the Configuration tab in the right.
4. Select Storage Adapters from the Hardware box on the left.
5. Select the iSCSI Adapter you wish to configure and click Properties.
6. You will be presented with the iSCSI Initiator Properties window. Click the Static Discovery tab.
7. You will be presented with the Static Discovery tab for the iSCSI Initiator as shown in Figure 6-3. Click Add to add a new iSCSI server and target.
8. You will be presented with the Add Static Target Server window. Enter the DNS Name or IP Address of the iSCSI server you want to add and the iSCSI Target Name. Click OK to continue.
9. Confirm that your iSCSI server and target have been added and click Close to exit.

FIGURE 6-3

The iSCSI Static Discovery tab

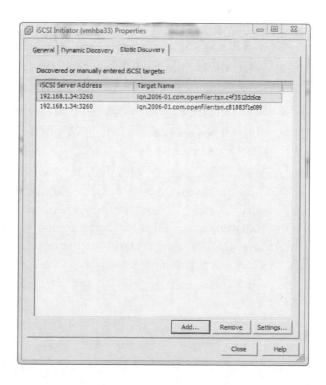

Configure CHAP Authentication

CHAP is an authentication protocol that is used by ESX/ESXi Hosts to authenticate to iSCSI storage. The authentication is based on a shared secret code between the Host and the iSCSI server. Two different types of CHAP authentication are used by vSphere Hosts:

- **One-way CHAP**   In one-way CHAP the iSCSI server authenticates the initiator but the initiator does not authenticate the iSCSI server.
- **Mutual CHAP**   In mutual CHAP the iSCSI server authenticates the initiator and the initiator authenticates the iSCSI server. Mutual CHAP is more secure but is currently supported only when using a software initiator.

When using the hardware initiator, CHAP can only be configured at the adapter level. This means that all of the targets that are connected to must use the same CHAP secret. When using the software initiator, CHAP can be configured on a per-target basis. Each iSCSI target can have a different secret. Because of this, software initiators can provide a greater level of security than hardware initiators.

To configure CHAP on a storage adapter, follow these steps:

1. Launch the vSphere Client and connect to your ESX Host.
2. In the navigation bar select Home | Inventory.
3. Select the Host in the left frame and click the Configuration tab in the right.
4. Select Storage Adapters from the Hardware box on the left.
5. Select the iSCSI Adapter you wish to configure and click Properties.
6. You will be presented with the iSCSI Initiator Properties window. Click CHAP to continue.
7. You will be presented with the CHAP Credentials window. You must determine if you want to use CHAP or Mutual CHAP. If you choose to use CHAP, select Use CHAP from the drop-down menu, check the box next to Use Initiator Name, and enter the Secret for this connection. If you wish to use Mutual CHAP, you must first configure CHAP and then configure Mutual CHAP. When you have entered the information, click OK to continue.
8. Click Close to exit.

Discover iSCSI LUNS

Now that we have configured the iSCSI initiator and set up discovery, we can go ahead and run a rescan of the iSCSI storage adapter to discover iSCSI targets.

To rescan an iSCSI storage adapter, follow these steps:

1. Launch the vSphere Client and connect to your ESX Host.
2. In the navigation bar select Home | Inventory.
3. Select the Host in the left frame and click the Configuration tab in the right.
4. Select Storage Adapters from the Hardware box on the left.
5. Select the iSCSI Adapter you wish to rescan and click Rescan.
6. If any targets were defined on the iSCSI Adapter, you will now see that the number of Connected Targets is no longer zero, as shown in Figure 6-4.

FIGURE 6-4

Notice that the iSCSI Connected Targets value is now set to 1.

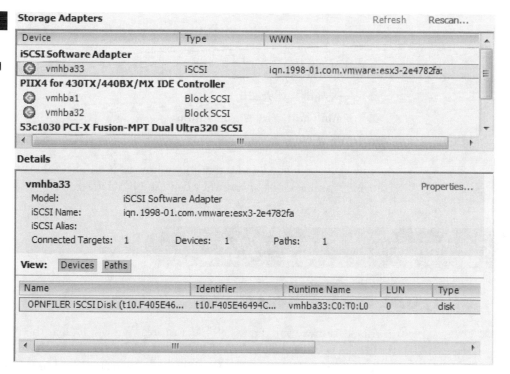

Identify iSCSI Addressing in the Context of the Host

ESX and ESXi Hosts use unique names to identify each iSCSI storage adapter. These names are defined by the format

iqn:yyyy-mm.naming-authority:unique name

where

- **yyyy-mm**   This is the four-digit year and two-digit month when the naming authority was established.
- **naming-authority**   This is the Internet name of the authority that created the iSCSI adapter given in reverse order.
- **unique name**   This is a user-defined unique name.

An example would be

iqn.1998-01.com.vmware:esx3-2e4782fa

In this example,

- **yyyy-mm** = 1998-01
- **naming-authority** = com.vmware
- **unique name** = esx3-2e4782fa

Now that you a good understanding of how ESX and ESXi Hosts use iSCSI storage, let's take a look at how they can use NFS datastores.

CERTIFICATION OBJECTIVE 6.03

Configure NFS Datastores

In this section we will discuss NFS datastores. We will look at the types of hardware that make up NFS datastores and how networking is configured to allow a Host to connect to an NFS datastore. We will finish the section by discussing how to add an NFS datastore to an ESX Host.

Identify NFS Hardware Components

An NFS datastore comprises a number of hardware components that work together to present storage to an ESX/ESXi Server or shared storage to a number of ESX/ESXi Servers at the same time. These hardware components include

- **NFS Server**   The NFS Server is the server or device that contains and manages NFS shares.
- **NFS shares**   NFS shares are the actual unit of storage that is provided by an NFS Server.
- **Network switch**   NFS uses standard network switches to provide storage over IP. It is recommended that separate physical switches or VLANs be used for network and IP storage traffic.

Explain ESX Exclusivity for NFS Mounts

ESX exclusivity is a method for preventing multiple ESX/ESXi Hosts from attempting to run the same virtual machine on a shared NFS mount. When a Host attempts to run a virtual machine that is on NFS storage, it will look for a lock file in the same directory as the disk file for the virtual machine. If it finds this lock file, it will not start the virtual machine, since another Host is running it. If it does not find a lock file, it will create one and start the virtual machine. Since there is now a lock file, no other Host will attempt to start the virtual machine.

Configure ESX/ESXi Network Connectivity to the NAS Device

Now that you have a basic understanding of the hardware components of an NFS datastore, let's go ahead and set up network connectivity for a NAS device.

To configure a VMkernel network connection for NFS storage, follow these steps:

1. Launch the vSphere Client and connect to your ESX Host.
2. In the navigation bar select Home | Inventory.
3. Select the Host in the left frame and click the Configuration tab in the right.
4. Select Networking from the Hardware box on the left.
5. Select Add Networking.

6. You will be presented with the Connection Type window. Check the radio box next to VMkernel and click Next to continue.

7. You will be presented with the VMkernel – Network Access window. Check the radio box next to Create A Virtual Switch to create a new switch or check the radio box to Use An Existing vSwitch and click Next to continue.

8. You will be presented with the VMkernel – Connection Settings window. Enter a meaningful Network Label and click Next to continue.

9. You will be presented with the VMkernel – IP Connection Settings window. Enter an IP Address and Subnet Mask for the new network connection.

10. You will be presented with the Ready To Complete window. Click Finish to create the new port group and exit.

Create an NFS Datastore

Now that we have configured a VMkernel network connection for NFS, we can go ahead and add an NFS datastore.

To add an NFS datastore, follow these steps:

1. Launch the vSphere Client and connect to your ESX Host.

2. In the navigation bar select Home | Inventory.

3. Select the Host in the left frame and click the Configuration tab in the right.

4. Select Storage from the Hardware box on the left.

5. Select Add Storage.

6. You will be presented with the Select Storage Type window. Check the radio box next to Network File System and click Next to continue.

7. You will be presented with the Locate Network File System window as shown in Figure 6-5. Enter the name of the NFS Server, the Share Name, and a new name for the datastore. Click Next to continue.

8. You will be presented with a summary window. Click Finish to create the new datastore and exit.

FIGURE 6-5

The Locate
Network File
System window

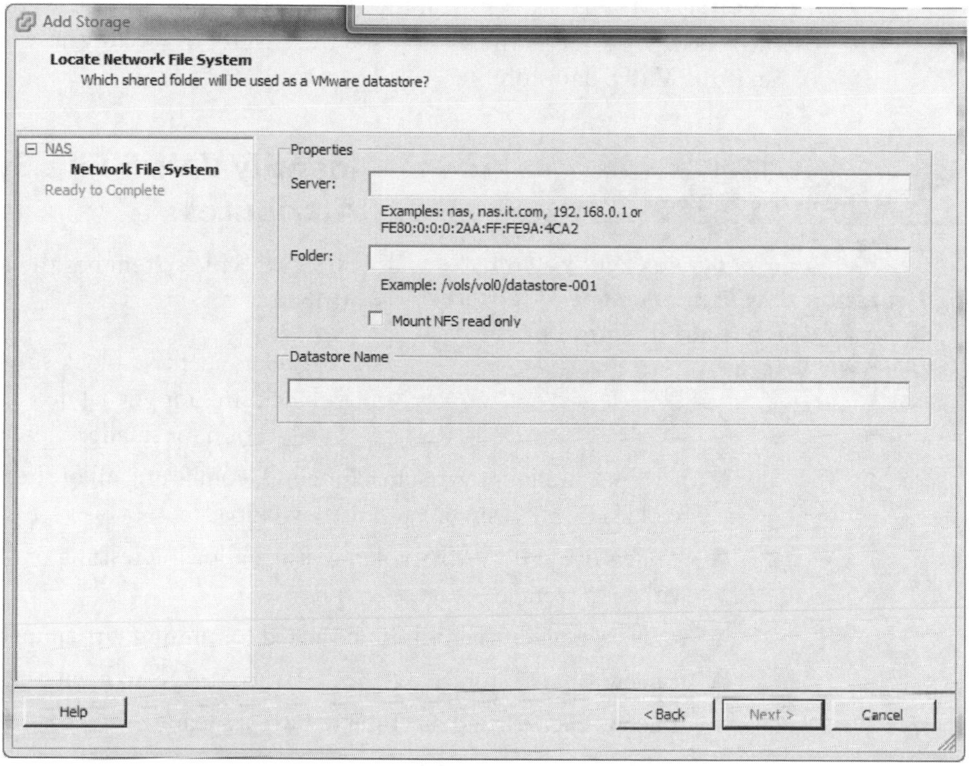

CERTIFICATION OBJECTIVE 6.04

Configure and Manage VMFS Datastores

VMFS datastores are storage locations that are used to store the files that make up virtual machines. In this section we will look at how to configure and manage VMFS datastores. We will discuss the attributes that make up a VMFS datastore and determine the best datastore location for given virtual machines. We will then look at usage cases for multiple VMFS datastores. We will then review how to add existing VMFS datastores to an ESX Host and how to manage them once they are attached. We will end the section and the chapter by looking at ways to grow an existing VMFS datastore.

For the exam you may see a question that lists a number of features and asks which is not a feature of the VMFS file system.

Identify VMFS File System Attributes

The VMFS file system has the following attributes:

- It offers adaptive block sizing to use large block sizes for virtual disk I/O and sub-block allocation for smaller files and directories.
- It is optimized for virtual machine I/O, combining all of the virtual machine workloads into a single optimized workload.
- It offers dynamic VMFS volume sizing, allowing resizing of VMFS volumes without a storage outage.
- It allows new virtual disks to be added to running virtual machines.
- It allows shared storage over iSCSI or FC SANs to create Host Clusters.
- It allows each virtual machine to have a separate directory where its files are stored.

Determine the Appropriate Datastore Location/Configuration for Given Virtual Machines

There are a number of conditions to consider when determining the appropriate datastore for a given virtual machine:

- **Available space**   Before a virtual machine can be created on a datastore you need to make sure there is enough space for it. Virtual machines can use either thick or thin provisioning. If a virtual machine uses thin provisioning the size of its disk file will start out small and grow as it needs additional space. If it uses thick provisioning, all of the space for the disk file will be allocated up front.

■ **Performance** Different types of storage offer different levels of performance. In general FC LUNs will provide the best performance but at the highest cost. iSCSI storage provides slightly lower performance than FC SANs but generally costs significantly less. NFS datastores can be the least expensive storage option, but they also provide the weakest performance.

■ **Storage options** Microsoft Clustering Service is not supported on NFS datastores. If you have a virtual machine that will be a part of a Microsoft Cluster, you will not be able to use NFS and will need to use either iSCSI or FC SAN storage.

Determine Usage Cases for Multiple VMFS Datastores

There are certain instances where a Host could benefit by using multiple VMFS datastores. A Host can reduce the amount of disk contention for a single VMFS datastore by adding additional VMFS datastores and moving some of the virtual machines to them. Having fewer virtual machines on each datastore means that more disk throughput will be available to each virtual machines. Also by using multiple datastores, a Host can segregate the virtual machines it manages to storage that is a best fit for the VM, given its performance requirements.

INSIDE THE EXAM

Microsoft Clustering

In the past VMware has put an emphasis on how virtual machines can be used to implement Microsoft Clustering. It could be important for the exam to know that Microsoft Clustering is not supported on NFS datastores and that clustered VMDKs must be thick-provisioned.

Create/Configure VMFS Datastores

Before we can start managing VMFS datastores, let's take a look at how to create a new one.

To create a new VMFS datastore on local storage, follow these steps:

1. Launch the vSphere Client and connect to your Host or vCenter Server.
2. In the navigation bar select Home | Inventory.
3. Select the Host in the left frame and click the Configuration tab in the right.
4. Select Storage from the Hardware box on the left.
5. Select Add Storage.
6. You will be presented with the Select Storage Type window. Select the radio box next to Disk/LUN and click Next to continue.
7. You will be presented with the Select Disk/LUN window. Select the LUN where you want to create the new VMFS datastore and click Next to continue.
8. You will be presented with the Current Disk Layout window. Click Next to create a partition and continue.
9. You will be prompted to enter a name for the new datastore. Enter a meaningful name and click Next to continue.
10. You will be prompted to enter a Block Size and Capacity for the new VMFS partition. The block size you enter will determine the maximum file size you will be able to create. Enter this information and click Next to continue.
11. You will be presented with a summary screen. Confirm that the information is correct and click Finish to create the new VMFS datastore and exit.

Attach an Existing VMFS Datastore to a New ESX Host

To utilize shared storage between multiple ESX/ESXi Hosts, it is often necessary to add an existing VMFS datastore to a new Host. This is generally a two-step process. First the datastore must be presented to the ESX Host, and then a rescan must be performed on the Host's storage adapter so that it can see the new datastore. The presentation of the datastore will depend on the type of storage it exists on. If it resides on an FC SAN, the zoning will need to be properly configured. If it resides on an iSCSI target or NFS share, access will need to be granted to the Host. Once the storage has been presented to the Host, a rescan of the storage adapter is required.

To rescan a storage adapter on a Host, follow these steps:

1. Launch the vSphere Client and connect to your Host or vCenter Server.
2. In the navigation bar select Home | Inventory.
3. Select the Host in the left frame and click the Configuration tab in the right.
4. Select Storage Adapters from the Hardware box on the left.
5. Right-click the Storage Adapter you wish to rescan and select Rescan from the drop-down menu.
6. Once the rescan is complete, select Storage from the Hardware box on the left.

If the storage was presented correctly, you should now see the new datastore.

Manage VMFS Datastores: Group/Unmount/Delete

There are a number of actions you may need to perform when managing your VMFS datastores. In this section we will look at grouping VMFS datastores together, unmounting VMFS datastores, and deleting VMFS datastores that are no longer needed. Let's start by grouping VMFS datastores.

Group VMFS Datastores

Using vCenter VMFS datastores can be grouped together to make their management easier. Once datastores are grouped together, permissions and alarms can be configured on the entire group, ensuring that they will be consistent across all of the datastores.

To create groups of VMFS datastores, follow these steps:

1. Launch the vSphere Client and connect to your vCenter Server.
2. In the navigation bar select Home | Inventory | Datastores.

3. Right-click the datacenter in the left frame and click New Folder from the drop-down menu.

4. Enter a name for the new folder.

5. Select each datastore that you want to add to the group and drag it into the new folder.

You will now be able to manage all of the datastores in the folder as a single unit.

Unmount VMFS Datastores

Datastores can be unmounted from select ESX/ESXi Hosts. If a datastore is unmounted, its contents will not be lost but the Hosts that it has been unmounted from will no longer be able to access it. NFS datastores can be unmounted and VMFS datastores that have been mounted without resignaturing can be unmounted.

To unmount a VMFS datastore, follow these steps:

1. Launch the vSphere Client and connect to your vCenter Server.

2. In the navigation bar select Home | Inventory | Datastores.

3. Right-click the datastore that you wish to unmount in the left frame and click Unmount from the drop-down menu.

4. If this is a shared datastore, you will be presented with a list of Hosts that currently access the datastore. All of the Hosts in this list are selected by default. Deselect the Hosts that you wish to continue to have access to the datastore and click Next to continue.

5. You will be presented with a confirmation window. Click Finish to unmount the datastore and exit.

Delete VMFS Datastores

Once a datastore is no longer needed, you may want to delete it so that you can reclaim the storage space for other uses. Unlike when a datastore is unmounted, when a datastore is deleted, the information contained on it is no longer available.

To delete a VMFS datastore, follow these steps:

1. Launch the vSphere Client and connect to your Host or vCenter Server.

2. In the navigation bar select Home | Inventory | Datastores.

3. Right-click the datastore that you wish to delete and select Delete from the drop-down menu.

4. You will be presented with a confirmation window. Click Finish to delete the datastore and exit.

Grow VMFS Volumes

As your virtual environment grows and the number of virtual machines increases, you may need to expand the size of your VMFS volumes. This can be accomplished by adding an extent to your existing VMFS volume. An *extent* is essentially additional storage space that is added onto a volume to increase its size.

To add an extent to a VMFS volume, follow these steps:

1. Launch the vSphere Client and connect to your Host or vCenter Server.

2. In the navigation bar select Home | Inventory.

3. Select the Host in the left frame and click the Configuration tab in the right.

4. Select Storage from the Hardware box on the left.

5. Select the datastore with the volume that you wish to expand and click Properties.

6. You will be presented with the Datastore Properties window as shown in Figure 6-6. Click Increase under Volume Properties to increase the size of the volume.

7. You will be prompted to select a LUN on which you want to create the extent. Select a LUN from the list and click Next to continue.

8. You will be presented with the current disk layout of the LUN you choose. Select the space where you want to create the new extent and click Next to continue.

9. You will be presented with the Extent Size window. On this window you can choose to use all of the storage to create the new extent or to specify the amount of storage you wish to use. Make your selection and click Next to continue.

10. You will be presented with a summary screen. Confirm that the information is correct and click Finish to create the new extent and exit.

FIGURE 6-6

The Datastore
Properties
window

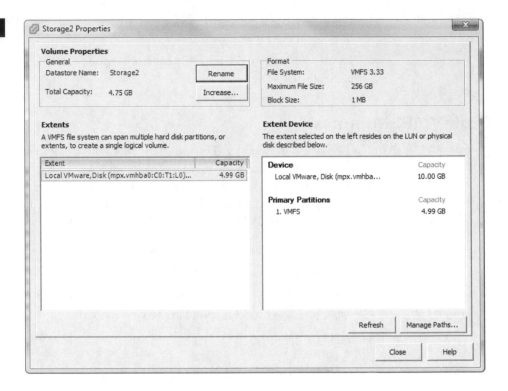

CERTIFICATION SUMMARY

We started this chapter by looking at Fibre Channel SANs. We looked at the types of hardware that make up FC SANs and how ESX Servers are connected to them. We discussed FC SAN addressing and then we discussed zoning and LUN masking. We then went through the steps of scanning for new LUNs and discussed the available multipathing policies for FC SANs. We ended the section by talking about NMP and MPP.

In the next section we looked at iSCSI SAN storage. We discussed the types of hardware that make up iSCSI SANs and looked at the differences between hardware and software iSCSI initiators. We then looked at dynamic and static discovery of iSCSI targets and went through the steps of configuring both. We then discussed the CHAP authentication protocol that is used by iSCSI. We ended the section by reviewing iSCSI addressing.

The next section looked at NFS datastores and the hardware components that they use. We briefly discussed ESX NFS exclusivity and then configured network connectivity for a Host to access an NFS datastore. We ended the section by going through the steps to create a new NFS datastore.

The last section of the chapter dealt with configuring and managing VMFS datastores. We looked at the unique attributes of the VMFS file system and discussed the placement of virtual machines onto VMFS volumes. We then created a new VMFS datastore for a Host and discussed how to add an existing VMFS datastore to a new Host. We then discussed how to perform management tasks on VMFS datastores like grouping, unmounting, and deleting them. We ended the section and the chapter by discussing how to increase the size of an existing VMFS volume.

✓ TWO-MINUTE DRILL

Configure FC SAN Storage

❏ Host bus adapters are basically NICs for connecting to FC SANs.

❏ FC SAN switches are physical switches that connect FC networks.

❏ An FC SAN controller is a device that controls how FC storage is allocated and presented to Hosts.

❏ FC storage is presented to a Host as a LUN.

❏ FC SAN storage is addressed as Adapter:Channel:Target:LUN.

❏ Zoning is a way to hide LUNs from servers and is used on the FC switches and FC SAN controllers.

❏ LUN masking is a way to hide LUNs from a Host and is configured on the Host.

❏ A World Wide Name, or WWN, is a unique identifier for an HBA.

❏ In the Fixed multipathing policy the first discovered path to a LUN is used. When it becomes unavailable, a new path is used. If the original path becomes available again, it is used. It is the default multipathing policy for LUNs presented by an active/active storage array.

❏ In the Most Recently Used multipathing policy the first discovered path to a LUN is used. When it becomes unavailable, a new path is used. If the original path becomes available again, it is not used. It is the default multipathing policy for LUNs presented by an active/passive storage array.

❏ In the Round Robin multipathing policy all of the available active paths are rotated through to achieve load balancing across all of the paths.

Configure iSCSI SAN Storage

❏ The iSCSI initiator is the system that is requesting storage from the iSCSI SAN.

❏ The iSCSI software initiator is a standard NIC connection on the Host.

❏ The iSCSI hardware initiator is an additional piece of hardware that is installed in the Host.

❑ The iSCSI target is the disk controller that manages the storage array.

❑ iSCSI uses standard network switches to provide storage over IP.

❑ iSCSI software initiators are cheap and are already installed in many servers.

❑ iSCSI hardware initiators are more expensive but allow some storage processing to be offloaded to the initiator.

❑ When using static discovery, connection information for each LUN needs to be manually entered.

❑ CHAP is an authentication protocol that is used by ESX/ESXi Hosts to connect to iSCSI SANs.

❑ In one-way CHAP the iSCSI server authenticates the initiator.

❑ In mutual CHAP the iSCSI server authenticates the initiator and the initiator authenticates the iSCSI server.

❑ Mutual CHAP is only supported using the software initiator.

Configure NFS Datastores

❑ An NFS Server is a server or device that contains and manages NFS shares.

❑ NFS shares are the unit of storage that is provided by an NFS Server.

❑ NFS uses standard network switches to provide storage over IP.

❑ ESX/ESXi Hosts use a lock file to maintain ESX exclusivity for NFS mounts.

Configure and Manage VMFS Datastores

❑ The VMFS file system uses adaptive block sizing.

❑ The VMFS file system is optimized for virtual machine I/O.

❑ The VMFS file system allows the resizing of VMFS volumes without an outage.

❑ The VMFS file system allows each virtual machine to be contained in a separate directory.

❑ If a VMFS datastore is unmounted, its data is not lost.

❑ If a VMFS datastore is deleted, its data is lost.

❑ VMFS volumes can be grown using extents.

SELF TEST

The following questions will help you measure your understanding of the material presented in this chapter. Read all the choices carefully and remember that there is only one best answer for each question.

Configure FC SAN Storage

1. Which ESX storage type requires special switches?
   A. FC SAN
   B. iSCSI SAN
   C. NFS datastores
   D. Local SCSI storage

2. In the following FC SAN address what is the target vmhba0:1:2:3?
   A. 0
   B. 1
   C. 2
   D. 3

3. Which of the following techniques can be used to hide an FC LUN from a non-VMware server?
   A. LUN masking
   B. LUN shadowing
   C. Zoning
   D. LUN hiding

4. In which storage multipathing policy will pathing return to the original path if it has failed and then become available again?
   A. Fixed
   B. Most Recently Used
   C. First Used
   D. Round Robin

Configure iSCSI SAN Storage

5. Which of the following is not a component of an iSCSI SAN?
    A. iSCSI initiator
    B. iSCSI target
    C. Fibre Channel HBA
    D. Network switch

6. The iSCSI hardware initiator is supported under ESX 4.0.
    A. True
    B. False

7. Which of the following is not a true statement about the iSCSI software initiator?
    A. The iSCSI software initiator uses a standard NIC port.
    B. The iSCSI software initiator requires more overhead from the VMkernel than the iSCSI hardware initiator.
    C. The iSCSI software initiator is less expensive than the iSCSI hardware initiator.
    D. The iSCSI software initiator requires less overhead from the VMkernel than the iSCSI hardware initiator.

8. In which type of CHAP authentication does the iSCSI initiator authenticate the iSCSI server?
    A. One-way CHAP
    B. Dual CHAP
    C. Two-way CHAP
    D. Mutual CHAP

Configure NFS Datastores

9. How is ESX exclusivity implemented on an NFS mount?
    A. Virtual SCSI locking
    B. A lock file
    C. Mount locking
    D. IP locking

Configure and Manage VMFS Datastores

10. Which of the following storage types does not support Microsoft Clustering?
   A. FC SAN
   B. iSCSI SAN
   C. NFS datastore
   D. Both B and C

11. Which of the following storage technologies generally provides the lowest performance level?
   A. iSCSI SAN
   B. NFS datastores
   C. FC SAN
   D. Local SCSI storage

12. If a datastore is unmounted from an ESX Host, the data in the datastore will be lost.
   A. True
   B. False

SELF TEST ANSWERS

Configure FC SAN Storage

1. ☑ **A.** FC SANs require special Fibre Channel switches.
    ☒ **B, C,** and **D** are incorrect. iSCSI SANs and NFS datastores use standard network switches. Local SCSI storage does not require a switch.

2. ☑ **C.** FC SAN addresses follow the naming standard Adapter:Channel:Target:LUN.
    ☒ **A, B,** and **D** are incorrect. 0 is the adapter. 1 is the Channel. 3 is the LUN.

3. ☑ **C.** Zoning is configured on the Fibre switches and can be used to hide LUNs from both VMware Hosts and non-VMware Servers.
    ☒ **A, B,** and **D** are incorrect. LUN masking is configured on an ESX/ESXi Host and is used to hide LUNs from the Host. LUN shadowing and LUN hiding are not actual technologies.

4. ☑ **A.** In the Fixed storage multipathing policy the original path will be used if it has failed and then become available again.
    ☒ **B, C,** and **D** are incorrect. In the MRU multipathing policy the original path will not be used if it has failed and then become available again. First Used is not a multipathing policy. The Round Robin multipathing policy uses all of the active paths one after the other.

Configure iSCSI SAN Storage

5. ☑ **C.** Fibre Channel HBAs are used for FC SANs, not for iSCSI SANs.
    ☒ **A, B,** and **D** are incorrect. The iSCSI initiator, iSCSI target, and network switches are all components of an iSCSI SAN.

6. ☑ **A.** Under ESX 4.0 the iSCSI hardware initiator is supported.
    ☒ **B** is incorrect. In earlier versions of ESX the iSCSI hardware initiator was not supported, but it is under ESX 4.0.

7. ☑ **D.** The iSCSI software initiator requires more overhead from the VMkernel than the iSCSI hardware initiator.
    ☒ **A, B,** and **C** are incorrect. The iSCSI software initiator uses a standard NIC port. The iSCSI software initiator requires more overhead from the VMkernel than the iSCSI hardware initiator. The iSCSI software initiator is less expensive than the iSCSI hardware initiator.

8. ☑ **D.** In mutual CHAP the iSCSI server authenticates the iSCSI initiator and the iSCSI initiator authenticates the iSCSI server.

⊠ **A, B,** and **C** are incorrect. In one-way CHAP the iSCSI server authenticates the iSCSI initiator. Dual CHAP and two-way CHAP are not actually types of CHAP authentication.

Configure NFS Datastores

9. ☑ **B.** A lock file located in the same directory as the virtual machine files is used to implement ESX exclusivity.
☒ **A, C,** and **D** are incorrect. Virtual SCSI locking, mount locking, and IP locking are not NFS technologies.

Configure and Manage VMFS Datastores

10. ☑ **C.** Microsoft Clustering is not supported on NFS datastores.
☒ **A, B,** and **D** are incorrect. Microsoft Clustering is supported on both FC SANs and iSCSI SANs.

11. ☑ **B.** NFS datastores generally provide lower performance than the other storage technologies.
☒ **A, C,** and **D** are incorrect. iSCSI SANs, FC SANs, and local SCSI drives generally provide better performance than NFS datastores.

12. ☑ **B.** When a datastore is unmounted from an ESX Host the data it contains is not lost.
☒ **A** is incorrect.

7

Create, Deploy, and Manage Virtual Machines and vApps

Welcome to Chapter 7. In this chapter we will learn about virtual machines and vApps. We will start by discussing what virtual machines are and how they can be used. We will look at the types of hardware that virtual machines can use and various ways to create virtual machines. We will then discuss the various settings and options that can be configured for virtual machines. We will then end the chapter by discussing how to deploy and configure vApps. By the end of this chapter you will be able to start deploying virtual machines and vApps in your vSphere environment.

CERTIFICATION OBJECTIVE 7.01

Create and Deploy Virtual Machines

Virtual machines are servers and desktops that operate just like physical servers and desktops except that they are implemented in software. They have the same components as physical servers and workstations and operate in complete isolation from each other even though they run on the same physical hardware. In this section we will discuss multiple methods for creating and deploying virtual machines. We will start by looking at virtual machine hardware maximums and then create our first virtual machine. We will then work with templates and virtual machine customization.

Virtual Machine Hardware Maximums

Before we can begin creating and deploying virtual machines, we need to understand their hardware limitations. Under ESX 4.0 a virtual machine can have only so many SCSI controllers or GBs of RAM. VMware refers to these limitations as *virtual machine hardware maximums*. The following table lists the available virtual devices and the maximum of each that can be used by a virtual machine. You will need to memorize these for the exam.

Device	Maximum	Device	Maximum
Virtual CPU	8	RAM	255GB
Swap file size	255GB	Max disk size	2TB minus 512B
SCSI adapters	4	IDE controllers/VM	1
SCSI targets per SCSI adapter	15	IDE devices/VM	4
SCSI targets/VM	60	Floppy controllers	1
Virtual NICs	10	Floppy devices	2
Parallel ports	3	Serial ports	4

INSIDE THE EXAM

Hardware Maximums

To test your knowledge of virtual machines, you should expect to see at least one or two questions that ask about hardware maximums. These values will need to be memorized to give you the best chance of passing the exam.

Now that you understand the hardware maximums for virtual machines, let's go ahead and create a new virtual machine.

Create a Virtual Machine

There are a number of different ways to create virtual machines in a vSphere environment. For our first virtual machine we will create a Typical virtual machine using the New Virtual Machine Wizard. Once we have the first build under our belt, we will go ahead and create a custom virtual machine using the wizard.

A Typical virtual machine is easier to set up and includes the most common settings for a virtual machine. To create a Typical virtual machine using the New Virtual Machine Wizard, follow these steps:

1. Launch the vSphere Client and connect to your ESX Host or vCenter Server.

2. In the navigation bar select Home | Inventory if you connected to your ESX Host or Home | Inventory | Hosts if you connected to your vCenter Server.

3. Select the Host you want to create the virtual machine on.

4. From the File menu select New and then Virtual Machine. You will now see the New Virtual Machine Wizard as shown in Figure 7-1.

5. Select the radio button for Typical and click Next to continue.

6. You will be prompted to enter a name for the new virtual machine. Enter a meaningful name and click Next to continue.

7. You will be prompted to enter a datastore where you want to place the new virtual machine. Select a datastore and click Next to continue.

8. You will be prompted to select the Guest Operating System and Version. Enter this information and click Next to continue.

9. You will be prompted to create a new disk for the virtual machine. You will need to specify the disk size and determine if you want to use Thin provisioning in which disk space is allocated as needed or Thick provisioning where all of the disk space is allocated now. You will also need to determine if you want the disk to be compatible with advanced clustering features. Selecting this option will cause the disk to take longer to create but will make it more flexible in the future. Make these selections and click Next to continue.

10. You will be presented with a summary screen. Click Finish to create the virtual machine.

FIGURE 7-1

The New Virtual
Machine Wizard
screen

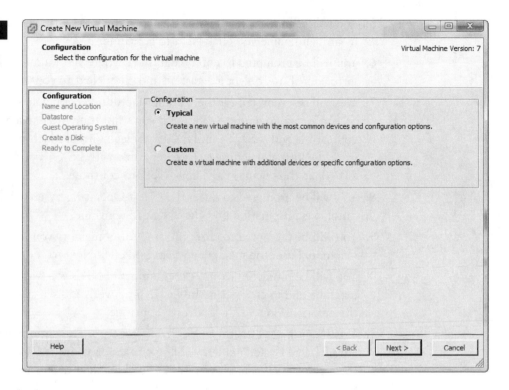

Creating a Custom virtual machine allows you more control over how the virtual machine will be created but is slightly more complicated. To create a Custom virtual machine using the New Virtual Machine Wizard, follow these steps:

1. Launch the vSphere Client and connect to your ESX Host or vCenter Server.
2. In the navigation bar select Home | Inventory if you connected to your ESX Host or Home | Inventory | Hosts if you connected to your vCenter Server.
3. Select the Host you want to create the virtual machine on.
4. From the File menu select New and then Virtual Machine. Select the radio button for Custom and click Next to continue.

5. You will be prompted to enter a name for the new virtual machine. Enter a meaningful name and click Next to continue.

6. You will be prompted to enter a datastore where you want to place the new virtual machine. Select a datastore and click Next to continue.

7. You will be prompted for the Virtual Machine Version you want to deploy. Select Virtual Machine Version 4 if you want the virtual machine to be compatible with ESX 3.x and EX 4.x. Select Virtual Machine Version 7 if you want the virtual machine to be compatible with ESX 4.x and VMware Server 2.0. Make the selection and click Next to continue.

8. You will be prompted to select the Guest Operating System and Version. Enter this information and click Next to continue.

9. You will be prompted to enter the amount of memory you want for the virtual machine. Enter the memory amount and click Next to continue.

10. You will be prompted to enter the number of NICs you want for the virtual machine and to connect each NIC to a network and select a NIC type. Enter this information and click Next to continue.

11. You are prompted to enter a SCSI adapter type. The options are Buslogic Parallel, LSI Logic Parallel, LSI Logic SAS, or VMware Paravirtual. Select the type of SCSI adapter you want and click Next to continue.

12. You will be prompted to select a disk type for the virtual machine. The options are Create A New Virtual Disk, Use An Existing Virtual Disk, Raw Device Mappings (these are links to RAW LUNs attached to the Host), or Do Not Create Disk. Select Create A New Virtual Disk and click Next to continue.

13. You will be prompted to create a new disk for the virtual machine. You will need to specify the disk size and determine if you want to use Thin provisioning, in which disk space is allocated as needed, or Thick provisioning, where all of the disk space is allocated now. You will also need to determine if you want the disk to be compatible with advanced clustering features. Selecting this option will cause the disk to take longer to create but will make it more flexible in the future. Make these selections and click Next to continue.

14. You will be prompted to enter some advanced options. You need to select a Virtual Device Node and the disk mode. We will review these settings later in the chapter. For now select the defaults and click Next to continue.

15. You will be presented with a summary screen. Click Finish to create the virtual machine.

Now that you have created a few virtual machines, let's look at installing the VMware Tools on them.

Install VMware Tools

The VMware Tools package is a collection of utilities, scripts, and drivers that you can install on a guest operating system on a virtual machine to improve its performance and make it easier to manage. Installing VMware Tools on each of your virtual machines is an easy way to boost the performance and manageability of your virtual environment and is required to utilize some of the advanced features of vSphere.

To install VMware Tools on a Windows virtual machine, follow these steps:

1. Launch the vSphere Client and connect to your ESX Host or vCenter Server.

2. In the navigation bar select Home | Inventory if you connected to your ESX Host or Home | Inventory | Hosts if you connected to your vCenter Server.

3. Select the virtual machine you want to install VMware Tools on.

4. Make sure the virtual machine is powered on.

5. Right-click the virtual machine and select Guest from the drop-down menu and the select Install/Upgrade VMware Tools.

6. You will be presented with the Install VMware Tools window. Click OK to continue.

7. Select the Console tab to view the console of the virtual machine.

8. Log on to the virtual machine.

9. If autorun is enabled on your Guest operating system, the install will begin automatically. If you do not have autorun enabled, you will need to go to My Computer and double-click the CD-ROM drive to begin the installation.

10. You will be presented with a window asking to launch the VMware Tools installer. Click OK to allow the installer to launch.

11. You will be presented with a welcome screen. Click Next to continue.

12. You will be prompted to enter the Setup Type for the VMware Tools installation. The options are Typical, Complete, and Custom. Select Typical if you only intend to use this virtual machine on ESX Server. Select Complete if you want to be able to use this virtual machine on other VMware platforms. Choose Custom if you are an advanced user. Make your selection and click Next to continue.

13. You will be presented with a summary screen. Click Next to continue.

14. You will be presented with a completion window informing you that the VMware Tools have been installed. Click Finish to exit. You will need to reboot the virtual machine before VMware Tools will be fully installed.

Now that you have VMware Tools installed on your virtual machine, you will see a significant performance boost.

Guest Customization

VMware allows you to save settings that are used to customize new virtual machines when they are created using the Guest Customization Wizard. These settings can then be applied to a new virtual machine when it is created from a template or when it is cloned from an existing virtual machine.

Requirements for Windows Guest Customization

Before a Windows virtual machine can be customized, the following requirements must be met:

■ Microsoft SYSPREP must be installed on the vCenter Server.
 ■ The clone or template must be one of the following Windows versions:
 ■ Windows 2000 Server
 ■ Windows XP Professional
 ■ Windows Server 2003
 ■ Windows Server 2008
 ■ Windows Vista

- The Guest cannot be a primary domain controller or backup domain controller.
- The clone or template must have the VMware Tools installed.

Installing Microsoft SYSPREP on Your vCenter Server

One of the requirements for using Guest Customization when creating Windows Guests is to have Windows SYSPREP installed on your vCenter Server.

To install Microsoft SYSPREP on your vCenter Server, follow these steps:

1. Download the SYSPREP version for the types of virtual machines you are creating from Microsoft to a folder on your vCenter Server.
2. Open a command prompt and navigate to the folder you downloaded SYSPREP to.
3. Extract the files from the file you downloaded by typing **<*filename.exe*> /x**, where *filename* is the name of the file you downloaded.
4. Use Windows Explorer to locate the deploy.cab file you extracted. Select it and you will be presented with the file contained in the .cab file.
5. Copy these files to the appropriate directory on your vCenter Server based on the version of SYSPREP you are configuring and the Windows version of your vCenter Server as shown in the table that follows.

   - For vCenter installed on Windows 2003 Server <directory> = C:\ Documents and Settings\All Users\Application Data\VMware\ VMware VirtualCenter\sysprep\
   - For vCenter installed on Windows 2008 Server <directory> = C:\ ProgramData\VMware\VMware VirtualCenter\sysprep

SYSPREP Version	Folder Location
Windows 2000 Server SP4	<directory>\1.1
Windows XP Pro SP2	<directory>\xp
Windows XP x64	<directory>\xp-64
Windows 2003 Server	<directory>\srv2003
Windows 2003 x64	<directory>\srv2003-64

Requirements for Linux Guest Customization

Before a Linux virtual machine can be customized, the following requirements must be met:

- The root volume of the clone or template must be formatted with ext2, ext3, or ReiserFS.
- The clone or template must be one of the following Linux versions:
  - Debian 4.0
  - Red Hat Desktop versions 3 and 4
  - Red Hat Enterprise Linux 5
  - Red Hat Enterprise Linux 5 Desktop
  - Red Hat Enterprise Linux AS versions 2.1, 3, 4, and 4.5
  - Red Hat Enterprise Linux ES versions 2.1, 3, and 4
  - Ubuntu 8.04
- The Guest operating system must have Perl installed on it.
- The clone or template must have the VMware Tools installed.

Create a Windows Guest Customization Specification

A Windows Guest Customization Specification contains all of the customization information that applies to a Windows virtual machine. It can be created in advance and can be used later when creating a new Windows virtual machine from a template or by cloning an existing virtual machine.

To create a Windows Guest Customization Specification, follow these steps:

1. Launch the vSphere Client and connect to your vCenter Server.

2. From the View menu select Management and then Customization Specifications Manager. You will be presented with the Customization Specifications Manager window as shown in Figure 7-2.

3. Click New at the top of the window to create a new Customization Specification. You will be presented with the New Customization Specification Wizard.

FIGURE 7-2   The Customization Specifications Manager window

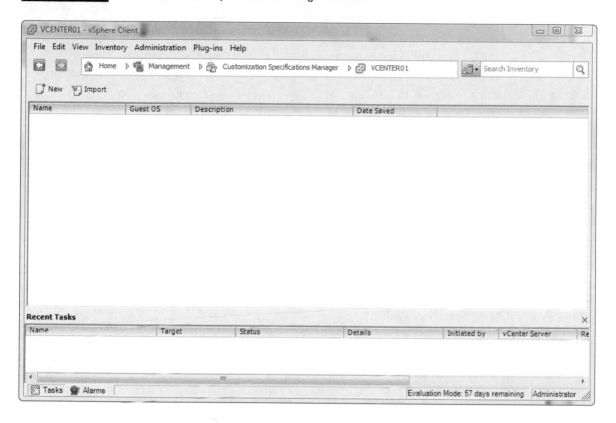

4. You will be prompted for the Target Virtual Machine OS (Windows or Linux), a name for the new customization specification, and a description. Select Windows, enter a descriptive name, and add a brief description. Click Next to continue.

5. You will be prompted to enter an Owner's name and Organization for the new virtual machine. Enter this information and click Next to continue.

6. You will be prompted to enter a NetBIOS name for the new virtual machine. Enter this information and click Next to continue. I recommend using the same name as you used for the virtual machine name.

7. You will be prompted to enter a Product Key and Server License Mode for the new virtual machine. Enter this information and click Next to continue.

8. You will be prompted to enter a password for the Administrator account and confirm the password. Enter this information and click Next to continue.

9. You will be prompted to enter a Time Zone for the new virtual machine. Enter this information and click Next to continue.

10. You will be prompted to enter any run-once commands for the new virtual machine. If you have any commands, enter them here and click Next to continue.

11. You will be prompted to enter Network Settings for the new virtual machine. Enter this information and click Next to continue.

12. You will be prompted to select whether the virtual machine will be in a workgroup or a domain. If you select workgroup, you need to enter the workgroup. If you select domain, you will need to enter the domain and a username and password that has authority to add the new virtual machine to the domain. Enter this information and click Next to continue.

13. You will be prompted to select if you want a new SID to be generated for the new virtual machine. Enter this information and click Next to continue.

14. You will be presented with a summary screen. Click Finish to create the Guest Customization Specification.

Create a Linux Guest Customization Specification

A Linux Guest Customization Specification contains all of the customization information that applies to a Linux virtual machine. Like its Windows counterpart, it can be created in advance and can be used later when creating a new Linux virtual machine from a template or by cloning an existing virtual machine.

To create a Linux Guest Customization Specification, follow these steps:

1. Launch the vSphere Client and connect to your vCenter Server.

2. From the View menu select Management and then Customization Specifications Manager. You will be presented with the Customization Specifications Manager window.

3. Click New at the top of the window to create a new Customization Specification. You will be presented with the New Customization Specification Wizard.

4. You will be prompted for the Target Virtual Machine OS (Windows or Linux), a name for the new customization specification, and a description. Select Linux, enter a descriptive name, and add a brief description. Click Next to continue.

5. You will be prompted to enter a name and a domain for the new virtual machine. Enter this information and click Next to continue.

6. You will be prompted to enter a Time Zone for the new virtual machine. Enter this information and click Next to continue.

7. You will be prompted to enter Network Settings for the new virtual machine. Enter this information and click Next to continue.

8. You will be prompted to enter DNS Settings for the new virtual machine. Enter this information and click Next to continue.

9. You will be presented with a summary screen. Click Finish to create the Guest Customization Specification.

Create and Convert Templates

A *template* is a gold image copy of a virtual machine that can be used to create new virtual machines that are configured exactly the same. The template contains all of the virtual machine settings, the guest operating system with customized settings, and any additional software that is installed on the guest OS. Templates can streamline the deployment of virtual machines by allowing you to quickly deploy new virtual machines with consistent configurations without having to reinstall additional software packages on the guest operating systems. There are two different ways to make a template from a virtual machine. You can convert a virtual machine into a template or clone a virtual machine into a template. If you convert a virtual machine into a template, the original virtual machine is changed into a template and can no longer be used as a virtual machine. If you clone a virtual machine into a template, the original virtual machine is not changed.

To convert a virtual machine into a template, follow these steps:

1. Launch the vSphere Client and connect to your vCenter Server.

2. In the navigation bar select Home | Inventory | VMs and Templates.

3. Select the virtual machine you want to convert into a template.

4. Make sure the virtual machine is powered off.

5. Right-click the virtual machine and select Template from the drop-down menu and then select Convert To Template. At this point, a new template will be created.

To clone a virtual machine into a template, follow these steps:

1. Launch the vSphere Client and connect to your vCenter Server.

2. In the navigation bar select Home | Inventory | VMs And Templates.

3. Select the virtual machine you want to convert into a template.

4. Make sure the virtual machine is powered off.

5. Right-click the virtual machine and select Template from the drop-down menu and then select Clone To Template.

6. You will be prompted to enter a name for the new template and for a location to store the template. Enter this information and click Next to continue.

7. You are prompted to select the Host or Cluster on which you want the new template to reside. Select the default and click Next to continue.

8. You are prompted to select the Datastore where you want the virtual machine files to reside. Select a Datastore and click Next to continue.

9. You are prompted to select the virtual disk format that will be used by the template. The choices are: Same Format As Source, where the template will use the same format as the virtual machine; Thin Provisioned Format, where the disk will be allocated as needed; or Thick Format, where the entire virtual disk will be allocated. Enter your selection and click Next to continue.

10. You are presented with a summary screen. Click Finish to create the new template and exit.

Deploy Virtual Machines from Templates

Now that we have created a few templates, let's look at how to deploy a virtual machine from a template.

To deploy a virtual machine from a template, follow these steps:

1. Launch the vSphere Client and connect to your vCenter Server.

2. In the navigation bar select Home | Inventory | VMs And Templates.

3. Select the template you want to use to deploy a virtual machine.

4. Right-click the template and select Deploy Virtual Machine From This Template.

5. You are prompted to enter a name and an inventory location for the new virtual machine. Enter this information and click Next to continue.

6. You are prompted to select a Host or cluster to place the new virtual machine on. We will discuss clusters later, so for now select a Host and click Next to continue.

7. You are prompted to select a Datastore for the new virtual machine. Select a Datastore and click Next to continue.

8. You are prompted to select the virtual disk format that will be used by the template. The choices are Same Format As Source, where the template will use the same format as the virtual machine; Thin Provisioned Format, where the disk will be allocated as needed; or Thick Format, where the entire virtual disk will be allocated. Enter your selection and click Next to continue.

9. On this screen you can perform Guest Customization on your Guest. The options are Do Not Customize, Customize Using The Customization Wizard, and Customize Using An Existing Customization Specification. Select Do Not Customize if you do not want to perform any guest customization. Select Customize Using The Customization Wizard and you will be prompted to enter customization information. Select Customize Using An Existing Customization Specification to use a customization specification that you created earlier. Make your selection and perform guest customization; then click Next to continue.

10. You are presented with a summary screen. Click Finish to create the new template and exit.

on the **job**

The vast majority of virtual machines that I deploy for my clients are deployed from a template. By using a template, I will only have to manually install all of the ancillary software that my clients require on their servers once.

Clone a Virtual Machine

Another way to create a virtual machine is to clone an existing virtual machine. The new virtual machine will be identical to the virtual machine it is cloned from. You can perform customizations on the new virtual machine as it is being created.

To deploy a virtual machine from a template, follow these steps:

1. Launch the vSphere Client and connect to your vCenter Server.

2. In the navigation bar select Home | Inventory | VMs and Templates.

3. Select the virtual machine you want to make a clone of.

4. Right-click the virtual machine and select Clone.

5. You will be presented with the Clone Virtual Machine Wizard.

6. You are prompted to enter a name and an inventory location for the new virtual machine. Enter this information and click Next to continue.

7. You are prompted to select a Host or cluster to place the new virtual machine on. We will discuss clusters later, so for now select a Host and click Next to continue.

8. You are prompted to select a Datastore for the new virtual machine. Select a Datastore and click Next to continue.

9. You are prompted to select the virtual disk format that will be used by the template. The choices are Same Format As Source, where the template will use the same format as the virtual machine; Thin Provisioned Format, where the disk will be allocated as needed; or Thick Format, where the entire virtual disk will be allocated. Enter your selection and click Next to continue.

10. On this screen you can perform Guest Customization on your Guest. The options are Do Not Customize, Customize Using The Customization Wizard, and Customize Using An Existing Customization Specification. Select Do Not Customize if you do not want to perform any guest customization. Select Customize Using The Customization Wizard and you will be prompted to enter customization information. Select Customize Using An Existing Customization Specification to use a customization specification that you created earlier. Make your selection and perform guest customization; then click Next to continue.

11. You are presented with a summary screen. Click Finish to create the new template and exit.

CERTIFICATION OBJECTIVE 7.02

Manage Virtual Machine Configurations

Now that you know how to create virtual machines, let's take a look at the different settings and options that can be changed on an existing virtual machine. In this section we will look at adding hardware to a virtual machine and modifying existing hardware, configuring virtual machine options, and managing virtual machine resources. Let's start by looking at adding new hardware to a virtual machine.

Add New Virtual Hardware and Modify Existing Virtual Hardware

Virtual hardware can be added to a virtual machine the same way that physical hardware can be added to a physical server. In this section we will look at all of the different types of hardware that make up a virtual machine and discuss how to add them to a virtual machine. The following types of hardware can be included in a virtual machine:

- CPU
- Floppy drives
- Hard disks
- Memory
- Network adapters
- Parallel ports
- SCSI controllers
- Serial ports
- USB controllers
- Video card

The first step to configuring existing hardware or adding additional hardware to a virtual machine is to launch the Virtual Machine Properties window on the virtual machine you wish to edit.

To access the Virtual Machine Properties Hardware window for a virtual machine, follow these steps:

1. Launch the vSphere Client and connect to your ESX Host or vCenter Server.
2. In the navigation bar select Home | Inventory if you connected to your ESX Host or Home | Inventory | Hosts if you connected to your vCenter Server.
3. In the left-hand frame right-click the virtual machine you wish to edit and select Edit Settings from the drop-down menu.
4. Select the Hardware tab and you will be presented with the Virtual Machine Properties window for the virtual machine as shown in Figure 7-3.

FIGURE 7-3

The Virtual Machine Properties Hardware window of a virtual machine

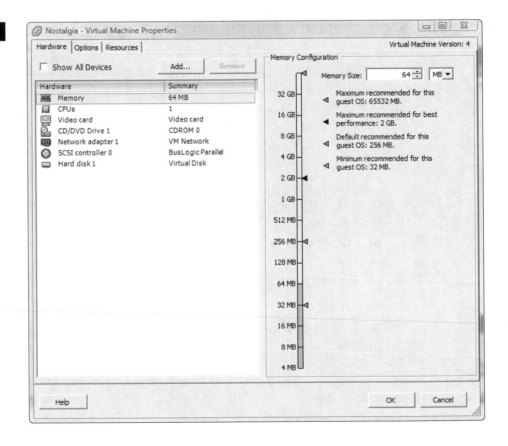

From the Virtual Machine Properties window you can view the existing hardware that is on the virtual machine, add additional hardware, and configure the virtual machine's options and resource settings.

Change the Number of Virtual CPUs on a Virtual Machine

Under vSphere a virtual machine can have up to eight virtual CPUs. The number of CPUs can be set during the creation of the virtual machine and can also be increased or decreased using the Virtual Machine Properties window.

To change the number of virtual CPUs on a virtual machine, follow these steps:

1. Launch the Virtual Machine Properties window for the virtual machine you want to edit.
2. Select the Hardware tab.
3. Select CPUs from the list of hardware devices.
4. Choose the number of virtual CPUs you want from the drop-down box for Number of virtual processors on the right side of the window.
5. Click OK to save the changes and exit.

Change the Configured Memory on a Virtual Machine

Under vSphere a virtual machine can have a maximum of 255GB of memory. The actual amount of memory you will be able to configure for your virtual machines will depend on the amount of memory you have available on your Hosts and the number of virtual machines you run on each Host. ESX/ESXi Hosts support memory overcommitment. Using overcommitment, you can assign more memory to your virtual machines than you actually have on the Host. This can be very useful but can also lead to memory swapping that can affect performance.

To change the amount of memory on a virtual machine, follow these steps:

1. Launch the Virtual Machine Properties window for the virtual machine you want to edit.
2. Select the Hardware tab.
3. Select Memory from the list of hardware devices.
4. Choose the amount of memory you want from the drop-down box for Memory Size on the right side of the window.
5. Click OK to save the changes and exit.

Modify the Video Card of a Virtual Machine

Each virtual machine has one virtual video card. You can configure the following settings for the video card:

- **Maximum Number of Displays**   This setting controls the maximum number of displays that can be configured for the virtual machines.
- **Memory Required for Displays**   This setting allows you to reserve video memory for the virtual machine. There are three options for configuring video memory. You can allow the system to auto-detect the video memory, specify the resolution and color depth, or specify a fixed amount for total video memory.

To modify the video card settings on a virtual machine, follow these steps:

1. Launch the Virtual Machine Properties window for the virtual machine you want to edit.
2. Select the Hardware tab.
3. Select the video card from the list of hardware devices.
4. Select the options you want to set on the right side of the window.
5. Click OK to save the changes and exit.

Modify or Add a Floppy Drive to a Virtual Machine

Under vSphere a virtual machine can have up to two virtual floppy drives. You can configure the following settings for a floppy drive:

- **Device Status**   This setting controls when the floppy drive is connected and can have the following values:
  - **Connected**   This value causes the floppy device to be connected immediately.
  - **Connect at power on**   This value causes the floppy device to connect when the virtual machine is powered on.
- **Device Type**   This setting controls which floppy device the virtual floppy is connected to and can have the following values:
  - **Client Device**   This value causes the virtual floppy device to connect to the floppy drive of the system using the vSphere Client to connect to the virtual machine.

- **Host Device**   This value causes the virtual floppy device to connect to the physical floppy drive on the Host.
- **Use existing floppy image in datastore**   This value causes the virtual floppy device to connect to a floppy disk image on a datastore connected to the Host.
- **Create new floppy image in datastore**   This value causes the virtual floppy device to connect to a new floppy disk image that you create on a datastore connected to the Host.

To modify the floppy drive settings on a virtual machine, follow these steps:

1. Launch the Virtual Machine Properties window for the virtual machine you want to edit.
2. Select the Hardware tab.
3. Select the floppy drive from the list of hardware devices.
4. Select the options you want to set on the right side of the window.
5. Click OK to save the changes and exit.

To add a new floppy drive to a virtual machine, follow these steps:

1. Launch the Virtual Machine Properties window for the virtual machine you want to edit.
2. Select the Hardware tab.
3. Click the Add button at the top of the window.
4. Select Floppy Drive from the device list and click Next to continue.
5. Select the type of media you would like the floppy drive to access and click Next to continue. You can choose to use a physical floppy device, use an existing floppy image, or create a blank floppy image.
6. Depending on the choice you made on the last screen, you will be asked to either select a physical floppy disk on the client or Host or to enter the path for a floppy image. Enter this information and click Next to continue.
7. You will be presented with a summary window showing the type of floppy drive you are about to create.
8. Click Finish to create the new floppy drive.
9. Click OK to save the changes and exit.

Modify or Add a Parallel Port to a Virtual Machine

Under vSphere a virtual machine can have up to three virtual parallel ports. You can configure the following settings for a parallel port:

- **Device Status** This setting controls when the floppy drive is connected and can have the following values:
  - **Connected** This value causes the parallel port to be connected immediately.
  - **Connect at power on** This value causes the parallel port to connect when the virtual machine is powered on.
- **Connection** This setting controls whether the parallel port uses a physical connection or an output file and can have the following values:
  - **Use physical parallel port** This value causes the virtual parallel port to use a physical port on the Host that you select from a drop-down menu.
  - **Use output file** This value causes the virtual parallel port to send its output to a file that you specify.

To modify the parallel port settings on a virtual machine, follow these steps:

1. Launch the Virtual Machine Properties window for the virtual machine you want to edit.
2. Select the Hardware tab.
3. Select the parallel port from the list of hardware devices.
4. Select the options you want to set on the right side of the window.
5. Click OK to save the changes and exit.

To add a new parallel port to a virtual machine, follow these steps:

1. Launch the Virtual Machine Properties window for the virtual machine you want to edit.
2. Select the Hardware tab.
3. Click the Add button at the top of the window.
4. Select Parallel Port from the device list and click Next to continue.
5. You are prompted to either use a physical parallel port on the Host or output to file. Select the connection type for the parallel port and click Next to continue.

6. If you selected a connection type using a physical parallel port on the Host, you will be prompted to select the port from a drop-down menu. If you selected a connection type of output to file, you will be prompted to enter the output file path. You will also see that Connect At Power On is checked by default. Enter this information and click Next to continue.

7. You will be presented with a summary window showing the type of parallel port you are about to create. Click Finish to create the new parallel port.

8. Click OK to save the changes and exit.

Modify or Add a Serial Port to a Virtual Machine

Under vSphere a virtual machine can have up to four virtual serial ports. You can configure the following settings for a serial port:

- **Device Status**   This setting controls when the floppy drive is connected and can have the following values:
  - **Connected**   This value causes the virtual serial port to be connected immediately.
  - **Connect at power on**   This value causes the virtual serial port to connect when the virtual machine is powered on.
- **Connection**   This setting controls whether the parallel port uses a physical connection or an output file and can have the following values:
  - **Use physical serial port**   This value causes the virtual serial port to use a physical port on the Host that you select from a drop-down menu.
  - **Use output file**   This value causes the virtual serial port to send its output to a file that you specify.
  - **Use Named Pipe**   This value causes the virtual serial port to send its output to a named pipe that you enter.
- **I/O Mode**   This setting controls whether the guest operating system can use this serial port in polled mode as opposed to interrupt mode and can have the following value:
  - **Yield CPU on poll**   This value causes the guest operating system to be able to use the serial port in polled mode.

To modify the serial port settings on a virtual machine, follow these steps:

1. Launch the Virtual Machine Properties window for the virtual machine you want to edit.
2. Select the Hardware tab.
3. Select the serial port from the list of hardware devices.
4. Select the options you want to set on the right side of the window.
5. Click OK to save the changes and exit.

To add a new serial port to a virtual machine, follow these steps:

1. Launch the Virtual Machine Properties window for the virtual machine you want to edit.
2. Select the Hardware tab.
3. Click the Add button at the top of the window.
4. Select Serial Port from the device list and click Next to continue.
5. You are prompted to either use a physical serial port on the Host, output to file, or connect to a named pipe. Select the connection type for the parallel port and click Next to continue.
6. If you chose to use a physical serial port on the Host, you will be prompted to select the port from a drop-down menu. If you chose to output to a file, you will be prompted to enter the output file path. If you chose to connect to a named pipe, you will be prompted for the pipe name. You will also see that Connect At Power On and Yield CPU On Poll are checked by default. Enter this information and click Next to continue.
7. You will be presented with a summary window showing the type of parallel port you are about to create. Click Finish to create the new serial port.
8. Click OK to save the changes and exit.

Add a USB Controller to a Virtual Machine

Under vSphere a virtual machine can have one virtual USB controller. There are no configuration settings for a USB controller.

To add a new serial port to a virtual machine, follow these steps:

1. Launch the Virtual Machine Properties window for the virtual machine you want to edit.

2. Select the Hardware tab.
3. Click the Add button at the top of the window.
4. Select USB Controller from the device list and click Next to continue.
5. You will be presented with a window telling you that a two-port USB controller is being added to the virtual machine. Click Next to continue.
6. You will be presented with a summary window showing the type of USB controller you are about to create. Click Finish to create the new USB controller.
7. Click OK to save the changes and exit.

Modify a SCSI Controller on a Virtual Machine

Under vSphere a virtual machine can have up to four virtual SCSI controllers. You can configure the following settings for a SCSI controller:

- **SCSI Controller Type** This setting controls when the floppy drive is connected; it can have the following values:
  - **BusLogic Parallel** This value causes the virtual serial port to be connected immediately.
  - **LSI Logic Parallel** This value causes the virtual serial port to connect when the virtual machine is powered on.
- **SCSI Bus Sharing** This setting controls whether the parallel port uses a physical connection or an output file; it can have the following values:
  - **None** This value does not allow virtual disks to be shared across virtual machines.
  - **Virtual** This value allows virtual disks to be shared across virtual machines on the same Host.
  - **Physical** This value allows virtual disks to be shared across virtual machines on different Hosts.

To modify the SCSI controller settings on a virtual machine, follow these steps:

1. Launch the Virtual Machine Properties window for the virtual machine you want to edit.
2. Select the Hardware tab.
3. Select the SCSI Controller from the list of hardware devices.

4. Select the options you want to set on the right side of the window.

5. Click OK to save the changes and exit.

SCSI controllers are added to a virtual machine by adding a new disk to the virtual machine and using a new, unused SCSI Bus number.

Modify or Add a Network Adapter to a Virtual Machine

Under vSphere a virtual machine can have up to ten virtual network adapters. You can configure the following settings for a network adapter:

- **Adapter Type** This setting controls when the floppy drive is connected and can have the following values:
  - **Flexible** This value is for 32-bit guest operating systems that were created with ESX Server 3.0 or higher.
  - **e1000** This value is the default for 64-bit operating systems.
  - **Enhanced vmxnet** This value requires that VMware Tools be installed on the virtual machine and provides enhancements over the older vmxnet adapter.
  - **vmxnet 3** This value is an even more enhanced version of the older vmxnet adapter that requires that VMware Tools be installed on the virtual machine and that the virtual machine have a hardware level 7 or greater.
- **Network Connection** This setting controls which network the new network adapter will connect to and can have the following values:
  - **Network Label** This value causes the virtual network adapter to use a named network on the Host that you select from a drop-down menu.
  - **Specify Port** This value causes the virtual network adapter to use a legacy network that you specify.
- **Device Status** This setting controls when the floppy drive is connected; it can have the following value:
  - **Connect at power on** This value causes the network adapter to connect when the virtual machine is powered on.
- **MAC Address** This setting controls how the MAC address of the virtual machine will be assigned; it can have the following values:
  - **Automatic** This value causes the MAC address of the virtual machine to be set automatically by the Host.
  - **Manual** This value causes the MAC address of the virtual machine to be set to a value you assign.

To modify the network interface settings on a virtual machine, follow these steps:

1. Launch the Virtual Machine Properties window for the virtual machine you want to edit.
2. Select the Hardware tab.
3. Select the network adapter from the list of hardware devices.
4. Select the options you want to set on the right side of the window.
5. Click OK to save the changes and exit.

To add a new network interface to a virtual machine, follow these steps:

1. Launch the Virtual Machine Properties window for the virtual machine you want to edit.
2. Select the Hardware tab.
3. Click the Add button at the top of the window.
4. Select Ethernet Adaptor from the device list and click Next to continue.
5. You are prompted to enter the Adapter Type, Network Connection, and Device Status for the new Ethernet Adaptor. Enter this information and click Next to continue.
6. You will be presented with a summary window showing the type of network adapter you are about to create. Click Finish to create the new network adapter.
7. Click OK to save the changes and exit.

Modify or Add a Hard Disk to a Virtual Machine

Under vSphere a virtual machine can have up to 60 virtual SCSI hard disks. You can configure the following settings for a hard disk:

- **Disk File** This setting shows the location of the virtual machine's disk file.
- **Disk Provisioning** This setting controls how the virtual disk is provisioned and can have the following values:
  - **Type** This value determines if the disk is provisioned as Thick or Thin. A Thin provisioned disk is only as large as the space it is using and grows as additional space is needed. A Thick provisioned disk uses its entire space when it is created and does not expand.

- **Provisioned Size** This value controls the size of the virtual disk.
- **Virtual Device Node** This value controls the virtual SCSI path to the disk drive.
- **Mode** This setting controls how changes to the disk file are handled and how the disk will be affected by snapshots; it can have the following value:
  - **Independent** This value causes the disk file to be unaffected by snapshots. An Independent disk can be either Persistent or Non-Persistent. A Persistent disk file will operate as a normal disk, and changes to the disk will still be there after a power cycle of the virtual machine. A Non-Persistent disk file also appears to operate as a normal disk, but after a power cycle of the virtual machine the disk will return to the state it was in when it was set to Non-Persistent and all changes to the disk will be lost.

To modify the network interface settings on a virtual machine, follow these steps:

1. Launch the Virtual Machine Properties window for the virtual machine you want to edit.
2. Select the Hardware tab.
3. Select the Hard Disk from the list of hardware devices.
4. Select the options you want to set on the right side of the window.
5. Click OK to save the changes and exit.

To add a new hard disk to a virtual machine, follow these steps:

1. Launch the Virtual Machine Properties window for the virtual machine you want to edit.
2. Select the Hardware tab.
3. Click the Add button at the top of the window.
4. Select Hard Disk from the device list and click Next to continue.
5. You are prompted to select the type of disk to use. Select either Create A New Virtual Disk, Use An Existing Virtual Disk, or Raw Device Mapping. If you select Create A New Virtual Disk, you will be prompted for the new disk capacity, the disk provisioning type, and the location for the disk. If you select Use An Existing Virtual Disk, you will be prompted for the Disk File Path to the existing virtual disk. If you select Raw Device Mapping, you will

be prompted for the LUN to use to connect the Raw Device Mapping, a data-store, and the compatibility mode for the Raw Device Mapping. The physical compatibility mode allows the guest operating system to have direct access to the SAN LUN to use specialized SAN management software for optimal performance, while the virtual compatibility mode allows the use of snapshots on LUN volumes. Enter this information and click Next to continue.

6. You will be prompted to enter the virtual device node and the disk mode. Enter this information and click Next to continue.

7. You will be presented with a summary window showing the type of hard disk you are about to create. Click Finish to create the new hard disk.

8. Click OK to save the changes and exit.

Now that you understand the different types of hardware that can be included in a virtual machine, let's take a look at the different options that can be configured for a virtual machine.

Configure Virtual Machine Options

There are a large number of options that can be configured for a virtual machine. These options control the various options for virtual machines such as the virtual machine name and location of its configuration files, how it reacts to VMware Tools operations, how it handles power management, and a number of other advanced options. Virtual machine settings fall under the following classes:

- General Options
- VMware Tools
- Power Management
- Advanced | General
- Advanced | CPUID Mask
- Advanced | Boot Options
- Advanced | Paravirtualization
- Advanced | CPU/MMU Virtualization
- Advanced | Swapfile Location

In this section we will review each of these classes of virtual machine options and discuss the settings available under each class. The first step to managing virtual machine options is to launch the Virtual Machine Properties Options window on the virtual machine you wish to edit.

To access the Virtual Machine Properties Options window for a virtual machine, follow these steps:

1. Launch the vSphere Client and connect to your ESX Host or vCenter Server.

2. In the navigation bar select Home | Inventory if you connected to your ESX Host or Home | Inventory | Hosts if you connected to your vCenter Server.

3. In the left-hand frame right-click the virtual machine you wish to edit and select Edit Settings from the drop-down menu.

4. Select the Options tab and you will be presented with the Virtual Machine Properties Options window for the virtual machine as shown in Figure 7-4.

FIGURE 7-4

The Virtual Machine Properties Options window of a virtual machine

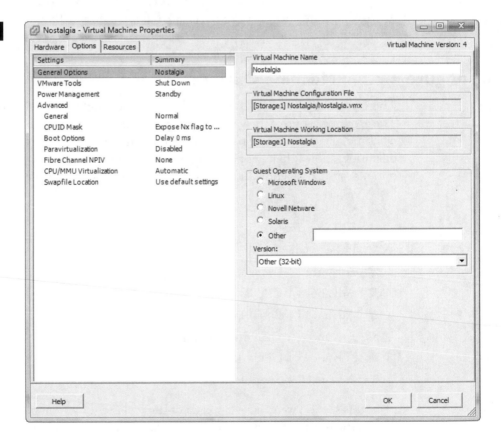

Now that you know how to access the Virtual Machine Properties Options window, let's take a look at each of the options classes.

General Options

The General Options class of virtual machine options contains settings that define the basic information for a virtual machine such as the location of its configuration file. You can configure the following options for a virtual machine under General Options:

- **Virtual Machine Name**　This option controls the display name of the virtual machine.
- **Virtual Machine Configuration File**　This option displays the location of the virtual machine's configuration file.
- **Virtual Machine Working Location**　This option displays the working folder for the virtual machine.
- **Guest Operating System**　This option displays the operating system and version for the guest operating system.

VMware Tools

The VMware Tools class of virtual machine options contains settings that define how the virtual machine reacts to VMware Tools operations. You can configure the following options for a virtual machine under VMware Tools:

- **Stop Button Action**　This option controls the action the virtual machine will take when the VMware Tools Stop button is pressed. It can be set to Shutdown Guest, Power Off, or System Default.
- **Pause Button Action**　This option controls the action the virtual machine will take when the VMware Tools Pause button is pressed. It can be set to Suspend or System Default.
- **Restart Button Action**　This option controls the action the virtual machine will take when the VMware Tools Restart button is pressed. It can be set to Reset, Restart Guest, or System Default.
- **Run VMware Tools Script**　This option controls when VMware Tools Scripts are run. It can be set to After Powering On, After Resuming, Before Suspending, or Before Shutting Down Guest.

■ **Check and upgrade Tools before each power on** If this option is selected, the version of VMware Tools running on the virtual machine will be checked each time the virtual machine is powered on.

■ **Synchronize guest time with Host** If this option is selected, the guest operating system will set its time to match the time of the Host.

Power Management

The Power Management class of virtual machine options contains a setting that defines how the virtual machine will respond when the guest operating system is placed on standby. You can configure the following option for a virtual machine under Power Management:

■ **Guest Power Management** This option controls how the virtual machine will respond when the guest operating system is placed on standby. It can be set to "Suspend the virtual machine" or "Put the guest OS into standby mode and leave the virtual machine powered on."

Advanced | General

The Advanced | General class of virtual machine options contains settings that define the more advanced information for a virtual machine. You can configure the following options for a virtual machine under Advanced | General:

■ **Disable acceleration** If this option is selected, acceleration will be disabled.

■ **Enable logging** If this option is selected, logging will be enabled.

■ **Debugging and Statistics** This option controls how the virtual machine manages debugging and statistics. It can be set to Run Normally, Record Debugging Information, Record Statistics, or Record Statistics and Debugging Information.

■ **Configuration Parameters** This option controls advance configuration parameters and should only be used by experienced administrators.

Advanced | CPUID Mask

The Advanced | CPUID Mask class of virtual machine options contains a setting that controls how the NX/XD flag of the processor is handled. You can configure the following option for a virtual machine under Advanced | CPUID Mask:

- **CPU Identification Mask**   This option controls how the NX/XD CPU flag is managed. It can be set to "Hide the NX/XD flag from the guest" or "Expose the NX/XD flag to the guest." By hiding the NX/XD flag from the guest, you can increase VMotion compatibility but can cause decreased performance for the guest OS.

Advanced | Boot Options

The Advanced | Boot Options class of virtual machine options contains settings that define the actions of the virtual machine during bootup. You can configure the following options for a virtual machine under Advanced | Boot Options:

- **Power-on Boot Delay**   This option controls how long the virtual machine will delay during bootup and is set in milliseconds.
- **Force BIOS Setup**   If this option is selected, the virtual machine will enter the BIOS setup screen the next time it is rebooted.

Advanced | Paravirtualization

The Advanced | Paravirtualization class of virtual machine options contains a setting that controls how the virtual machine handles paravirtualization. You can configure the following option for a virtual machine under Advanced | Paravirtualization:

- **Support VMI Paravirtualization**   If this option is selected and the operating system of the guest supports VMI paravirtualization, the guest can see significant performance increases but at the risk of VMotion compatibility issues with other Hosts.

Advanced | CPU/MMU Virtualization

The Advanced | CPU/MMU Virtualization class of virtual machine options contains a setting that controls how the virtual machine handles CPU/MMU virtualization. You can configure the following option for a virtual machine under Advanced | CPU/MMU Virtualization:

- **CPU/MMU Virtualization**   This option controls how a virtual machine determines if it should use hardware virtualization support. It can be set to Automatic, "Use software for instruction set and MMU virtualization," "Use Intel VT-x/AMD-V for instruction set virtualization and software for MMU virtualization," or "Use Intel VT-x/AMD-V for instruction set virtualization and Intel EPT/AMD RVI for MMU virtualization."

Advanced | Swapfile Location

The Advanced | Swapfile Location class of virtual machine options contains a setting that controls where the virtual machine will store its swapfile. You can configure the following option for a virtual machine under Advanced | Swapfile Location:

- **Swapfile location**   This option controls where a virtual machine will store its swapfile. It can be set to Default, "Always store with the virtual machine," or "Store in the host's swapfile datastore."

Configure Virtual Machine Resource Settings

There are a number of resource settings that can be configured for a virtual machine. These settings control how CPU, memory, and disk resources are allocated to the virtual machine. Virtual machine resources settings fall under the following classes:

- CPU
- Memory
- Disk
- Advanced CPU

In this section we will review each of these classes of virtual machine resources and discuss the configurations available under each class. The first step to managing virtual machine resources is to launch the Virtual Machine Properties Resources window on the virtual machine you wish to edit.

To access the Virtual Machine Properties Resources window for a virtual machine, follow these steps:

1. Launch the vSphere Client and connect to your ESX Host or vCenter Server.
2. In the navigation bar select Home | Inventory if you connected to your ESX Host or Home | Inventory | Hosts if you connected to your vCenter Server.
3. In the left-hand frame right-click the virtual machine you wish to edit and select Edit Settings from the drop-down menu.
4. Select the Resources tab and you will be presented with the Virtual Machine Properties Resources window for the virtual machine as shown in Figure 7-5.

FIGURE 7-5

The Virtual
Machine
Properties
Resources
window of a
virtual machine

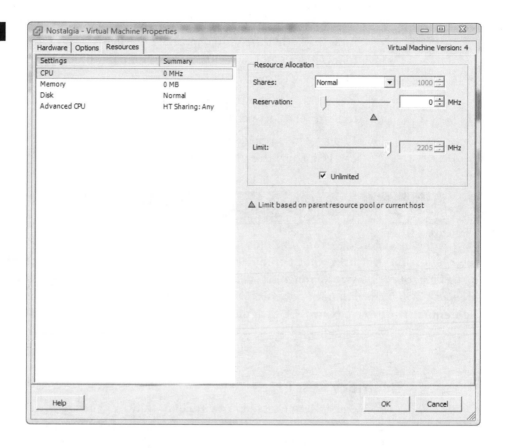

Now that you know how to access the Virtual Machine Properties Resources
window, let's take a look at each of the options classes.

CPU Resources

The CPU Resources class of virtual machine resource settings controls how CPU
resources are allocated to the virtual machine. You can configure the following
options for a virtual machine under CPU Resources:

- **Shares**   This setting controls the number of CPU shares that are allocated
  to the virtual machines. The number of CPU shares that are held by a virtual
  machine is used by the Host to allocate CPU resources to a virtual machine.
  The Host takes the total number of shares that are held by all of the virtual
  machines running on it and generates a total. The Host then allocates CPU

resources to individual virtual machines based on the percentage of the total shares that the virtual machine is assigned. This setting can have the following values: Low—500 Shares, Normal—1000 Shares, High—2000 Shares, or Custom.

- **Reservation**   This setting controls the minimum amount of CPU resources that are set aside specifically for this virtual machine.

- **Limit**   This setting controls the maximum amount of CPU resources that can be used by this virtual machine.

e x a m
ⓦatch

For the exam you may see a question that asks what percentage of CPU resources a virtual machine will receive given a set number of shares. Remember that the CPU will be assigned based on the percentage of CPU shares a virtual machine has when compared to the shares held by all of the virtual machines running on a Host.

Memory Resources

The Memory Resources class of virtual machine resource settings controls how memory resources are allocated to the virtual machine. You can configure the following options for a virtual machine under Memory Resources:

- **Shares**   This setting controls the number of memory shares that are allocated to the virtual machines. The number of memory shares that are held by a virtual machine is used by the Host to allocate memory resources to a virtual machine. The Host takes the total number of shares that are held by all of the virtual machines running on it and generates a total. The Host then allocates memory resources to individual virtual machines based on the percentage of the total shares that the virtual machine is assigned. This setting can have the following values: Low, Normal, High, or Custom.

- **Reservation**   This setting controls the minimum amount of memory resources that are set aside specifically for this virtual machine.

- **Limit**   This setting controls the maximum amount of memory that can be used by this virtual machine.

Disk Resources

The Disk Resources class of virtual machine resource settings controls how access to shared Host disk resources is allocated to the virtual machines that reside on the shared disk. You can configure the following option for a virtual machine under Disk Resources:

- **Shares**   This setting controls how CPU hyperthreading is handled. The number of disk shares that are held by a virtual machine is used by the Host to allocate disk access to a virtual machine. The Host takes the total number of shares that are held by all of the virtual machines running on it and generates a total. The Host then allocates access to shared Host disks to individual virtual machines based on the percentage of the total shares that the virtual machine is assigned. This setting can have the following values: Low, Normal, High, or Custom.

Advanced CPU Resources

The Advanced CPU Resources class of virtual machine resource settings controls how CPU hyperthreading is handled by the virtual machine. You can configure the following option for a virtual machine under Advanced CPU Resources:

- **Hyperthreading Core Sharing Mode**   This setting controls how CPU cores are shared when hyperthreading is supported on the physical Host. This setting can have the following values: Any—CPU cores are shared, None—CPU cores are not shared, or Internal—CPU cores are not shared between different virtual machines but are shared internally.

CERTIFICATION OBJECTIVE 7.03

Deploy and Manage vApps

vApps are collections of virtual machines that together provide an application or application suite. A *virtual appliance* is a virtual machine that is configured with a guest operating system and an application that can be imported or exported for easy installation. Before we can begin creating vApps and virtual appliances, let's take a look at the OVF or Open Virtualization Format.

What Is the Open Virtualization Format (OVF)?

The Open Virtualization Format, or OVF, is a standard for the configuration and exchange of virtual machines and vApps that are composed of multiple virtual machines. It is intended to be an open, vendor-neutral specification for packaging and trading virtual appliances that provides users with a simple automated method for creating and installing virtual appliances.

Export and Import Virtual Appliances

A virtual appliance is a single virtual machine that provides access to an application that is running on it. To create a virtual appliance, simply create a virtual machine, install a guest operating system, and install an application on it. Once you have created a virtual appliance, you will want to export it so that it can be used by people in their virtual environments.

To export a virtual appliance, follow these steps:

1. Launch the vSphere Client and connect to your vCenter Server.
2. In the navigation bar select Home | Inventory | Hosts And Clusters.
3. Select the virtual machine that you wish to export.
4. From the File menu select Export and then Export OVF Template. You will be presented with the Export OVF Template window as shown in Figure 7-6.
5. On the Export OVF Template window enter a name for the exported virtual appliance and enter a description of the virtual appliance.
6. On the Export OVF Template window select a directory to export the virtual appliance to.
7. You will need to determine if you want to optimize the OVF template for the Web or for Physical Media. If you select Web, the OVF template will be saved as a collection of files that are optimized for distribution over the Web. If you select Physical Media, the OVF template will be saved as a single file that is optimized for distribution on physical media. Enter your selection and click OK to continue.

The Export OVF
Template window

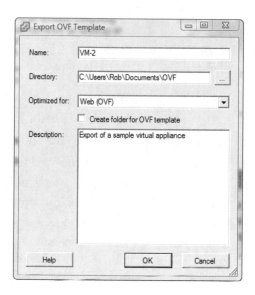

You may want to import a virtual appliance that has been created by someone else. VMware has created the VA Marketplace as a centralized marketplace for virtual appliances.

To import a virtual appliance, follow these steps:

1. Launch the vSphere Client and connect to your vCenter Server.

2. In the navigation bar select Home | Inventory | Hosts And Clusters.

3. From the File menu select Browse VA Marketplace. You will be presented with the Virtual Appliance Marketplace.

4. Search the marketplace to find a virtual appliance you wish to import. When you have found a virtual appliance, select it and click Next to continue.

5. You will be prompted for a name for the virtual appliance and an inventory location. Enter this information and click Next to continue.

6. You will be prompted for a Host to place the virtual appliance on. Select a Host and click Next to continue.

7. You will be prompted for a Datastore for the virtual appliance. Select a Datastore and click Next to continue.

8. You will be presented with a summary screen. Click OK to continue and import the virtual appliance.

Create a vApp

Now that you know what a vApp is, let's go ahead and create one.
To create a vApp, follow these steps:

1. Launch the vSphere Client and connect to your vCenter Server.
2. In the navigation bar select Home | Inventory | Hosts And Clusters.
3. Select the Host you want to create the vApp under.
4. From the File menu select New and then vApp.
5. You will be prompted for the name of the new vApp you want to create. Enter the name and click Next to continue.
6. You will be prompted to enter resource allocations for the new vApp. You can enter the Shares, Reservation, and Limit for CPU and Memory for the vApp. Enter this information and click Next to continue.
7. You will be presented with a summary screen. Click Finish to create the vApp.

We have now created a new vApp, but by itself a vApp doesn't do very much. The next step will be to add virtual machines into the vApp.

Add Virtual Machines to a vApp

Now that we have a vApp created, the next step is to add virtual machines to it.
To add an existing virtual machine to a vApp, follow these steps:

1. Launch the vSphere Client and connect to your vCenter Server.
2. In the navigation bar select Home | Inventory | Hosts And Clusters.
3. Select the virtual machine you want to add to the vApp.
4. Left-click the virtual machine and drag it over the vApp.
5. Release the mouse button and the virtual machine will now appear under the vApp. In Figure 7-7 you can see the virtual machines VM-1 and VM-2 under the vApp Sample vApp1.

FIGURE 7-7

VM-1 and VM-2 have been added to the vApp Sample vApp1.

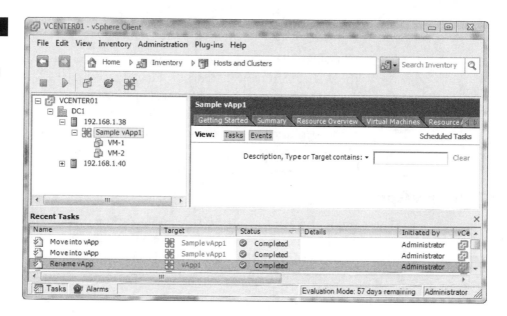

Export vApps

Now that we have a fully configured vApp, we can share it with other users. To make it easy to share the vApp, we will export it into the OVF format.

To export an existing vApp, follow these steps:

1. Launch the vSphere Client and connect to your vCenter Server.

2. In the navigation bar select Home | Inventory | Hosts And Clusters.

3. Select the vApp that you wish to export.

4. From the File menu select Export and then Export OVF Template. You will be presented with the Export OVF Template window.

5. On the Export OVF Template window enter a name for the exported vApp and enter a description of the vApp.

6. On the Export OVF Template window select a directory to export the vApp to.

7. You will need to determine if you want to optimize the OVF template for the Web or for Physical Media. If you select Web, the OVF template will be saved as a collection of files that are optimized for distribution over the web. If you select Physical Media, the OVF template will be saved as a single file that is optimized for distribution on physical media. Enter your selection and click OK to continue.

Clone a vApp

There are times when you may want to create a vApp that is very similar to an existing vApp. One way to do this is to clone the existing vApp and then make changes to its settings or the virtual machines it contains.

To clone an existing vApp, follow these steps:

1. Launch the vSphere Client and connect to your vCenter Server.

2. In the navigation bar select Home | Inventory | Hosts And Clusters.

3. Select the vApp that you wish to clone. Right-click the vApp and select Clone from the drop-down menu.

4. You will be prompted to select a Host for the new vApp. Select a Host and click Next to continue.

5. You will be prompted for the name of the new vApp you want to create. Enter the name and click Next to continue.

6. You will be prompted to enter the storage location for the new vApp. Select a Datastore and click Next to continue.

7. You will be presented with a summary screen. Click Finish to create the vApp. Figure 7-8 shows the newly created clone.

FIGURE 7-8   Notice the new vApp Clone of Sample vApp1.

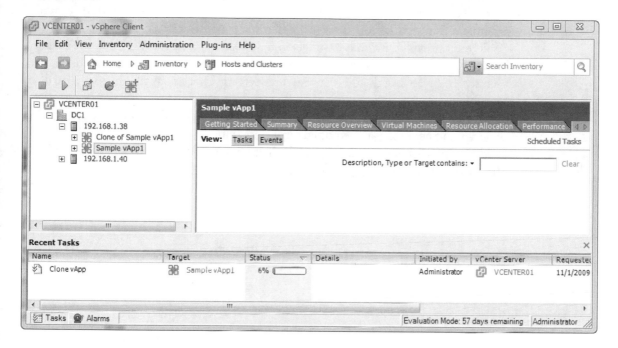

CERTIFICATION SUMMARY

We started this chapter by looking at virtual machines. We discussed what they are and the hardware maximums they are constrained by. We then created a few virtual machines using the New Virtual Machine Wizard. Once we had a few virtual machines, we discussed installing the VMware Tools and guest customization. We then used our existing virtual machines to create a template and deploy a new virtual machine from the template. We ended the section by creating a new virtual machine by cloning an existing virtual machine.

In the next section we looked at the various types of hardware that make up virtual machines. We discussed how to add new hardware and reviewed the available configuration settings for each type of hardware. We then looked at all of the different options that can be configured for a virtual machine. We discussed each class of options and reviewed the settings available under each class. We ended the section by reviewing the different resource settings that are available for a virtual machine.

We ended the chapter by looking at vApps. We discussed the Open Virtualization Format and imported and exported virtual appliances. We then created a vApp and added some virtual machines to it. We then reviewed how to export a vApp and how to create a new vApp by cloning an existing vApp.

TWO-MINUTE DRILL

Create and Deploy Virtual Machines

❑ A virtual machine is just like a physical machine except that it is implemented in software.

❑ A virtual machine can have a maximum of eight virtual CPUs.

❑ A virtual machine can have a maximum of 255GB of RAM.

❑ A virtual machine can have a maximum swap file size of 255GB.

❑ A virtual machine can have a maximum of four virtual SCSI adapters.

❑ A virtual machine can have a maximum of 15 virtual SCSI targets per SCSI adapter.

❑ A virtual machine can have a maximum of 60 virtual SCSI targets.

❑ A virtual machine can have a maximum disk size of 2TB minus 512B.

❑ A virtual machine can have only one virtual IDE controller.

❑ A virtual machine can have a maximum of four virtual IDE devices.

❑ A virtual machine can have a maximum of one virtual floppy controller.

❑ A virtual machine can have a maximum of two virtual floppy devices.

❑ A virtual machine can have a maximum of ten virtual NICs.

❑ A virtual machine can have a maximum of three virtual parallel ports.

❑ A virtual machine can have a maximum of four virtual serial ports.

❑ VMware Tools is a package of utilities, scripts, and drivers that are installed on a virtual machine to improve performance and management.

❑ A template is a gold image copy of a virtual machine that can be used to create new virtual machines that are configured exactly the same.

❑ A virtual machine can be converted into a template or cloned into a template.

❑ Virtual machines can be created from templates.

❑ Virtual machines can be created by cloning an existing virtual machine.

Manage Virtual Machine Configurations

❑ Virtual machines can have the following hardware: CPU, floppy drives, hard disks, memory, NICs, parallel ports, SCSI controllers, serial ports, USB controllers, and a video card.

❑ Virtual hardware can be added to a virtual machine in the Virtual Machine Properties Hardware window.

❑ A virtual disk that is provisioned as Thick uses its entire space as soon as it is created and does not grow with use.

❑ A virtual disk that is provisioned as Thin starts out small and grows as more space is used.

❑ If a virtual disk has a mode of Independent it is not affected by snapshots and can be Persistent or Non-Persistent. If it is Persistent, changes to the disk are maintained after a power cycle. If it is Non-Persistent, changes are lost after a power cycle.

❑ Virtual machine options can be changed in the Virtual Machine Properties Options window.

❑ The General Options class of virtual machine options contains settings that define the basic information for a virtual machine such as the location of its configuration file.

❑ The VMware Tools class of virtual machine options contains settings that define how the virtual machine reacts to VMware Tools operations.

❑ The Power Management class of virtual machine options contains a setting that defines how the virtual machine will respond when the guest operating system is placed on standby.

❑ The Advanced | General class of virtual machine options contains settings that define the more advanced information for a virtual machine.

❑ The Advanced | CPUID Mask class of virtual machine options contains a setting that controls how the NX/XD CPU flag is handled by the virtual machine.

❑ The Advanced | Boot Options class of virtual machine options contains settings that define the actions of the virtual machine during bootup.

❑ The Advanced | Paravirtualization class of virtual machine options contains a setting that controls how the virtual machine handles paravirtualization.

❑ The Advanced | CPU/MMU Virtualization class of virtual machine options contains a setting that controls how the virtual machine handles CPU/MMU virtualization.

❑ The Advanced | Swapfile Location class of virtual machine options contains a setting that controls where the virtual machine will store its swapfile.

❑ CPU Shares is a setting offering a method for assigning CPU resources to a virtual machine based on the percentage of total CPU shares that are held by all of the virtual machines running on a Host.

❑ CPU Reservation is the minimal amount of CPU resources that are set aside specifically for a virtual machine.

❑ CPU Limit is the maximum amount of CPU resources that can be used by a virtual machine.

❑ Memory Shares is a setting offering a method for assigning memory resources to a virtual machine based on the percentage of total memory shares that are held by all of the virtual machines running on a Host.

❑ Memory Reservation is the minimal amount of memory resources that are set aside specifically for a virtual machine.

❑ Memory Limit is the maximum amount of memory resources that can be used by a virtual machine.

❑ Disk Shares is a setting offering a method for assigning disk resources to a virtual machine based on the percentage of total disk shares that are held by all of the virtual machines running on a Host.

❑ The Hyperthreading Core Sharing Mode setting controls how CPU cores are shared when hyperthreading is supported on the physical Host.

Deploy and Manage vApps

❑ vApps are collections of virtual machines that together provide an application or application suite.

❑ The Open Virtualization Format, or OVF, is a standard for the configuration and exchange of virtual machines and vApps.

❑ Virtual appliances can be imported from the VA Marketplace.

SELF TEST

The following questions will help you measure your understanding of the material presented in this chapter. Read all the choices carefully and remember that there is only one best answer for each question.

Create and Deploy Virtual Machines

1. What is the maximum number of virtual CPUs per virtual machine?
   A. 2
   B. 4
   C. 8
   D. 16

2. What is the maximum number of virtual parallel ports per virtual machine?
   A. 1
   B. 2
   C. 3
   D. 4

3. What is the maximum number of serial ports per virtual machine?
   A. 1
   B. 2
   C. 3
   D. 4

4. Which of the following is a method for creating a new virtual machine?
   A. The New Virtual Machine Wizard
   B. Cloning an existing virtual machine
   C. Creating a virtual machine from a template
   D. All of the above

5. Which of the following is not an available choice for a virtual disk format when cloning a virtual machine into a template?
   A. Thin Format
   B. Thick Format
   C. Same Format As Source
   D. Extensible

Manage Virtual Machine Configurations

6. Which of the following is not a valid device type for a floppy device on a virtual machine?
   A. Client Device
   B. Remote Device
   C. Host Device
   D. Use Existing Floppy Image In Datastore

7. Which of the following is not a valid connection setting for a serial port on a virtual machine?
   A. Use Physical Serial Port
   B. Use Output File
   C. Use Named Pipe
   D. Client Device

8. Which of the following is the default network adapter for 64-bit operating systems?
   A. Flexible
   B. e1000
   C. Enhanced vmxnet
   D. vmxnet 3

9. A _____ provisioned disk is small when it is created and expands as additional space is used by the guest operating system.
   A. Thin
   B. Thick
   C. Persistent
   D. Non-Persistent

10. Which of the following is not an available setting for the Restart Button Action under the VMware Tools class of virtual machine options?
    A. Reset
    B. Power-Cycle
    C. Restart Guest
    D. System Default

11. If the CPU Shares value is set to Normal and there is one vCPU, how many shares does it have?
    A. 500
    B. 1000
    C. 2000
    D. 3000

Deploy and Manage vApps

12. Which of the following is a standard proposed by VMware for the configuration and exchange of virtual machines and vApps?

    A. Open Virtual Application Format

    B. Open Virtualization Format

    C. Virtual Application Standard

    D. Open Virtualization Standard

SELF TEST ANSWERS

Create and Deploy Virtual Machines

1. ☑ **C.** A virtual machine can have a maximum of eight virtual CPUs.

☒ **A, B,** and **D** are incorrect. Eight virtual CPUs is the only acceptable answer.

2. ☑ **C.** A virtual machine can have a maximum of three virtual parallel ports.

☒ **A, B,** and **D** are incorrect. Three virtual parallel ports is the only possibility.

3. ☑ **D.** A virtual machine can have a maximum of four virtual serial ports.

☒ **A, B,** and **C** are incorrect. Four virtual serial ports is the only possibility.

4. ☑ **D.** Virtual machines can be created by running the New Virtual Machine Wizard, by cloning an existing virtual machine, or from a template.

☒ **A, B,** and **C** are incorrect. There can only be one best answer, and D is the best answer.

5. ☑ **D.** Extensible is not an available choice for a virtual disk format when cloning a virtual machine into a template.

☒ **A, B,** and **C** are incorrect. Thin Format, Thick Format, and Same Format As Source are available choices for a virtual disk format when cloning a virtual machine into a template.

Manage Virtual Machine Configurations

6. ☑ **B.** Remote Device is not a valid device type for a floppy device on a virtual machine.

☒ **A, C,** and **D** are incorrect. Client Device, Host Device, and Use Existing Floppy Image In Datastore are all valid device types for a floppy device on a virtual machine.

7. ☑ **D.** Client Device is not a valid connection setting for a serial port on a virtual machine.

☒ **A, B,** and **C** are incorrect. Use Physical Serial Port, Use Output File, and Use Named Pipe are valid connection settings for a serial port on a virtual machine.

8. ☑ **B.** The e1000 NIC is the default network adapter for 64-bit operating systems.

☒ **A, C,** and **D** are incorrect. Flexible, Enhanced vmxnet, and vmxnet 3 are not the default network adapters for 64-bit operating systems.

9. ☑ **A.** Thin provisioned disks start out small and expand as additional space is used by the guest operating system.

☒ **B, C,** and **D** are incorrect. Thick provisioned disks allocate all of their space when they are created. Persistent and Non-Persistent are not types of disk provisioning.

10. ☑ **B.** Power-Cycle is not an available setting for the Restart Button Action under the VMware Tools class of virtual machine options.

☒ **A, C,** and **D** are incorrect. Reset, Restart Guest, and System Default are all available settings for the Restart Button Action under the VMware Tools class of virtual machine options.

11. ☑ **B.** For CPU Shares a value of normal represents 1000 shares.

☒ **A, C,** and **D** are incorrect. For CPU Shares a value of normal represents 1000 shares.

Deploy and Manage vApps

12. ☑ **B.** The Open Virtualization Format is a standard proposed by VMware for the configuration and exchange of virtual machines and vApps.

☒ **A, C,** and **D** are incorrect. These are not standards proposed by VMware for the configuration and exchange of virtual machines and vApps.

8
Managing Compliance

W elcome to Chapter 8. In this chapter we will review the methods that VMware provides with vSphere to help us keep our ESX Hosts and virtual machines in compliance when it comes to patch management and consistent configurations. We will take a deeper look at the vCenter add-on, vCenter Update Manager, which we installed in Chapter 4, and you will learn how to use it to perform patch management for our ESX Hosts and virtual machines. You will then learn about Host Profiles and how you can use them to keep our ESX Host configurations consistent across our entire vSphere environment. Let's start the chapter by taking a look at vCenter Update Manager.

CERTIFICATION OBJECTIVE 8.01

Configure and Manage VMware vCenter Update Manager

In Chapter 4 we briefly discussed vCenter Update Manager and reviewed its installation process as a part of our vCenter installation. As a review, vCenter Update Manager is an add-on utility for vCenter Server that allows vSphere administrators to perform patch management on ESX Hosts and the virtual machines running on them. In this section we will discuss how to fully configure vCenter Update Manager, and you will learn how to use it to create patch management baselines for our ESX Hosts and our virtual machines. Since we have already installed vCenter Update Manager on the vCenter Server, the next step is to enable it on a vSphere Client.

Enable Update Manager on a vSphere Client

Before you can work with Update Manager, you need to enable the Update Manager plug-in on the vSphere Client that you will use to manage it. In this section we will go through the process of enabling Update Manager on our vSphere Client.

To enable the Update Manager plug-in on a vSphere Client, follow these steps:

1. Launch the vSphere Client and connect to your vCenter Server.
2. From the Plug-ins drop-down menu select Manage Plug-ins.
3. You will be presented with the Plug-ins Manager window. Under the Plug-in Name column find VMware vCenter Update Manager Extension. When you have located the extension, click Download And Install.
4. The download and installation will take a few minutes. When it is completed, click Finish and then close the Plug-in Manager window.

Now that we have the Update Manager enabled on our vSphere Client, we can move on to configuring the Update Manager.

Configure VMware vCenter Update Manager

Now that we have installed vCenter Update Manager on our vCenter Server and have enabled our vSphere Client to work with Update Manager, we can start to configure it for our environment. There are six classes of settings that can be configured for vCenter Update Manager:

■ Network Connectivity
■ Patch Download Settings
■ Patch Download Schedule
■ Virtual Machine Settings
■ ESX Host Settings
■ vApp Settings

INSIDE THE EXAM

vSphere Update Manager

To test your knowledge of the installation process for vSphere Update Manager, you may see a question that asks the installation steps. Remember that there are two different steps to the install. You need to install both the server and client components before you will be able to use vSphere Update Manager.

We will look at each of these classes of settings in the following sections. To begin configuring the vCenter Update Manager, follow these steps to access the vCenter Update Manager Configuration window:

1. Launch the vSphere Client and connect to your vCenter Server.
2. Click the Home icon in the navigation toolbar and then click Update Manager under Solutions And Applications.
3. You will be presented with the Update Manager Administration window. Click the Configuration tab to enter the Configuration window.

Now that we have reached the vCenter Update Manager Configuration window, let's take a look at each of the available classes of settings.

Network Connectivity Settings

There are a few network connectivity settings that can be customized under vCenter Update Manager. To configure these settings, go to the Update Manager Configuration window and select Network Connectivity from the Settings box on the left side of the window. You will then see the Network Connectivity window as shown in Figure 8-1.

In this window you will see that there are three network configuration settings that can be customized:

■ **SOAP Port**   Using this setting, you can change the SOAP port that is used by vCenter Update Manager.
■ **Server Port**   This is the port that the patch store service uses for connectivity between ESX/ESXi Hosts and the Update Manager Patch Store.
■ **IP address or host name for the patch store**   This is the name or address that can be used by vCenter Update Manager to connect to a different server that contains a patch store.

The patch store is the physical location where downloaded patches are stored. In large environments that have multiple vCenter Servers the patch store can be kept on a separate server that is then accessed by all of the vCenter Servers. For our sample environment the patch store is contained on the vCenter Server.

FIGURE 8-1   The vCenter Update Manager Network Connectivity window

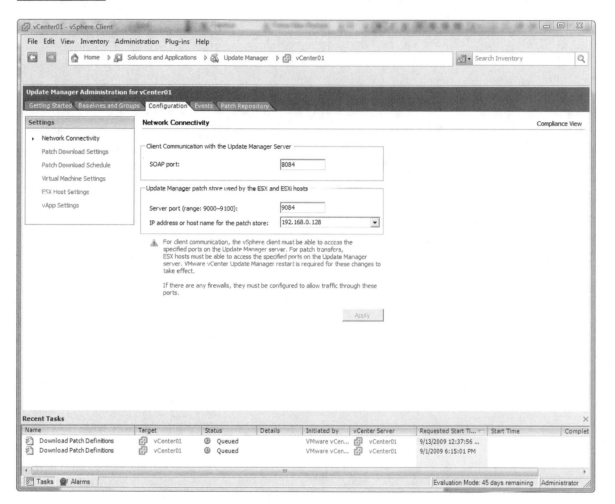

Patch Download Settings

There are a number of settings that can be customized under vCenter Update Manager relating to patch downloads. To configure these settings go to the Update Manager Configuration window and select Patch Download Settings from the Settings box on the left side of the window. You will then see the Patch Download Settings window as shown in Figure 8-2.

FIGURE 8-2 The vCenter Update Manager Patch Download Settings window

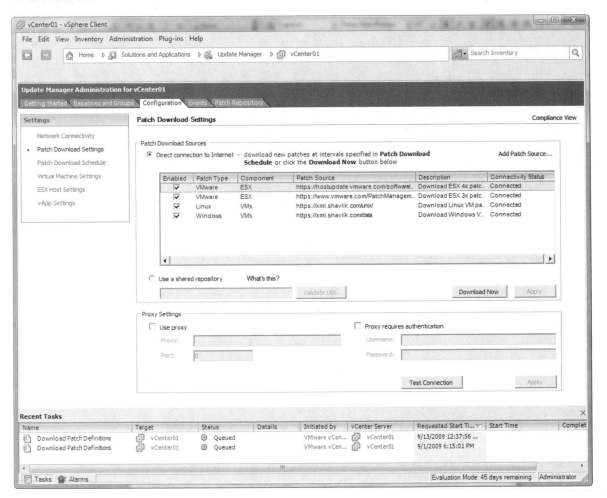

In this window the following Patch Download configuration settings can be customized:

■ **The method to connect to Patch Download sources** This can be either a direct connection to the Internet or a link to a server that is internal to your network that has been configured as a patch store.

- **Proxy Settings** If your vCenter Server uses a proxy to connect to the Internet, you enter the proxy address and port here. You can also enter a username and password if your proxy requires them.

For our environment we will use a direct connection to the Internet that does not require a proxy server. You can also view and add Patch Sources on this window. Patch Sources are web sites where operating system patches are available to be downloaded. The default installation contains Patch Sources for the following operating systems:

- VMware ESX 4.*x* Hosts
- VMware ESX 3.*x* Hosts
- Linux
- Windows

As additional Patch Sources are made available for vCenter Update Manager, you will be able to add them on this window.

Patch Download Schedule

On the Patch Download Schedule window you can view or change the frequency with which vCenter Update Manager connects to Patch Sources and downloads patches. To configure these settings, go to the Update Manager Configuration window and select Patch Download Schedule from the Settings box on the left side of the window. You will then see the Patch Download Schedule window as shown in Figure 8-3.

To change the frequency of patch downloads, click Edit Patch Downloads. You will be presented with a window where you can change the frequency and start time of downloads.

Virtual Machine Settings

On the Virtual Machine Settings window you can elect to have Update Manager make a snapshot of virtual machines before patches are applied and determine how long those snapshots will be maintained. To configure these settings, go to the Update Manager Configuration window and select Virtual Machine Settings

FIGURE 8-3   The vCenter Update Manager Patch Download Schedule window

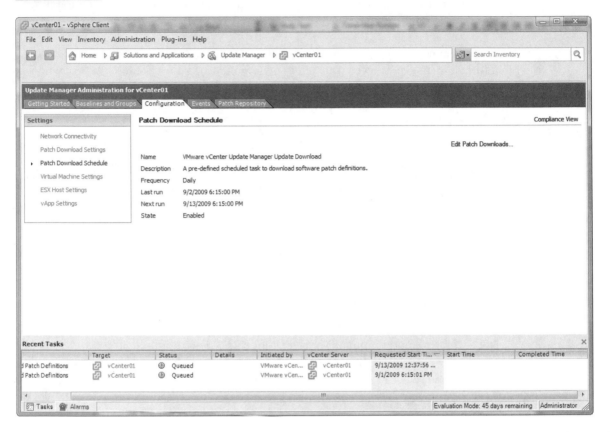

from the Settings box on the left side of the window. You will then see the Virtual Machine Settings window as shown in Figure 8-4.

To have a snapshot created of the virtual machine, make sure that the check box next to "Snapshot the virtual machines before remediation to enable rollback" is checked. You can then set how many hours you want to keep the snapshots or that you want to keep them indefinitely. Creating a snapshot before installing patches on a virtual machine can be a very good idea. In the past certified patches from vendors have caused systems to become unstable. If you have a snapshot of the virtual machine before the patch is installed, you can easily revert to the snapshot if the patch causes issues.

FIGURE 8-4   The vCenter Update Manager Virtual Machine Settings window

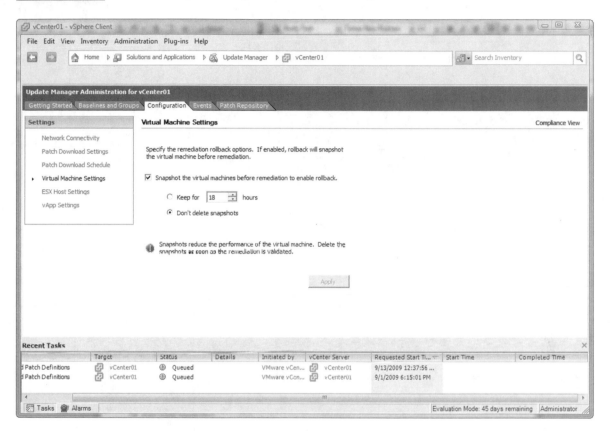

ESX Host Settings

On the ESX Host Settings window you can configure how Update Manager handles issues with trying to update ESX Hosts. To configure these settings, go to the Update Manager Configuration window and select ESX Host Settings from the Settings box on the left side of the window. You will then see the ESX Host Settings window as shown in Figure 8-5.

FIGURE 8-5　The vCenter Update Manager ESX Host Settings window

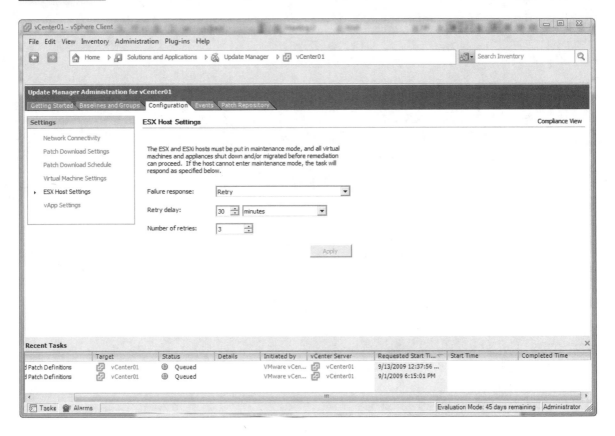

In this window you will see that there are three network configuration settings that can be customized:

- **Failure response**　Using this setting, you can change the action that Update Manager will take if there is a failure when trying to put an ESX Host into maintenance mode. You can configure it to retry, Power Off virtual machines and retry, Suspend virtual machines and retry, or Fail the task.

- **Retry delay**　This is the amount of time Update Manager will wait before trying to put an ESX Host into maintenance mode after a failure.

- **Number of retries**　This is the number of times Update Manager will attempt to put an ESX Host into maintenance mode after a failure.

An ESX Host must not have powered-on virtual machines on it when patches are installed. The fastest way to remove running virtual machines from an ESX Host is to put it into maintenance mode. When an ESX Host is placed into maintenance mode, all of the virtual machines running on it will be moved to a different ESX Host automatically using vMotion.

vApp Settings

On the vApp Settings window you can select to enable or disable smart reboot after remediation. To configure this setting, go to the Update Manager Configuration window and select vApp Settings from the Settings box on the left side of the window. You will then see the vApp Settings window as shown in Figure 8-6.

FIGURE 8-6   The vCenter Update Manager Update Manager vApp Settings window

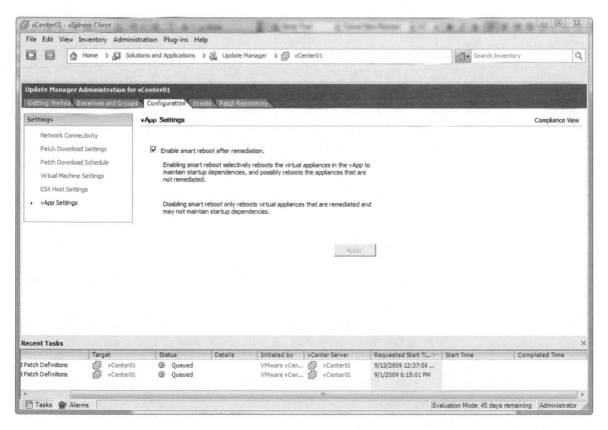

Smart reboot allows the virtual appliances that are contained in a vApp to be rebooted in a specified order. If you allow smart reboot some of the virtual appliances that were not remediated may still be rebooted to maintain startup dependencies. If you do not allow smart reboot, only the virtual appliances that have been remediated will be restarted.

You should now have a good idea of the available settings for configuring vCenter Update Manager. Now let's move on and take a look at Baselines.

Creating and Managing Baselines

Baselines are collections of patches or upgrades that can be used to check ESX Hosts and virtual machines for compliance and then can be used for remediation of missing patches. These baselines can be either patch baselines or upgrade baselines. By default vCenter Update Manager contains four patch baselines and four upgrade baselines that cannot be edited or deleted.

The four default patch baselines are

- **Critical Host Patches**   This baseline contains all of the patches that are considered critical by VMware for ESX Hosts.
- **Non-Critical Host Patches**   This baseline contains all of the patches that are considered non-critical by VMware for ESX Hosts.
- **Critical VM Patches**   This baseline contains all of the patches that are considered critical for Linux and Windows virtual machines.
- **Non-Critical VM Patches**   This baseline contains all of the patches that are considered non-critical for Linux and Windows virtual machines.

The four default upgrade baselines are

- **VMware Tools Upgrade to Match Host**   This baseline compares the version of VMware tools that is running on virtual machines against the version that is contained on the ESX Host where the virtual machine is running.
- **VM Hardware to Match Host**   This baseline compares the version of VMware hardware that is running on virtual machines against the version that is supported on the ESX Host where the virtual machine is running.
- **VA Upgrade to Latest**   This baseline compares the version of a virtual appliance against the latest available version of the virtual appliance.

- **VA Upgrade to Latest Critical** This baseline compares the version of a virtual appliance against the latest available critical version of the virtual appliance.

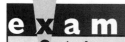

W a t c h   *For the exam you may see a question that asks which default baseline would be used in a given situation. Be careful that the answers are actually default baselines. They may include an answer that sounds like a default baseline but is not.*

These default baselines are very powerful, but they may not meet all of your needs. In the next section we will look at how to create our own baselines.

Create Baselines

Most of the time the default baselines that are provided with vSphere will be sufficient to meet your needs, but occasionally you may want to create a baseline that is customized to your specific environment. vSphere allows you to create and save customized baselines that you can then use just like the default baselines.

To create a baseline, follow these steps:

1. Launch the vSphere Client and connect to your vCenter Server.
2. Click the Home icon in the navigation toolbar and then click Update Manager under Solutions And Applications.
3. You will be presented with the Update Manager Administration window. Click the Baselines And Groups tab to enter the Baselines And Groups window.
4. Click Create in the top-right corner of the window to begin making a new baseline.
5. You will be presented with the Baseline Name And Type window. In this window enter a name for your new baseline, a brief description, and the type of baseline you want to create. The type options are Host Patch, Host Upgrade, VM Patch, and Virtual Appliance Upgrade. Select VM Patch to create a new patch baseline for virtual machines. Click Next to continue.

6. You will be presented with the Patch Options window. On this window you can choose to make your baseline Fixed or Dynamic. A fixed baseline will not be updated if new patches are downloaded, while a dynamic baseline will be updated as new patches are downloaded. Select Dynamic and click Next to continue.

7. You will be presented with the Dynamic Baseline Criteria window. On this window you can select the patches that you want to include in the baseline from the list of all of the available patches that have been downloaded. Select the patches you want to include and click Next to continue.

8. You will be presented with a summary window of the new baseline. Click Finish to complete the new baseline. Your newly created baseline will now be available on the Baselines And Groups window as shown in Figure 8-7.

FIGURE 8-7   The newly created Custom VM Patch Baseline

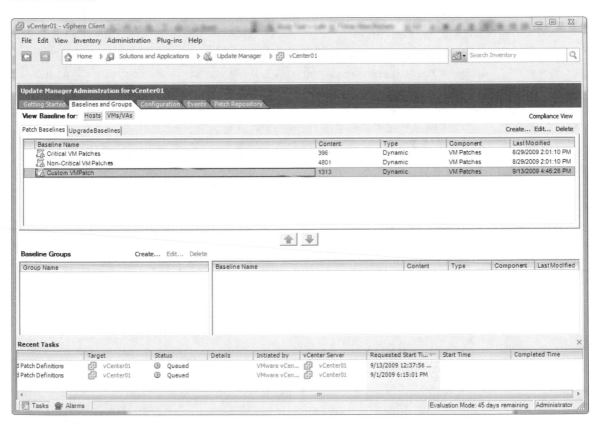

Baseline Groups

Baseline groups are sets of baselines that are combined together. Baseline groups allow multiple baselines to be compared against your vCenter objects at the same time. If you have multiple baselines that you need to periodically run against your virtual environment, you can save time by combining them into a baseline group and then just running that group.

Attach Baselines to vCenter Inventory Objects

Before you can use a baseline to scan an ESX Host or virtual machine, you must attach the baseline to the vCenter Object you wish to scan. You can attach a baseline to a single object like a virtual machine, but it is easier to attach the baseline to the container that hold the objects you wish to scan. By attaching to a container instead of an object, you will be able to scan multiple objects at the same time.

To attach a baseline to a virtual machine, follow these steps:

1. Launch the vSphere Client and connect to your vCenter Server.
2. In the navigation bar select Home | Inventories | VMs And Templates.
3. Select the virtual machine on the left side of the screen that you wish to attach a baseline to.
4. Select the Update Manager tab in the vSphere Client window and click Attach to begin the process.
5. You will be presented with the Attach Baseline Or Group window. Select the baseline that you want to use and click Attach. You have now attached the baseline to your virtual machine.

To attach a baseline to an ESX Host, follow these steps:

1. Launch the vSphere Client and connect to your vCenter Server.
2. In the navigation bar select Home | Inventories | Hosts And Clusters.
3. Select the Host on the left side of the screen that you wish to attach a baseline to.
4. Select the Update Manager tab in the vSphere Client window and click Attach to begin the process.
5. You will be presented with the Attach Baseline Or Group window. Select the baseline that you want to use and click Attach. You have now attached the baseline to your Host.

Now that we have attached a baseline to a virtual machine and to an ESX Host, let's look at scanning these objects for compliance with the baselines.

Scan and Remediate ESX Hosts and Virtual Machines

Once you have attached baselines to your ESX Hosts and virtual machines, you will be able to begin scanning them for compliance. When you scan a Host, virtual machine, or virtual appliance, the baseline that you have attached to the object is compared against the configuration of the object itself.

To scan a virtual machine after a baseline has been attached to it, follow these steps:

1. Launch the vSphere Client and connect to your vCenter Server.
2. In the navigation bar select Home | Inventories | VMs And Templates.
3. Select the virtual machine you wish to scan.
4. Select the Update Manager tab in the vSphere Client window and click Scan. When the scan is complete, you will be presented with the results of the scan as shown in Figure 8-8.

FIGURE 8-8   The results of a baseline scan of a virtual machine

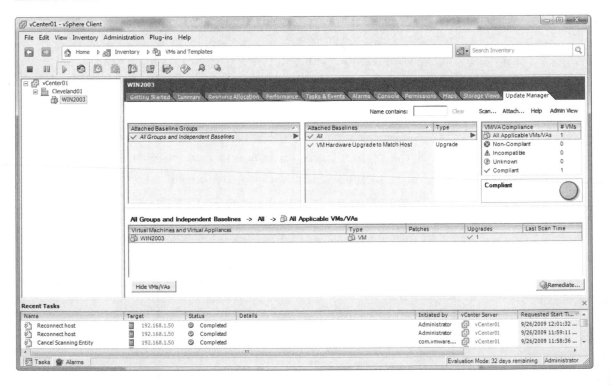

5. To remediate the issues that were discovered, simply press the Remediate button on the results frame.

CERTIFICATION OBJECTIVE 8.02

Establish and Apply ESX Host Profiles

Host Profiles are templates that contain all of the configuration information from a model ESX Host. Once these profiles are created, they can then be applied to new or existing ESX Hosts to simplify their configuration and guarantee that all of the Hosts across the vSphere environment have a consistent configuration. As ESX Hosts become larger and have more configured datastores and networks, their configurations can become very complex. Host Profiles help to reduce the chances of human error during the configuration process of these larger Hosts by allowing a standard configuration to simply be applied. Once the profile is applied, all of the configuration for the new Host is complete and consistent. Host Profiles also allow existing Hosts to be periodically compared to the profile to make sure no changes have been made to their configurations.

Before we can begin to use Host Profiles, we will need to review how to create them. In the next section we will look at how to create and delete Host Profiles.

A number of my clients use Host Profiles as an integral part of their disaster recovery plans. By having Host Profiles of each of their production systems, they can quickly restore their ESX Hosts at a disaster recovery site by just doing a basic ESX install and then applying the Host Profile.

Create/Delete Host Profiles

The first step to working with Host Profiles is to create one. Before you create your first Host Profile, you want to make sure you have a properly configured model host. This host should be checked and then checked again to make sure it is properly configured. Once you have your model Host configured, you are ready to begin creating your first Host Profile.

To create a new Host Profile, follow these steps:

1. Launch the vSphere Client and connect to your vCenter Server.
2. From the View menu select Management and then select Host Profiles. You will be presented with the Host Profiles view. From here you can Create new Host Profiles, Edit existing Host Profiles, Delete existing Host Profiles, and Attach Host Profiles. The Host Profiles view can be seen in Figure 8-9.

FIGURE 8-9 The Host Profiles view

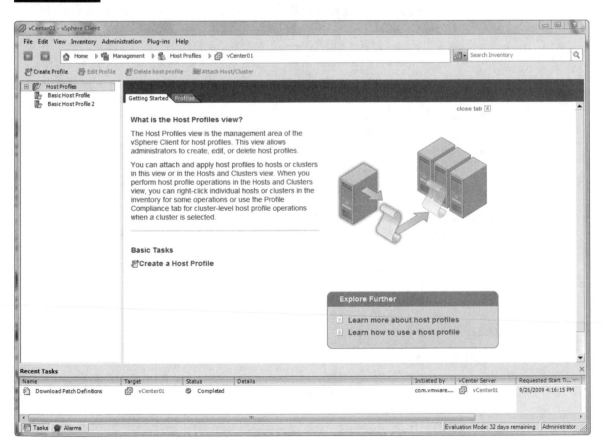

3. Click Create a Host Profile to start the Create Profile Wizard.

4. Select Create Profile From Existing Host and click Next to continue.

5. Select the Host you want to use as your model and click Next to continue.

6. Give your profile a descriptive name and a short description and click Next to continue.

7. You will be presented with a summary window that shows your selections. Click Finish to create a Host Profile.

To delete an existing Host Profile, follow these steps:

1. Launch the vSphere Client and connect to your vCenter Server.

2. From the View menu select Management and then select Host Profiles. You will be presented with the Host Profiles view.

3. Select the Host Profile you wish to delete from the left-hand frame and click Delete Host Profile from the top frame.

4. You will be prompted to confirm the deletion. Click Yes to continue and delete the Host Profile.

Export/Import Host Profiles

Now that we have a new Host Profile, we can start working with it. One of the first things we can do with a Host Profile is to export it to a file. By exporting the Host Profile, you will have a backup of the profile. If changes are later made to the profile that need to be rolled back, you can import the profile from the backup and the changes will be gone.

To export an existing Host Profile, follow these steps:

1. Launch the vSphere Client and connect to your vCenter Server.

2. From the View menu select Management and then select Host Profiles. You will be presented with the Host Profiles view.

3. Select the Host Profile you wish to export from the left-hand frame and click Export Host Profile from the right frame.

4. You will be presented with a Save As window. In this window select the location where you wish to save the Host Profile and give it a descriptive name. Notice that the file type is VMware profile format and the extension for a Host Profile is vpf. Click Save to finish the export.

To import a Host Profile, follow these steps:

1. Launch the vSphere Client and connect to your vCenter Server.

2. From the View menu select Management and then select Host Profiles. You will be presented with the Host Profiles view.

3. Click Create A Host Profile to start the Create Profile Wizard.

4. Select Import Profile and click Next to continue.

5. You will prompted for the location of a previously exported Host Profile. Enter the location and click Next to continue.

6. You will be prompted to enter a new name and description for the Host Profile. Enter this information and click Next to continue.

7. You will be presented with a summary window that shows you selections. Click Finish to import the Host Profile.

Edit Host Profile Policies

Once you have an existing Host Profile, you may want to change some of its settings due to changes in your Datacenter or due to changes in corporate policies. You can do this in two different ways. If you have a lot of changes, you may want to make them on your model Host and create a new Host Profile that represents these changes. If you only have a few changes, you can go in and edit your existing Host Profile.

To edit an existing Host Profile, follow these steps:

1. Launch the vSphere Client and connect to your vCenter Server.

2. From the View menu select Management and then select Host Profiles. You will be presented with the Host Profiles view.

3. Select the Host Profile you wish to edit from the left-hand frame and click Edit Profile from the top frame. You will be presented with the Edit Profile window as shown in Figure 8-10.

FIGURE 8-10   The Edit Profile window

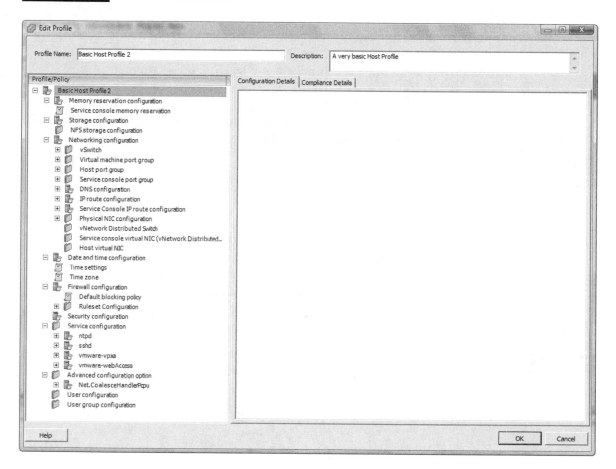

4. The Edit Profile window shows you all of the settings that can be changed on an ESX 4.0 Host in the left frame. To change a setting, select it in the left frame and make the change in the right frame. Once you have made your desired changes, click OK to save the changes and exit.

Attach a Host Profile to an ESX Host

Now that you have a basic understanding of how to create and edit Host Profiles, we will look at how to attach them to an ESX Host. You can attach a Host Profile to an ESX Host or to an entire ESX Cluster using the same procedure.

To attach an existing Host Profile to an ESX Host, follow these steps:

1. Launch the vSphere Client and connect to your vCenter Server.

2. From the View menu select Management and then select Host Profiles. You will be presented with the Host Profiles view.

3. Select the Host Profile you wish to attach from the left-hand frame and click Attach Host/Cluster from the top frame. You will be presented with the Attach Host/Cluster window.

4. In the left frame of the Attach Host/Cluster window select the Host that you wish to attach the Host Profile to and click Attach to attach the Host Profile. In the right frame you can see all of the Hosts and Clusters that are attached to this Host Profile. You can Detach a Host or Cluster from the Host Profile in this window. Figure 8-11 shows the Attach Host/Cluster window with the newly attached Host. Click OK to exit the window.

FIGURE 8-11

The Attach Host/
Cluster window

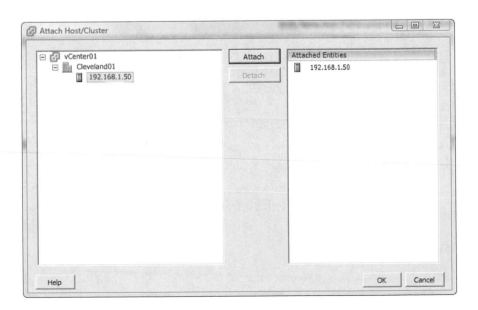

Apply Host Profiles

Now that you have a Host Profile attached to a Host, you are ready to take the next step and apply the Host Profile. Until now no changes have been made to the Host, but once you apply the Host Profile, it will change the configuration settings on the Host to match the Host Profile.

To apply a Host Profile to an ESX Host, follow these steps:

1. Launch the vSphere Client and connect to your vCenter Server.
2. Put the Host on which you want to apply a Host Profile into maintenance mode by right-clicking the Host and selecting Enter Maintenance Mode.
3. From the View menu select Management and then select Host Profiles. You will be presented with the Host Profiles view.
4. Select the Host Profile you wish to attach from the left-hand frame and select the Host you wish to apply it to from the right frame. Click Apply Profile to begin applying the profile.
5. You will be presented with a window that will show you the changes that will be applied to the Host. Click Finish to apply the changes.

For the exam make sure you understand the difference between attaching a Host Profile and applying a	*Host Profile. Attaching a Host Profile does not actually change any of the settings on the Host, while applying a Host Profile does.*

Check for Host Profile Compliance

Sometimes you may want to know what changes have occurred to a Host since the last time a Host Profile was applied to it. To review these changes, you can check the compliance of a Host against the Host Profile that is attached to it. You can then decide if you want to remove these changes by reapplying the Host Profile.

To check the compliance of an ESX Host against a Host Profile, follow these steps:

1. Launch the vSphere Client and connect to your vCenter Server.
2. From the View menu select Management and then select Host Profiles. You will be presented with the Host Profiles view.
3. Select the Host Profile you wish to check against from the left-hand frame and select the Host from the right frame. Click Check Compliance Now to begin the compliance check.
4. If there are differences between the Host's configuration and the Host Profile, they will be displayed in the bottom frame of the window titled Compliance Failures.

CERTIFICATION SUMMARY

We started this chapter by taking a deeper look at VMware vCenter Update Manager. We had installed vCenter Update Manager in a previous chapter, but now we have installed its client components and configured its network settings. We configured it to download patches, and we configured how it would apply patches to virtual machines and to ESX Hosts. We looked at the default baselines that are used by vSphere Update Manager and reviewed how to create additional baselines and how to use them to patch and upgrade ESX Hosts and virtual machines.

We then looked at ESX Host Profiles as a means to consistently apply configurations to our ESX Host environment. We discussed how to create and delete Host Profiles and how to import and export them. We then used them to push a configuration to an ESX Host. We finished the chapter by using a Host Profile to audit the compliance of an ESX Host against a model Host Profile.

✓ TWO-MINUTE DRILL

Configure and Manage VMware vCenter Update Manager

❑ vCenter Update Manager is a client/server application that must be installed on both the vCenter Server and the vSphere Client that will manage it.

❑ Patch downloads can be scheduled in vCenter Update Manager.

❑ By default vCenter Update Manager includes patch sources for ESX 4.*x* Hosts, ESX 3.*x* Hosts, Linux, and Windows.

❑ vCenter Update Manager can be configured to take a snapshot of a virtual machine before applying patches to it.

❑ Baselines are collections of packages or upgrades that can be applied to ESX Hosts or virtual machines.

❑ Critical Host Patches is a default patch baseline that contains all of the patches that are considered critical by VMware for ESX Hosts.

❑ Non-Critical Host Patches is a default patch baseline that contains all of the patches that are considered non-critical by VMware for ESX Hosts.

❑ Critical VM Patches is a default patch baseline that contains all of the patches that are considered critical for Linux and Windows virtual machines.

❑ Non-Critical VM Patches is a default patch baseline that contains all of the patches that are considered non-critical for Linux and Windows virtual machines.

❑ VMware Tools Upgrade to Match Host is a default upgrade baseline that compares the version of VMware tools that is running on virtual machines against the version that is contained on the ESX Host where the virtual machines are running.

❑ VMware Hardware to Match Host is a default upgrade baseline that compares the version of VMware hardware that is running on virtual machines against the version that is supported on the ESX Host where the virtual machines are running.

❑ VA Upgrade to Latest is a default upgrade baseline that compares the version of a virtual appliance against the latest available version of the virtual appliance.

❑ VA Upgrade to Latest Critical is a default upgrade baseline that compares the version of a virtual appliance against the latest available critical version of the virtual appliance.

❑ Baseline Groups are sets of baselines that are combined into a single group.

Establish and Apply ESX Host Profiles

❑ Host Profiles are templates that contain all of the configuration information from a model ESX Host.

❑ Host Profiles can be applied to individual ESX Hosts or to Clusters.

❑ Host Profiles can be exported and backed up to a file.

❑ Host Profiles can be used to automatically configure settings on ESX Hosts.

❑ Host Profiles can be used to audit ESX Host configurations for compliance to standards.

SELF TEST

The following questions will help you measure your understanding of the material presented in this chapter. Read all the choices carefully and remember that there is only one best answer for each question.

Configure and Manage VMware vCenter Update Manager

1. Which of the following is not a class of settings that can be configured for vCenter Update Manager?
   A. Network Connectivity
   B. Patch Download Schedule
   C. Virtual Machine Settings
   D. Storage Settings

2. Under which class of vCenter Update Manager settings can the Server Port be configured?
   A. Network Connectivity
   B. Patch Download Scheduler
   C. Virtual Machine Settings
   D. ESX Host Settings

3. Under which class of vCenter Update Manager settings can the Proxy Settings be configured?
   A. Network Connectivity
   B. Patch Download Settings
   C. Virtual Machine Settings
   D. ESX Host Settings

4. The default installation of vCenter Update Manager does not have a patch source for which of the following operating systems?
   A. VMware ESX 4.x Hosts
   B. VMware ESX 3.x Hosts
   C. VMware ESX 2.x Hosts
   D. Linux

5. What must be true of an ESX Host before vCenter Update Manager can apply patches to it?

  A. It must be in maintenance mode.

  B. It must not contain any powered-on virtual machines.

  C. It must not be a member of a cluster.

  D. It must have vMotion enabled on one of its virtual switches.

6. Which of the following is not a default patch baseline?

  A. Critical Host Patches

  B. Critical VM Patches

  C. VA Upgrade to Latest Critical

  D. Non-Critical VM Patches

7. Which of the following is not a default upgrade baseline?

  A. VM Hardware to Match Host

  B. VA Upgrade to Latest

  C. VA Upgrade to Latest Urgent

  D. VA Upgrade to Latest Critical

8. Which of the following are sets of baselines that can be run at the same time?

  A. Baseline Sets

  B. Baseline Collections

  C. Baseline Groups

  D. Baseline Templates

Establish and Apply ESX Host Profiles

9. Which of the following are templates that contains all of the configuration information from a model ESX Host?

  A. Host Profiles

  B. Host Baselines

  C. Host Configuration Tables

  D. Host Snapshots

10. When a Host Profile is exported to a file, what is the extension of the file?

  A. csv

  B. pdf

  C. vpf

  D. txt

SELF TEST ANSWERS

Configure and Manage VMware vCenter Update Manager

1. ☑ **D.** Storage Settings is not a class of settings for vCenter Update Manager.
☒ **A, B,** and **C** are incorrect. Network Connectivity, Patch Download Settings, and Virtual Machine Settings are all classes of settings that can be configured for vCenter Update Manager.

2. ☑ **A.** The Server Port is configured in the Network Connectivity class of settings.
☒ **B, C,** and **D** are incorrect. The Server Port is not configured in the Patch Download Settings, Virtual Machine Settings, or ESX Host Settings classes of settings.

3. ☑ **B.** The Proxy Settings are configured in the Patch Download Settings class of settings.
☒ **A, C,** and **D** are incorrect. The Proxy Settings are not configured in the Network Connectivity, Virtual Machine Settings, or ESX Host Settings classes of settings.

4. ☑ **C.** By default vCenter Update Manager does not include a patch source for VMware ESX 2.*x* Hosts.
☒ **A, B,** and **D** are incorrect. vCenter Update Manager includes default patch sources for ESX 4.*x* Hosts, ESX 3.*x* Hosts, Linux virtual machines, and Windows virtual machines.

5. ☑ **B.** An ESX Host must not have any powered-on virtual machines running on it for vCenter Update Manager to apply patches to it.
☒ **A, C,** and **D** are incorrect. vCenter Update Manager can deploy patches to Hosts that are not in maintenance mode and those that are part of a cluster. vCenter Update Manager does not use or rely on vMotion.

6. ☑ **C.** VA Upgrade to Latest Critical is not a default upgrade baseline.
☒ **A, B,** and **D** are incorrect. Critical Host Patches, Critical VM Patches, and Non-Critical VM Patches are all default patch baselines.

7. ☑ **C.** VA Upgrade to Latest Urgent is not a default upgrade baseline.
☒ **A, B,** and **D** are incorrect. VM Hardware to Match Host, VA Upgrade to Latest, and VM Upgrade to Latest Critical are all default upgrade baselines.

8. ☑ **C.** Baseline Groups are sets of baselines that are combined into a single group and can be run together.
☒ **A, B,** and **D** are incorrect. Baseline Sets, Baseline Collections, and Baseline Templates are all made up and are not a part of vCenter Update Manager.

Establish and Apply ESX Host Profiles

9. ☑ **A.** Host Profiles are templates that contains all of the configuration information from a model ESX Host.

☒ **B, C,** and **D** are incorrect. Host Baselines, Host Configuration Tables, and Host Snapshots are all made up and are not a part of vSphere.

10. ☑ **C.** The extension of an exported Host profile is vpf for VMware profile format.

☒ **A, B,** and **D** are incorrect. The extension of an exported Host Profile is not csv, pdf, or txt.

9

Establish Service Levels

Welcome to Chapter 9. In this chapter we will look at the various constructs in vSphere that allow us to establish and maintain service levels. In the first section we will discuss VMware Clusters. We will look at how VMware uses clusters to establish High Availability (HA), VMotion, and Dynamic Resource Scheduling (DRS). In the next section we will talk about Fault-Tolerant (FT) virtual machines. Then we will discuss resource pools and how they can be used to aggregate the resources of multiple Hosts into a single unified construct. In the next section we will look at the various methods to migrate virtual machines between Hosts and between datastores. We will then end the chapter by looking at different solutions for backing up and restoring virtual machines.

CERTIFICATION OBJECTIVE 9.01

Create and Configure VMware Clusters

In this section we will look at VMware Clusters. We'll start by creating a new cluster. Once we have a cluster, we will discuss how to add Hosts to it. We will then look at HA and DRS. We will then discuss Distributed Power Management (DPM), which can allow significant power savings for virtualized datacenters. Once you understand DPM, we will discuss Enhanced VMotion Compatibility (EVC) and finally end the section by looking at the swapfile options that are available when using clusters.

Create a New Cluster

The first step toward working with VMware Clusters is to create one. We do this through the vSphere Client connected to the vCenter Server.

To create a new cluster, follow these steps:

1. Launch the vSphere Client and connect to your vCenter Server.
2. In the navigation bar select Home | Inventory | Hosts And Clusters.
3. Right-click the Datacenter where you want to create the new cluster and select New Cluster from the drop-down menu.

4. You will be presented with the New Cluster Wizard. Enter a name for the new cluster. On this screen you can also enable VMware HA and VMware DRS. We will discuss these features later in the chapter. For now leave them blank and click Next to continue.

5. You will be presented with the VMware Enhanced VMotion Compatibility window. We will discuss VMware EVC later in the chapter. For now leave the choices blank and click Next to continue.

6. You will be presented with the Virtual Machine Swapfile Location window. We will discuss the placement of the swapfile later in the chapter. For now accept the default and click Next to continue.

7. You will be presented with a summary screen. Confirm that the information is correct and click Finish to create the new cluster and exit. You will now see the new cluster, Test_Cluster-1, as shown in Figure 9-1.

Add ESX/ESXi Hosts to a Cluster

Now that we have created a new cluster, the next step is to add Hosts to it. We do this through the vSphere Client connected to the vCenter Server.

To add a Host to a cluster, follow these steps:

1. Launch the vSphere Client and connect to your vCenter Server.

2. In the navigation bar select Home | Inventory | Hosts And Clusters.

3. Left-click the Host and drag it to the cluster you want to add it to.

FIGURE 9-1

The newly
created cluster
Test_Cluster-1

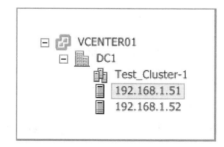

Configure High Availability Basic and Advanced Settings

VMware High Availability is a feature provided with vSphere that allows virtual machines that have failed to be restarted on a different ESX/ESXi Host in the same HA cluster. This failure can be caused by a failure of the virtual machine or of the Host on which it resides. When a failure is detected, there is an outage while the virtual machine is restarted on the new Host. There are three different classes of options that are available for a HA cluster. In the rest of this section we will look at these options in detail.

VMware HA General Options

The first class of HA options is the general options. The general options include the following:

- **Host Monitoring Status**   Host Monitoring Status can be either enabled or not enabled. If this option is enabled, all of the Hosts in a cluster will exchange network heartbeats that will allow them to determine if a Host has failed. If this option is not enabled, no heartbeats will be exchanged.

- **Admission Control**   Admission Control can be set to "Prevent VMs from being powered on if they violate availability constraints" or "Allow VMs to be powered on if they violate availability constraints." This policy is used by the cluster to ensure that there is sufficient capacity remaining in the cluster to perform failovers if there are Host failures. If it is set to "Prevent VMs from being powered on," any VM that would cause the remaining capacity to be insufficient to handle failover requirements would not be allowed to be powered on. If it is set to "Allow VMs to be powered on," VMs are allowed to be powered on even if they would cause the remaining capacity to be insufficient to handle failover requirements.

- **Admission Control Policy**   There are three settings under admission control policy. The first is "Host failures cluster tolerates." This setting defines the maximum number of Host failures that the cluster can tolerate at one time. The second is "Percentage of cluster resources reserved as failover spare capacity." This setting is given as a percentage and determines the amount of resources that are set aside for failover capability as a percentage of the capacity of the entire cluster. The last option is "Specify a failover host." This setting allows you to set aside an entire Host to be used as failover capacity.

To edit these settings, follow these steps:

1. Launch the vSphere Client and connect to your vCenter Server.
2. In the navigation bar select Home | Inventory | Hosts And Clusters.
3. Right-click the cluster you wish to edit and select Edit Settings from the drop-down menu.
4. You will be presented with the Cluster Settings window. Click VMware HA from the left-hand list and you will be presented with the VMware HA General Options window as shown in Figure 9-2.
5. Edit the settings you wish to change and click OK to exit.

FIGURE 9-2	

The VMware HA General Options window

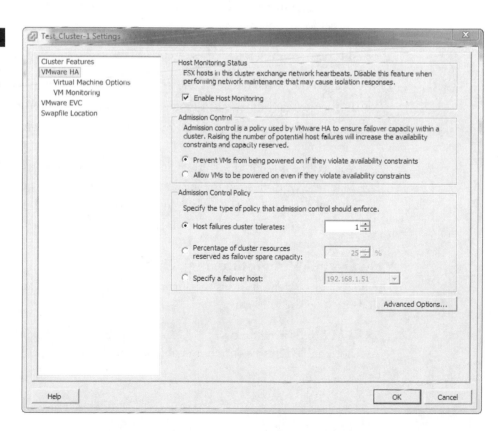

VMware HA Virtual Machine Options

The next class of HA options is the Virtual Machine options. The Virtual Machine options include the following:

- **VM restart priority**   The VM restart priority can have the following values: Disabled, Low, Medium, High. This setting is used by the HA cluster to determine the order that virtual machines will be brought back online when a failure occurs.

- **Host isolation response**   The Host isolation response can have the following values: Leave Powered On, Power Off, Shut Down. This setting determines what the cluster will do to virtual machines if the Host they reside on is not able to be reached through a console connection but is still functioning.

- **Virtual machine settings**   The virtual machine settings section allows individual virtual machines to have different settings than the defaults that are set for the cluster.

To edit these settings, follow these steps:

1. Launch the vSphere Client and connect to your vCenter Server.
2. In the navigation bar select Home | Inventory | Hosts And Clusters.
3. Right-click the cluster you wish to edit and select Edit Settings from the drop-down menu.
4. You will be presented with the Cluster Settings window. Click Virtual Machine Options from the left-hand list and you will be presented with the Virtual Machine Options window as shown in Figure 9-3.
5. Edit the settings you wish to change and click OK to exit.

VMware HA VM Monitoring

The next class of HA options is the Virtual Machine options. The Virtual Machine options include the following:

- **VM Monitoring Status**   VM Monitoring Status can be either enabled or not enabled. If this option is enabled, virtual machines will be restarted if

FIGURE 9-3

The VMware HA
Virtual Machine
Options window

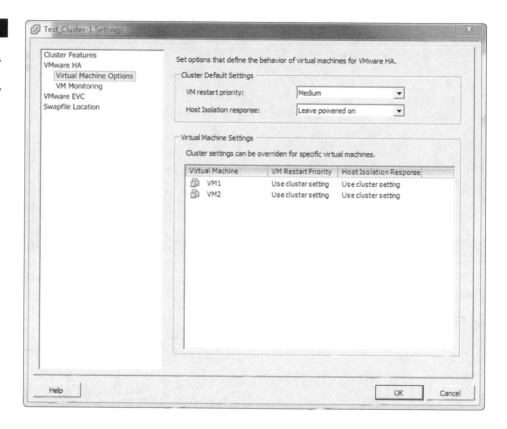

the cluster does not receive a heartbeat from the virtual machine within a
set time. The heartbeat is established using VMware Tools, which must be
installed on the guest virtual machines.

- **Monitoring Sensitivity** Monitoring Sensitivity can have the following
  values: Low, Medium, High, Custom. These settings determine the length of
  time HA will wait for a heartbeat signal from a VM and how many times it
  will restart the VM in a given time interval.

- **Virtual Machine Settings** The Virtual Machine Settings section allows
  individual virtual machines to have different settings than the defaults that
  are set for the cluster.

To edit these settings, follow these steps:

1. Launch the vSphere Client and connect to your vCenter Server.
2. In the navigation bar select Home | Inventory | Hosts And Clusters.
3. Right-click the cluster you wish to edit and select Edit Settings from the drop-down menu.
4. You will be presented with the Cluster Settings window. Click VM Monitoring from the left-hand list and you will be presented with the VM Monitoring window as shown in Figure 9-4.
5. Edit the settings you wish to change and click OK to exit.

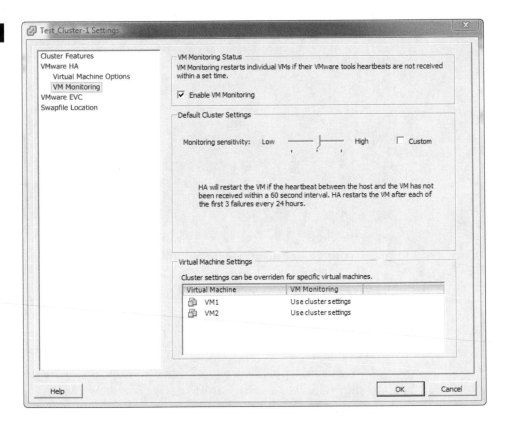

FIGURE 9-4

The VMware HA VM Monitoring window

Configure Distributed Resource Scheduler
Basic and Advanced Settings

VMware Distributed Resource Scheduler (DRS) is a feature provided with vSphere that allows a cluster to manage all of its Hosts as a single pool of resources. DRS also allows a cluster to assign virtual machines to Hosts in the cluster to balance computing loads and to enforce resource constraints. The VMware DRS options include the following:

1. **Automation Level**   The Automation Level of a DRS cluster can have the following values: Manual, Partially Automated, Fully Automated. If the Automation Level is set to Manual, vCenter will only make suggestions as to which Host new virtual machines should be placed on and when they should be migrated to different Hosts. If the Automation Level is set to Partially Automated, vCenter will automatically place new virtual machines on Hosts and will make recommendations on when a virtual machine should be migrated to a different Host. If the Automation Level is set to Fully Automated, vCenter will automatically place new virtual machines on Hosts and will automatically migrate virtual machines to different Hosts to balance workloads.

2. **Rules**   Rules can be configured to Keep Virtual Machines Together or to Separate Virtual Machines. If a rule is set to Keep Virtual Machines Together, DRS will always keep the virtual machines running on the same Host. These rules are generally referred to as virtual machine affinity rules. If a rule is set to Separate Virtual Machines, DRS will always keep the virtual machines on different Hosts. These rules are generally referred to as anti-affinity rules.

3. **Virtual Machine Settings**   The virtual machine settings section allows individual virtual machines to have different settings than the defaults that are set for the cluster.

To edit these settings, follow these steps:

1. Launch the vSphere Client and connect to your vCenter Server.
2. In the navigation bar select Home | Inventory | Hosts And Clusters.
3. Right-click the cluster you wish to edit and select Edit Settings from the drop-down menu.

4. You will be presented with the Cluster Settings window. Click VM DRS from the left-hand list and you will be presented with the Automation Level window, or select Rules from the left-hand list and you will be presented with the DRS Rules window.

5. Edit the settings you wish to change and click OK to exit.

Configure Distributed Power Management

Distributed Power Management is a feature provided with vSphere that allows a DRS-enabled cluster to move all of the virtual machines from a Host and then power off the Host to conserve energy when the cluster's resource utilization is low and power them back on when resource utilization rises. This feature can allow significant power cost savings for companies that have differing compute workloads during different times of the day. DPM uses the wake-on-LAN (WOL), ILO, or IPMI capabilities of modern NIC cards to power Hosts on and off. The Distributed Power Management options include the following:

- **Power Management Level**   The Power Management Level of a DRS cluster can have the following values: Off, Manual, Automatic. If the Power Management Level is set to Off, DPM will not be used for the cluster. If the Power Management Level is set to Manual, vCenter will make recommendations on which Hosts should have their virtual machines migrated and be powered down and when they should be powered back on. If the Power Management Level is set to Automatic, vCenter will automatically migrate virtual machines and power off Hosts when utilization is low and power them back on when utilization rises.

- **Host Options**   The Host Options section allows individual Hosts to have different settings than the defaults that are set for the cluster.

To edit these settings, follow these steps:

1. Launch the vSphere Client and connect to your vCenter Server.

2. In the navigation bar select Home | Inventory | Hosts And Clusters.

3. Right-click the cluster you wish to edit and select Edit Settings from the drop-down menu.

4. You will be presented with the Cluster Settings window. Click Power Management from the left-hand list and you will be presented with the Power Management window, or select Host Options from the left-hand list and you will be presented with the Host Options window.

5. Edit the settings you wish to change and click OK to exit.

Configure Enhanced VMotion Capability

Enhanced VMotion Compatibility (EVC) is a feature provided with vSphere that allows VMotion to occur between Hosts that share a common CPU baseline features. VMotion is the ability to migrate a running virtual machine from one Host to another without any interruption of the virtual machine. We will discuss VMotion further later in this chapter. Enhanced VMotion helps to maximize VMotion compatibility between Hosts by taking the CPU instruction set from the oldest processor in the cluster and dumbing down the other Hosts to match that instruction set. The Enhanced VMotion modes include the following:

- **Disable EVC** If this setting is selected, Enhanced VMotion will not be used by the cluster.
- **Enable EVC for AMD Hosts** If this setting is selected, Enhanced VMotion will be used by the cluster and will be optimized for Hosts with AMD processors.
- **Enable EVC for Intel Hosts** If this setting is selected, Enhanced VMotion will be used by the cluster and will be optimized for Hosts with Intel processors.

To configure Enhanced VMotion, follow these steps:

1. Launch the vSphere Client and connect to your vCenter Server.
2. In the navigation bar select Home | Inventory | Hosts And Clusters.
3. Right-click the cluster you wish to edit and select Edit Settings from the drop-down menu.
4. You will be presented with the Cluster Settings window. Click VMware EVC from the left-hand list and you will be presented with the Enhanced VMotion window. Click Change to change the EVC Mode.
5. You will be presented with the Change EVC Mode window as shown in Figure 9-5. Edit the settings you wish to change and click OK to exit.

FIGURE 9-5

The Change EVC
Mode window

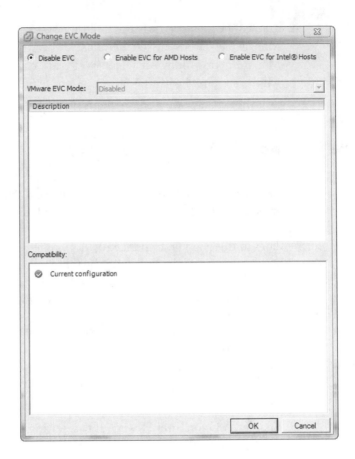

Many datacenters use a mix of Intel and AMD servers. Unfortunately VMotion is not supported between Hosts that have AMD processors and those that have Intel processors. VMware EVC does not currently allow this to occur.

Configure Swap File Location

By default virtual machine swap files are stored in the same directory as the other files that make up the virtual machine. In certain situations you may want to store these swap files in another location, such as lower-cost storage or storage with better performance characteristics. The Swapfile Policy can have the following settings:

- **Store the swapfile in the same directory as the virtual machine**   If this setting is selected, the virtual machine swap file will be stored with the other files that make up the virtual machine.
- **Store the swapfile in the datastore specified by the Host**   If this setting is selected, the virtual machine swap file will be stored on a datastore specified by the configuration of the Host.

To configure the Swap File location, follow these steps:

1. Launch the vSphere Client and connect to your vCenter Server.
2. In the navigation bar select Home | Inventory | Hosts And Clusters.
3. Right-click the cluster you wish to edit and select Edit Settings from the drop-down menu.
4. You will be presented with the Cluster Settings window. Click Swapfile Location from the left-hand list and you will be presented with the Swapfile Policy for Virtual Machines window.
5. Edit the settings you wish to change and click OK to exit.

CERTIFICATION OBJECTIVE 9.02

Enable a Fault-Tolerant Virtual Machine

Fault-Tolerant virtual machines are used by vSphere to enable greater uptime for a virtual machine by essentially creating a copy of the virtual machine and switching control to the copy in the event of a failure of the Host where the original VM resides or a failure of the virtual machine itself. High Availability would have the ability to restart the virtual machine on another Host, but there would be downtime on the virtual machine. Using Fault Tolerance, this downtime is greatly reduced.

In this section we will work with Fault-Tolerant virtual machines. We will review the requirements for Fault Tolerance and look at various usage cases for it. We will then set up a Fault Tolerance network and verify the operating system requirements for Fault Tolerance. Once you understand all of the requirements, we will enable and test Fault Tolerance for a virtual machine. We will end the section by discussing the special requirements for upgrading ESX Hosts that contain Fault-Tolerant virtual machines.

Identify FT Restrictions

There are a large number of restrictions that apply to virtual machine Fault Tolerance. For Fault Tolerance to work correctly, all of the following conditions will need to be met:

- Hardware virtualization must be enabled in the BIOS of both the primary and secondary Hosts.
- The primary and secondary Hosts must have access to the shared storage that contains the virtual machine.
- Both the primary and secondary Hosts must be contained in the same HA cluster.
- Both the primary and secondary Hosts must be running the same version of ESX.
- Both the primary and secondary Hosts must have the same CPU model, family, and stepping.
- Each VM that is using Fault Tolerance must have a single virtual CPU.
- Virtual machines must not have Thin provisioned disks.
- Virtual machines must not be configured to use the VMXNET3 NIC.
- Virtual machines must not be a part of a Microsoft Cluster.
- There can be a maximum of four virtual machine primaries or secondaries on any ESX/ESXi Host.
- The operating system of the virtual machine must be supported by Fault Tolerance.
- The guest operating system of the virtual machine must use NTP for time synchronization.

Before attempting to use Fault Tolerance, make sure that your configuration meets the preceding requirements.

Evaluate FT Usage Cases

Now that you understand the requirements for Fault Tolerance, let's take a look at its usage cases. The following are the main usage cases for VMware Fault Tolerance:

- **Hardware failures**   The main use for Fault Tolerance is to protect against failures on the ESX/ESXi Hosts. The main cause of Host failures is hardware failures.

- **Host OS failures**   If the ESX/ESXI Hosts experience a failure due to an OS issue, Fault Tolerance will enable critical virtual machines to continue functioning.

- **High availability for non–cluster aware applications**   Fault Tolerance can provide a high availability option for critical applications that are not cluster aware. If an application is cluster aware, it is recommended that clustering be used instead of Fault Tolerance.

Set Up an FT Network

Fault Tolerance uses a technology called vLockstep to keep the primary and secondary virtual machines synchronized during regular operation. This synchronization occurs over a VMkernel network port group. The first step to configuring Fault Tolerance is to set up a new VMkernel port group for Fault Tolerance traffic. You will need to do this on all of the Hosts that will participate in Fault Tolerance.

To configure a VMkernel port group for Fault Tolerance, follow these steps:

1. Launch the vSphere Client and connect to your vCenter Server.
2. In the navigation bar select Home | Inventory | Hosts And Clusters.
3. Select the Host you wish to configure from the left-hand menu and click the Configuration tab.

4. You will be presented with the Configuration window. Select Networking from the Hardware menu.

5. Select the virtual switch where you want to create the port group and click Properties.

6. You will be presented with the properties window for the virtual switch. Click Add to enter the Add Network Wizard.

7. Select the radio box next to VMkernel and click Next to continue.

8. You will be presented with the VMkernel | Connection Settings window as shown in Figure 9-6. Enter a network label for this port group and check the box next to "Use this port group for Fault Tolerance logging." You can also use this port group for VMotion, but it is not recommended. Click Next to continue.

9. You will be prompted to enter an IP address for the new port group. Enter an IP address and subnet mask and click Next to continue.

10. You will be presented with a summary screen. Click Finish to create the new port group and exit.

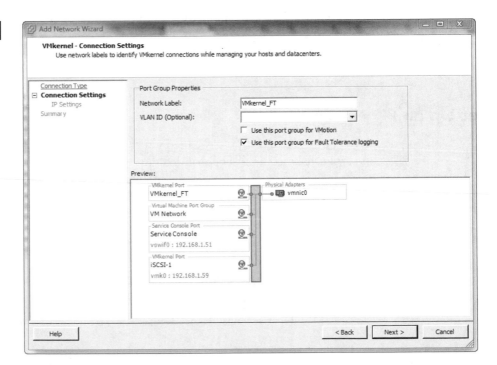

FIGURE 9-6

The VMkernel Connection Settings window

Enable FT for a Virtual Machine

There are two parts to using Fault Tolerance on a virtual machine: Turning on Fault Tolerance and Enabling Fault Tolerance. Turning on Fault Tolerance prepares the virtual machine for Fault Tolerance by converting any Thin-provisioned disks to Thick-provisioned and by resetting the memory reservation of the virtual machine to the memory size of the virtual machine.

To Turn On and Enable Fault Tolerance for a virtual machine, follow these steps:

1. Launch the vSphere Client and connect to your vCenter Server.
2. In the navigation bar select Home | Inventory | Hosts And Clusters.
3. Right-click the virtual machine you wish to prepare for Fault Tolerance and select Fault Tolerance and then Turn On Fault Tolerance from the drop-down menus.
4. You will be presented with the Turn On Fault Tolerance window. Click Yes to exit and prepare the virtual machine for Fault Tolerance.
5. If the virtual machine was powered on when Fault Tolerance was turned on, a secondary virtual machine will be created on another Host in the cluster and turned on if it passes admission control. The status of the primary virtual machine will now be set to Protected.
6. If the virtual machine was not powered on when Fault Tolerance was turned on, a secondary machine will be created on another Host in the cluster but will not be powered on. The status of the virtual machine will be Not Protected. Once the primary virtual machine is powered on, the secondary will also be powered on, and if it passes admission control, the status of the primary virtual machine will be set to Protected.

Test an FT Configuration

Once you have Fault Tolerance turned on and enabled for a virtual machine, you will want to test it to make sure it is working correctly. vSphere provides two different tests you can perform on a Fault-Tolerant virtual machine: Test Failover and Test Restart Secondary. The Test Failover option performs a failover making the secondary virtual machine into the primary and the primary virtual machine into the secondary. The Test Restart Secondary option performs a restart on the secondary virtual machine to make sure it is performing correctly.

To test Fault Tolerance for a virtual machine, follow these steps:

1. Launch the vSphere Client and connect to your vCenter Server.
2. In the navigation bar select Home | Inventory | Hosts And Clusters.
3. Right-click the virtual machine you wish to test for Fault Tolerance and select Fault Tolerance and then Test Failover or Test Restart Secondary from the drop-down menus.

Upgrade ESX Hosts Containing FT Virtual Machines

Fault-Tolerant virtual machines must be taken into account when performing Host upgrades. Since Fault Tolerance requires the primary and secondary virtual machines to be running on Hosts that have the same ESX version, upgrading a Host that holds the primary or secondary to a new version can cause issues.

To upgrade Hosts that contain Fault-Tolerant virtual machines, follow these steps:

1. Use VMotion to move all of the Fault-Tolerant virtual machines from two of the Hosts that are going to be upgraded. Remember to migrate the virtual machines to Hosts that meet the requirements of Fault Tolerance.
2. Upgrade the two Hosts that you have just moved the virtual machines from to the same version of ESX.
3. Disable Fault Tolerance on the primary virtual machine of a Fault-Tolerant pair and use VMotion to migrate it to one of the newly upgraded Hosts.
4. Re-enable Fault Tolerance on the virtual machine that you just migrated to the new Host. This will create a new secondary virtual machine on the other newly migrated Host.
5. Repeat Step 3 and Step 4 to remove all of the Fault-Tolerant virtual machines from two more Hosts.
6. Upgrade the two Hosts from which you just removed the Fault-Tolerant virtual machines.
7. Repeat Steps 3 through 6 until you have upgraded all of your Hosts.

CERTIFICATION OBJECTIVE 9.03

Create and Configure Resource Pools

A *resource pool* is a VMware construct that represents a collection of CPU and memory resources that are presented as a single pool. Resource pools can be used to segment your virtual computing resources into logical units and can be used to delegate access to different users or groups within your organization. Each resource pool can be managed as if it were a single computing resource, even though it can contain multiple virtual machines and even other resource pools.

In this section we will look at how resource pools are structured and how they use shares, reservations, and limits to control computing resources. We will then create a resource pool and discuss how to edit its settings once it is created. We will then talk about expandable reservations and then end the section by adding virtual machines to our new resource pool.

Describe Resource Pool Hierarchy

Resource pools can be cascaded within one another. A parent resource pool can have zero or more child resource pools that can each have zero or more child resource pools. In this way a resource pool is the child of the resource pools above it and a parent to the resource pools below it.

Evaluate Appropriate Shares, Reservations, and Limits in a Given Situation

Resource pools use shares, reservations, and limits to determine the amount of memory or CPU resources they have available to assign to virtual machines and to child resource pools.

■ **CPU Shares**   CPU Shares represent the percentage of the parent's CPU resources that a resource pool will have when weighed against the total number of CPU shares held by all of its peer resource pools. For example: If there are three resource pools at the same level, Pool-A has 2000 shares, and Pool-B and Pool-C have 1000 shares each, there are a total of 4000 shares. Since Pool-A has 2000 of the 4000 shares, it will receive 50 percent of the CPU resources.

■ **CPU Reservation**   The CPU Reservation indicates the minimum amount of CPU resources that will be guaranteed to the resource pool; it is expressed in MHz.

■ **CPU Limit**   The CPU Limit represents the maximum amount of CPU resources that will be given to the resource pool; it is expressed in MHz.

■ **Memory Shares**   Memory Shares represent the percentage of the parent's memory resources that a resource pool will have when weighed against the total number of memory shares held by all of its peer resource pools. For example: If there are three resource pools at the same level, Pool-A has 2000 shares, and Pool-B and Pool-C have 1000 shares each, there are a total of 4000 shares. Since Pool-A has 2000 of the 4000 shares, it will receive 50 percent of the memory resources.

■ **Memory Reservation**   A Memory Reservation indicates the minimum amount of memory resources that will be guaranteed to the resource pool; it is expressed in MB.

■ **Memory Limit**   The Memory Limit represents the maximum amount of memory resources that will be given to the resource pool; it is expressed in MB.

Define Expandable Reservation

When we created the resource pool earlier, there was a check box labeled Expandable Reservation, which was selected by default. If Expandable Reservation is checked, the resource pool will be able to use additional resources from its parent if they are available. If a virtual machine in a resource pool that does not have expandable reservations is attempting to power on and its reservation combined with the reservations of the other running virtual machines is more than the resource pool has available, the virtual machine will not be allowed to be powered on. If expandable reservations are enabled, the resource pool will attempt to use resources from its parent to allow the virtual machine to be powered on.

Create Resource Pools

Now that you know what a resource pool is and how to use it, the next step is to go ahead and create a new resource pool.

To create a resource pool, follow these steps:

1. Launch the vSphere Client and connect to your vCenter Server.
2. In the navigation bar select Home | Inventory | Hosts And Clusters.
3. You can create a resource pool under an ESX/ESXi Host, under a cluster, or under another resource pool. Right-click the inventory object you want to create the resource pool under and select New Resource Pool from the drop-down menu.
4. You will be presented with the Create Resource Pool window as shown in Figure 9-7. Enter a name for the resource pool and set shares, reservations, and limits for both CPU Resources and Memory Resources. Click OK to exit and create the resource pool.

FIGURE 9-7

The Create
Resource Pool
window

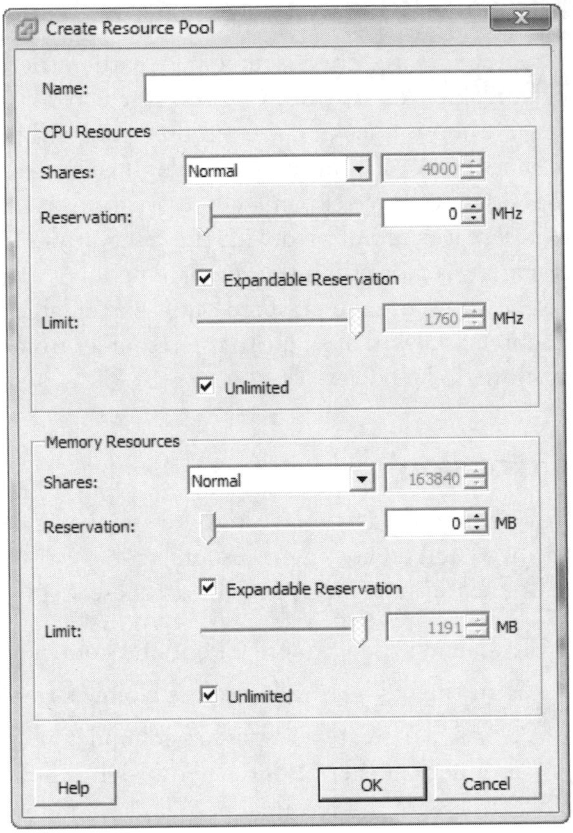

Set Resource Shares, Reservations, and Limits

You can set shares, reservations, and limits on a resource pool when it is created, but as your environment changes, you may need to make changes to these values.

To edit the settings of a resource pool, follow these steps:

1. Launch the vSphere Client and connect to your vCenter Server.

2. In the navigation bar select Home | Inventory | Hosts And Clusters.

3. Right-click the resource pool you want to edit and select Edit Settings from the drop-down menu.

4. You will be presented with the Edit Settings window for the resource pool. On this window you can change the name of the resource pool and the shares, reservation, and limit for both CPU and memory resources. You can also select to use expandable reservations for CPU and memory resources. Change the settings to their new values and click OK to exit.

Add Virtual Machines to a Pool

Before a resource pool can be useful, it will need to contain some virtual machines. You can create new virtual machines in a resource pool, or you can move existing virtual machines into a resource pool.

To move a virtual machine into a resource pool, follow these steps:

1. Launch the vSphere Client and connect to your vCenter Server.
2. In the navigation bar select Home | Inventory | Hosts And Clusters.
3. Click and hold the left mouse button on the virtual machine you wish to move into the resource pool and drag it over the existing resource pool. Release the button to add the virtual machine to the resource pool.
4. Expand the resource pool by clicking the + sign next to it and confirm that the virtual machine has been moved.

CERTIFICATION OBJECTIVE 9.04

Migrate Virtual Machines

In this section we will look at the different methods for migrating a virtual machine from one Host to another and from one datastore to another. We will start by looking at the different methods to migrate a virtual machine and describe the strengths and weaknesses of each method. We will then discuss usage cases for each migration method. We will end the section by performing virtual machine migrations using each available method.

Understand the Three Methods of Virtual Machine Migration

There are three methods that can be used to migrate virtual machines:

- **Cold migration** A cold migration is performed on a virtual machine that is powered off. The virtual machine is moved from residing on one Host to another Host. During a cold migration the files that are associated with the virtual machine can be migrated to a different datastore, and they are not required to be on shared storage.
- **VMotion** A VMotion migration allows a powered-on virtual machine to be moved from one Host to another without a loss of service from the virtual machine. In a VMotion migration the files that are associated with the virtual machine do not move to a different datastore, and they must be on shared storage that is accessible to both Hosts. A VMotion migration requires that the source and target Hosts have compatible CPUs.
- **Storage VMotion** A Storage VMotion allows a powered-on virtual machine to have its associated files moved from one datastore to another without a loss of service from the virtual machine. During a Storage VMotion the Host that the virtual machine is running on does not change.

Determine Migration Usage Cases

There are a number of usage cases where a virtual machine will need to be migrated.

- Usage Cases for Cold Migrations
  - Migrate powered-off VMs between Hosts without shared storage
- Usage Cases for VMotion Migrations
  - Used by maintenance mode to move VMs off of a Host
  - Used by DRS to load-balance VMs across Hosts
  - Used by DPM to move VMs off of a Host to be powered down

- Usage Cases for Storage VMotion
  - Used to move VMs from one datastore to another

Migrate a Virtual Machine Using VMotion

Before we can perform a migration using VMotion, we need to understand its requirements.

VMotion has the following requirements:

- Both Hosts must have access to the same shared storage.
- Both Hosts must share a Gigabit network connection.
- The network names for both Hosts must be the same.
- The Hosts must have processors that are from the same family.

Now that you understand the requirements for VMotion, let's go ahead and perform a migration using VMotion.

To migrate a virtual machine using VMotion, follow these steps:

1. Launch the vSphere Client and connect to your vCenter Server.
2. In the navigation bar select Home | Inventory | VMs And Templates.
3. Right-click the virtual machine you wish to migrate and select Migrate from the drop-down menu.
4. You will be presented with the Select Migration Type window as shown in Figure 9-8. Select the radio button next to Change Host and click Next to continue.

5. You will be presented with the Select Destination window. Select the target Host for the migration and click Next to continue.

6. You will be presented with the VMotion Priority window. On this window you can choose to "Reserve CPU for optimal VMotion performance" or to "Perform with available CPU resources." If you elect to reserve CPU resources, the VMotion will be faster but may fail if there are not sufficient resources for it to be initiated. Select to reserve CPU resources and click Next to continue.

7. You will be presented with a summary screen. Click Finish to perform the VMotion and exit.

FIGURE 9-8

The Select
Migration Type
window

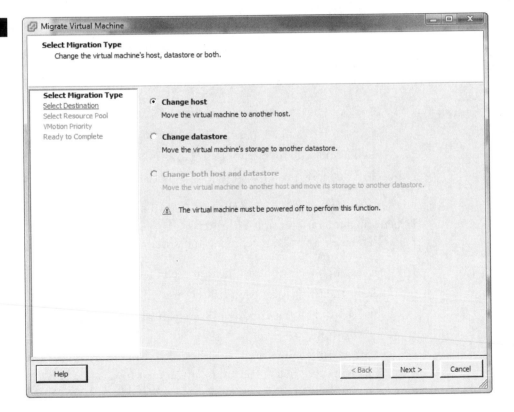

Migrate a Virtual Machine Using Storage VMotion

Storage VMotion is used to migrate virtual machines from one datastore to another without an outage.

To migrate a virtual machine using VMotion, follow these steps:

1. Launch the vSphere Client and connect to your vCenter Server.
2. In the navigation bar select Home | Inventory | VMs And Templates.
3. Right-click the virtual machine you wish to migrate and select Migrate from the drop-down menu.
4. You will be presented with the Select Migration Type window. Select the radio button next to Change Datastore and click Next to continue.
5. You will be presented with the Select Datastore window. Select the target datastore for the migration and click Next to continue.
6. You will be presented with the Disk Format window as shown in Figure 9-9. On this window you can choose the format that you want for the virtual

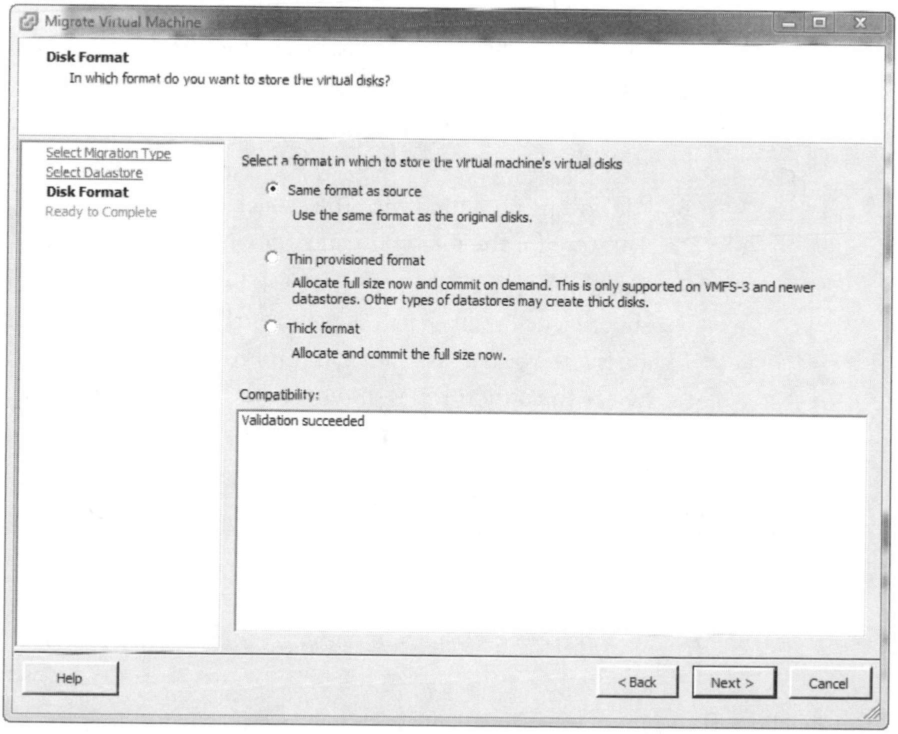

FIGURE 9-9

The Storage
VMotion Disk
Format window

machine's disks. Your options are Same Format As Source, Thin Provisioned Format, or Thick Format. Select the option you want and click Next to continue.

7. You will be presented with a summary screen. Click Finish to perform the Storage VMotion and exit.

Cold-Migrate a Virtual Machine

Cold migrations are used to move powered-off virtual machines from one Host to another. They do not require the source and target Hosts to have compatible CPUs or shared storage.

To cold-migrate a virtual machine, follow these steps:

1. Launch the vSphere Client and connect to your vCenter Server.
2. In the navigation bar select Home | Inventory | VMs And Templates.
3. Right-click the virtual machine you wish to migrate and select Migrate from the drop-down menu.
4. You will be presented with the Select Migration Type window. Select the radio button next to Change Both Host And Datastore and click Next to continue.
5. You will be presented with the Select Destination window. Select the target Host for the migration and click Next to continue.
6. You will be presented with the Select Datastore window. Select the target datastore for the migration and click Next to continue.
7. You will be presented with the Disk Format window. On this window you can choose the format that you want for the virtual machine's disks. Your options are Same Format As Source, Thin Provisioned Format, or Thick Format. Select the option you want and click Next to continue.
8. You will be presented with a summary screen. Click Finish to perform the Cold Migration and exit.

CERTIFICATION OBJECTIVE 9.05

Back Up and Restore Virtual Machines

In this section we will look at different ways to back up and restore virtual machines. We will start by reviewing the different types of backup and restore strategies that are used with virtual machines. We will then look at the idea of virtual machine snapshots. Once you understand snapshots, we will download and configure a backup solution from VMware called vCenter Data Recovery. We will finish the section and the chapter by running a number of backups and restores with vCenter Data Recovery.

Describe Different Backup and Restore Procedures and Strategies

Companies use a number of different strategies to back up and restore their servers. When backing up physical servers, most companies use some type of centralized backup server that communicates with an agent that is installed on each server that needs backed up to back up all of the files on the server. This system has been working for a long time and is widely used, but it does have some issues. These backups can take a long time to perform and can often have issues with open files not being backed up properly. In addition to these issues, restoring from these backups can be very time consuming. VMware has introduced VMware Data Recovery to try to resolve some of these issues.

There are two main types of backups that can be performed on virtual machines: file-level backups and image backups.

- **File-level backups** File-level backups are the traditional way that physical servers are currently backed up. File-level backups have the advantage of being very familiar to server administrators, since they most likely already use this type of backups for their physical servers.

- **Image backups** Image backups are basically backups of the files that make up the virtual machine. By making backups of the relatively small number of files that make up a virtual machine, administrators can perform backups very quickly and without some of the problems associated with traditional backups and without having to install an agent on each virtual machine.

Later in the chapter we will look at VMware Data Recovery to see how it can help to automate backups for our virtual environment.

Create, Delete, and Restore Snapshots

Snapshots are a feature of vSphere that allows you to take point-in-time images of a virtual machine. Once a snapshot is taken of a virtual machine, it can be easily returned to the exact state it was in when the snapshot was taken. Snapshots can be a very powerful tool when performing software upgrades or applying patches to virtual machines. If a snapshot is taken before the software upgrades are performed and there are problems after the upgrade, the virtual machine can quickly be returned to the exact state it was in before the upgrade. Now that you have a basic understanding of what snapshots are, let's look at how to create snapshots, delete snapshots, and restore a virtual machine to a snapshot.

To create a snapshot of a virtual machine, follow these steps:

1. Launch the vSphere Client and connect to your vCenter Server.
2. In the navigation bar select Home | Inventory | VMs And Templates.
3. Right-click the virtual machine you wish to snapshot and select Snapshot and then Take Snapshot from the drop-down menu.
4. You will be presented with the Take Virtual Machine Snapshot window. Enter a descriptive name for the snapshot and enter a description. You have the following options on this window: "Snapshot the virtual machine's memory" and "Quiesce guest file system." If you choose to "Snapshot the virtual machine's memory," the contents of the virtual machine's memory will be copied. If you choose to "Quiesce guest file system," all running processes on the virtual machine will be paused and the virtual machine will be in a known consistent state when the snapshot is taken. Click OK to create the snapshot and exit.

To delete a snapshot of a virtual machine, follow these steps:

1. Launch the vSphere Client and connect to your vCenter Server.
2. In the navigation bar select Home | Inventory | VMs And Templates.
3. Right-click the virtual machine you wish to snapshot and select Snapshot and then Snapshot Manager from the drop-down menu.

4. You will be presented with the Snapshot Manager window as shown in Figure 9-10. Select the snapshot you wish to delete and click Delete.

5. You will be presented with a confirmation window. Click Yes to continue and delete the snapshot.

To revert a virtual machine to a snapshot, follow these steps:

1. Launch the vSphere Client and connect to your vCenter Server.

2. In the navigation bar select Home | Inventory | VMs And Templates.

3. Right-click the virtual machine you wish to snapshot and select Snapshot and then Revert To Current Snapshot from the drop-down menu.

4. You will be presented with a confirmation window. Click Yes to continue and revert the virtual machine to the most current snapshot.

on the
! () o b

Snapshots can be an extremely valuable tool when applying patches to a virtual machine. Before applying an untested patch to a virtual machine, take a snapshot. If the patch then causes issues for the virtual machine, you can easily revert to the snapshot. This has saved me a number of times when patches or upgrades caused virtual machine problems.

FIGURE 9-10

The Snapshot
Manager window

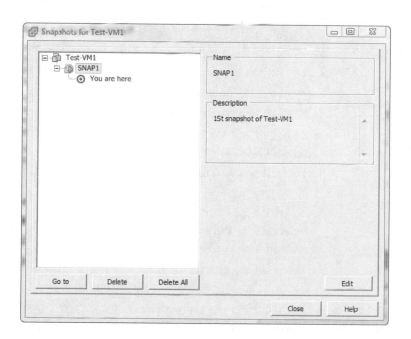

VMware Data Recovery

VMware Data Recovery is a product from VMware that can be used to perform backups and restores of virtual machines. It is a client/server application that has two parts: the Backup and Recovery Appliance that is installed as an OVF appliance, and the vCenter Data Recovery Plug-in that is installed as a plug-in for the vSphere Client. VMware Data Recovery supports the volume shadow copy service to enable it to create seamless backups of Windows virtual machines, and since it integrates with the vCenter Server, it can back up virtual machines even if they have been migrated to different Hosts.

on the **Job**

There are a large number of backup applications for virtual machines. The main drawback to many of these applications is that they are not able to find virtual machines after they have been migrated to different Hosts. An advantage of VMware Data Recovery is its ability to follow virtual machines as they move between Hosts.

Install Backup and Recovery Appliance

Now that you know a little about Data Recovery, let's go ahead and install it. The first step is to install the Backup and Recovery Appliance.

To install the Backup and Recovery Appliance, follow these steps:

1. Download the VMware Data Recovery template and save it to your workstation.
2. Launch the vSphere Client and connect to your vCenter Server.
3. From the File menu select Deploy OVF Template.
4. You will be presented with the Deploy OVF Template Wizard. Select the radio button next to Deploy From File. Click Browse and navigate to the template you downloaded in Step 1. Click Next to continue.
5. You will be presented with a details window for the template. Click Next to continue.
6. You will be presented with the Name And Location window for the template. Select a location for the virtual appliance from the Inventory Location frame and click Next to continue.
7. You will be presented with the Datastore window for the template. Select a datastore for the virtual appliance and click Next to continue.
8. You will be presented with a summary screen. Confirm that the information is correct and click Finish to exit and install the virtual appliance.

INSIDE THE EXAM

VMware Data Recovery

To test your knowledge of the installation process for VMware Data Recovery, you may see a question that asks where each piece of the Data Recovery package is installed.

Remember that there are two different steps to the install. You need to install both the Appliance on a Host and the Plug-In on your workstation before you will be able to use VMware Data Recovery.

Install vCenter Data Recovery Plug-In

Now that we have the Backup and Recovery Appliance installed, the next step is to install the vCenter Data Recovery Plug-in.

To install the vCenter Data Recovery Plug-in, follow these steps:

1. Copy the VMwareDataRecoveryPlugin.msi file to your workstation.
2. Navigate to the location where you saved the msi file and double-click it.
3. You will be presented with an installation wizard. Follow the prompts of the wizard to complete the install.

Create a Backup Job with vCenter Data Recovery

The two main functions of vCenter Data Recovery is to perform backups and restores of your virtual machines. In this section we will create a backup job for a virtual machine, and in the next section we will perform a restore.

To create a backup job with vCenter Data Recovery, follow these steps:

1. Launch the vSphere Client and connect to your vCenter Server.
2. In the navigation bar select Home | Solutions And Applications | VMware Data Recovery.
3. You will be presented with the VMware Data Recovery window. Select New Backup Job.
4. You will be presented with the Virtual Machines window. On this window select the virtual machine you wish to back up. You can either select a

single virtual machine or select a group of virtual machines by selecting the container they are in. Once you have made your selection, click Next to continue.

5. You will be presented with the Backup Window window. On this window select the backup window in which you want the backup to run and click Next to continue.

6. You will be presented with the Retention Policy window. On this window select the retention policy you want for the backup and click Next to continue.

7. You will be presented with a summary screen. Confirm that the information is correct and click Finish to create the backup job.

Perform Rehearsal and Production Restores Using vCenter Data Recovery

Using vCenter Data Recovery, you can perform two different types of restores: rehearsal and production. A *rehearsal* restore is basically a dry run of a restore where you can test your backups to make sure they will restore correctly. During a rehearsal restore a new virtual machine is created but the original virtual machine is not replaced. This allows the newly restored machine to be fully tested without altering the original virtual machine. A *production* restore returns the original virtual machine to the state it was in when the backup job was run.

To perform a rehearsal restore with vCenter Data Recovery, follow these steps:

1. Launch the vSphere Client and connect to your vCenter Server.

2. In the navigation bar select Home | Solutions And Applications | VMware Data Recovery.

3. You will be presented with the VMware Data Recovery window. Right-click the virtual machine that you wish to restore and select Restore Rehearsal.

4. You will be presented with the Virtual Machine Restore Wizard. Click Restore to finish and restore the virtual machine.

5. Once the restore is complete, you will see the new virtual machine in the inventory.

To perform a production restore with vCenter Data Recovery, follow these steps:

1. Launch the vSphere Client and connect to your vCenter Server.

2. In the navigation bar select Home | Solutions And Applications | VMware Data Recovery.

3. You will be presented with the VMware Data Recovery window. Enter the name of the Backup and Recovery Appliance you configured earlier and click Connect.

4. Once you are connected to the appliance, select the Restore tab and click Restore.

5. You will be presented with the Source Selection window. On this window select the virtual machine or virtual machines you wish to restore. Once you have made this selection, click Next to continue.

6. You will be presented with the Destination Selection window. On this window select the datastore and virtual disk node you wish to restore to. You must also decide if the restored virtual machine will have its NIC connected to the network and whether or not the virtual machine will be powered on. Once you have made these selections, click Next to continue.

7. You will be presented with a summary screen. Confirm that the information is correct and click Finish to run the restore.

CERTIFICATION SUMMARY

We started this chapter by taking a look at VMware Clusters. We discussed how to create new clusters and add Hosts to them. We then talked about VMware High Availability (HA) and the Distributed Resource Scheduler (DRS) and how they can be configured and used on a cluster. Then we discussed Distributed Power Management (DPM) and saw how it can provide significant power savings for your datacenter. We ended the section by implementing Enhanced VMotion Compatibility (EVC) and discussing virtual machine swap files and how they can be located in a cluster.

In the next section we looked at Fault-Tolerant virtual machines. We reviewed the many requirements for Fault Tolerance and discussed usage cases where it could provide real advantages. Once you understood Fault Tolerance, we configured our network to allow it and enabled it on one of our virtual machines. We then discussed the different options for testing Fault Tolerance and ended the section by looking at the special requirements for upgrading Hosts that have Fault-Tolerant virtual machines running on them.

We then took a look at resource pools. We discussed how resource pools can be used and looked at shares, reservations, and limits for both CPU and memory resources. We then went ahead and created a new resource pool and configured its CPU and memory resources. We finished the section by adding virtual machines to our newly created resource pool.

In the next section we reviewed the various methods for migrating virtual machines. We then discussed usage cases for each type of migration. We ended the section by performing a cold migration, a VMotion migration, and a storage VMotion migration.

In the final section we discussed the various ways to back up and restore virtual machines. We started by discussing the current methods that are used to perform backups and restores. We then looked at the concept of snapshots and created, deleted, and restored snapshots. We finished the section and the chapter by installing and working with the VMware Data Recovery product.

✓ TWO-MINUTE DRILL

Create and Configure VMware Clusters

❑ VMware High Availability (HA) is a feature provided with vSphere that allows virtual machines on a failed Host to be restarted on a different ESX/ESXi Host.

❑ The VM restart priority determines the order in which virtual machines will be brought back online when a failure occurs.

❑ HA Admission Control can be set to "Prevent VMs from being powered on if they violate availability constraints" or "Allow VMs to be powered on if they violate availability constraints."

❑ The Host isolation response determines what the cluster will do to virtual machines if the Host they reside on is not able to be reached through a console connection but is still functioning.

❑ Individual virtual machines can have different HA settings than those of the cluster they are in.

❑ If VM Monitoring Status is set to enabled for a virtual machine, the virtual machine will be restarted if the cluster does not receive a heartbeat from the virtual machine within a set time.

❑ DRS can have the following automation levels: Manual, Partially Automated, Fully Automated.

❑ If the DRS Automation Level is set to Manual, vCenter will only make suggestions on which Host new virtual machines should be placed and when they should be migrated to different Hosts.

❑ If the DRS Automation Level is set to Partially Automated, vCenter will automatically place new virtual machines on Hosts and will make recommendations on when a virtual machine should be migrated to a different Host.

❑ If the DRS Automation Level is set to Fully Automated, vCenter will automatically place new virtual machines on Hosts and will automatically migrate virtual machines to different Hosts to balance workloads.

❑ DRS affinity rules keep virtual machines running on the same Host.

❑ DRS anti-affinity rules keep virtual machines running on different Hosts.

❑ Distributed Power Management is a feature provided with vSphere that allows a DRS-enabled cluster to move all of the virtual machines from a Host and then power off the Host to conserve energy when the cluster's resource utilization is low and power them back on when resource utilization rises.

❑ Enhanced VMotion Compatibility (EVC) is a feature provided with vSphere that allows VMotion to occur between Hosts that share common CPU baseline features.

Enable a Fault-Tolerant Virtual Machine

❑ Fault-Tolerant virtual machines are used by vSphere to enable greater uptime for a virtual machine by essentially creating a copy of the virtual machine and switching control to the copy in the event of a failure of the Host where the original VM resides.

❑ Fault Tolerance uses a technology called vLockstep to implement virtual machine mirroring.

❑ For Fault Tolerance to work correctly, hardware virtualization must be enabled in the BIOS of both the primary and secondary Hosts.

❑ For Fault Tolerance to work correctly, the primary and secondary Hosts must have access to the shared storage that contains the virtual machine.

❑ For Fault Tolerance to work correctly, both the primary and secondary Hosts must be contained in the same HA cluster.

❑ For Fault Tolerance to work correctly, both the primary and secondary Hosts must be running the same version of ESX.

❑ For Fault Tolerance to work correctly, both the primary and secondary Hosts must have the same CPU model, family, and stepping.

❑ For Fault Tolerance to work correctly, each VM that is using Fault Tolerance must have a single virtual CPU.

❑ For Fault Tolerance to work correctly, virtual machines must not have thin-provisioned disks.

❑ For Fault Tolerance to work correctly, virtual machines must not be a part of a Microsoft Cluster.

❑ There can be a maximum of four virtual machine primaries or secondaries on any ESX/ESXi Host.

❑ To test Fault Tolerance for a virtual machine, right-click the virtual machine you wish to test for Fault Tolerance and select Fault Tolerance and then Test Failover or Test Restart Secondary from the drop-down menus.

Create and Configure Resource Pools

❑ A resource pool is a VMware construct that represents a collection of CPU and memory resources that are presented as a single pool.

❑ A parent resource pool can have zero or more child resource pools that can each have zero or more child resource pools.

❑ CPU Shares represent the percentage of the parent's CPU resources that a resource pool will have when weighed against the total number of CPU shares held by all of its peer resource pools.

❑ The CPU Reservation indicates the minimum amount of CPU resources that will be guaranteed to the resource pool; it is expressed in MHz.

❑ The CPU Limit represents the maximum amount of CPU resources that will be given to the resource pool; it is expressed in MHz.

❑ Memory Shares represent the percentage of the parent's memory resources that a resource pool will have when weighed against the total number of memory shares held by all of its peer resource pools.

❑ A Memory Reservation indicates the minimum amount of memory resources that will be guaranteed to the resource pool; it is expressed in MB.

❑ The Memory Limit represents the maximum amount of memory resources that will be given to the resource pool; it is expressed in MB.

Migrate Virtual Machines

❑ A cold migration is performed on a virtual machine that is powered off.

❑ During a cold migration, the files that are associated with the virtual machine can be migrated to a different datastore, and they are not required to be on shared storage.

❑ A VMotion migration allows a powered-on virtual machine to be moved from one Host to another without a loss of service from the virtual machine.

❑ A VMotion migration requires that the source and target Hosts have compatible CPUs and have shared storage.

❑ A Storage VMotion allows a powered-on virtual machine to have its associated files moved from one datastore to another without a loss of service from the virtual machine.

❑ During a Storage VMotion, the Host that the virtual machine is running on does not change.

Back Up and Restore Virtual Machines

❑ File-level backups are backups of all of the individual files that are contained on a virtual server.

❑ Image backups are basically backups of the files that make up the virtual machine.

❑ Snapshots are a feature of vSphere that allows you to take point-in-time images of a virtual machine.

❑ VMware Data Recovery is a product from VMware that can be used to perform backups and restores of virtual machines.

❑ VMware Data Recovery supports the volume shadow copy service to enable it to create seamless backups of Windows virtual machines.

SELF TEST

The following questions will help you measure your understanding of the material presented in this chapter. Read all the choices carefully and remember that there is only one best answer for each question.

Create and Configure VMware Clusters

1. Which of the following is not a setting for the HA Admission Control Policy?
   A. Host failures cluster tolerates
   B. Percentage of cluster resources reserved as failover spare capacity
   C. Hosts reserved for failover
   D. Specify a failover Host

2. Which of the following is not a setting for the HA Host isolation response?
   A. Leave powered on
   B. Power off
   C. Shut down
   D. Enter Standby

3. Under which of the following DRS Automation Levels will the administrator need to manually move virtual machines between Hosts?
   A. Manual
   B. Partially Automated
   C. Fully Automated
   D. Both A and B

4. Which of the following is not an Enhanced VMotion Compatibility (EVC) mode?
   A. Enable EVC for AMD Hosts
   B. Enable EVC for Intel Hosts
   C. Enable AMD/Intel Crossover
   D. Disable EVC

5. By default where are virtual machine swap files located?
   A. On a separate partition on the Host where the virtual machine is managed.
   B. In the same folder as the virtual machine files.
   C. In a datastore specified by the Host where the virtual machine is managed.
   D. On a folder on the vCenter Server.

Enable a Fault-Tolerant Virtual Machine

6. Which of the following is not a requirement for Fault Tolerance?

   A. Each VM that is using Fault Tolerance must use thin-provisioned disks.

   B. Both the primary and secondary Hosts must be contained in the same HA cluster.

   C. Both the primary and secondary Hosts must have the same CPU model, family, and stepping.

   D. Each VM that is using Fault Tolerance must have a single virtual CPU.

7. What is the maximum number of secondary Fault-Tolerant virtual machines that can be on a single Host?

   A. 2

   B. 4

   C. 6

   D. 8

8. Which of the following is not a usage case for VMware Fault Tolerance?

   A. Protect virtual machines against Host hardware failures.

   B. Protect virtual machines against Host OS failures.

   C. Improve virtual machine performance through load balancing.

   D. Provide high availability for non–cluster aware applications.

Create and Configure Resource Pools

9. If resource pool Pool-A has 2000 CPU shares and its peer resource pools Pool-B and Pool-C each have 3000 CPU shares, what percentage of the total CPU of the parent will be guaranteed to Pool-A?

   A. 20

   B. 25

   C. 30

   D. 50

10. Which of the following represents the minimum amount of memory that is guaranteed to a resource pool by its parent?

   A. Memory Shares

   B. Memory Reservation

   C. Memory Base

   D. Memory Limit

Migrate Virtual Machines

11. Which method of virtual machine migration can be used to change both the datastore that a virtual machine is using and the Host that is managing the virtual machine?
   A. Cold migration
   B. VMotion
   C. Storage VMotion
   D. None of the above

Back Up and Restore Virtual Machines

12. Which of the following backup methods is essentially taking a backup of the files that make up a virtual machine?
   A. File-level backups
   B. Snapshots
   C. Image backups
   D. None of the above

SELF TEST ANSWERS

Create and Configure VMware Clusters

1. ☑ **C.** "Hosts reserved for failover" is not a setting for the HA Admission Control Policy.
    ☒ **A, B,** and **C** are incorrect. "Host failures cluster tolerates," "Percentage of cluster resources reserved as failover spare capacity," and "Specify a failover Host" are all settings for the HA Admission Control Policy.

2. ☑ **D.** Enter Standby is not a setting for the HA Host isolation response.
    ☒ **A, B,** and **C** are incorrect. "Leave powered on," "Power off," and "Shut down" are all settings for the HA Host isolation response.

3. ☑ **D.** Under both the Manual and Partially Automated Automation Level vCenter will only make recommendations on where virtual machines should be moved for load balancing.
    ☒ **A, B,** and **C** are incorrect. Even though A and B are correct, D is a better answer. Under the Fully Automated Automation Level, DRS will automatically move virtual machines to different Hosts for both initial placement and load balancing.

4. ☑ **C.** Enhanced VMotion Compatibility (EVC) does not allow VMotion between AMD and Intel CPUs.
    ☒ **A, B,** and **D** are incorrect. Enable EVC For AMD Hosts, Enable EVC For Intel Hosts, and Disable EVC are all Enhanced VMotion Compatibility modes.

5. ☑ **B.** By default virtual machine swap files are stored in the same directory as the other files that make up the virtual machine.
    ☒ **A, C,** and **D** are incorrect. Virtual machine swap files can be configured to reside on a separate partition or datastore on the Host they are managed by, but they are not by default. Virtual machine swap files do not reside on the vCenter Server.

Enable a Fault-Tolerant Virtual Machine

6. ☑ **A.** Each VM using Fault Tolerance must not use thin-provisioned disks.
    ☒ **B, C,** and **D** are incorrect. For Fault Tolerance both the primary and secondary Hosts must be contained in the same HA cluster and must have the same CPU model, family, and stepping. Each VM that is using Fault Tolerance must have a single virtual CPU.

7. ☑ **B.** There can be a maximum of four virtual machine primaries or secondaries on any ESX/ESXi Host.
    ☒ **A, C,** and **D** are incorrect.

8. ☑ **C.** Even though multiple copies of the same virtual machine exist when using Fault Tolerance, they are not load balanced.

☒ **A, B,** and **D** are incorrect. The main usage cases for Fault Tolerance are: protect virtual machines against Host hardware failures, protect virtual machines against Host OS failures, and provide high availability for non–cluster aware applications.

Create and Configure Resource Pools

9. ☑ **B.** There are a total of 8000 CPU shares. Pool-A has 2000 CPU shares. 2000 is one fourth, or 25 percent, of 8000.

☒ **A, C,** and **D** are incorrect.

10. ☑ **B.** A Memory Reservation indicates the minimum amount of memory resources that will be guaranteed to the resource pool and is expressed in MB.

☒ **A, C,** and **D** are incorrect. Memory Shares represent the percentage of the parent's memory resources that a resource pool will have when weighed against the total number of memory shares held by all of its peer resource pools. Memory Base is not an actual resource pool setting. The Memory Limit represents the maximum amount of memory resources that will be given to the resource pool; it is expressed in MB.

Migrate Virtual Machines

11. ☑ **A.** During a cold migration, a virtual machine can be moved from one Host to another and its datastore can be relocated to the new Host.

☒ **B, C,** and **D** are incorrect. During a VMotion migration, the datastore of the virtual machine is not changed. During a Storage VMotion, the Host that is managing the virtual machine is not changed.

Back Up and Restore Virtual Machines

12. ☑ **C.** Image backups are basically backups of the files that make up the virtual machine.

☒ **A, B,** and **D** are incorrect. File-level backups are backups of each individual file that is contained on the virtual server. Snapshots are not actually backups but are point-in-time images of a virtual machine. Snapshots can be backed up but are not by themselves backups.

10

Basic
Troubleshooting and
Alarm Management

W elcome to Chapter 10. In this chapter we will look at the ways to troubleshoot some of the problems that can occur with vSphere and learn how to monitor our environment for alarms and performance. We will start by discussing how to troubleshoot issues with Hosts and clusters. We will then discuss troubleshooting issues with networking and storage. In the next section we will look at issues with HA, DRS, and VMotion. After that we will look at connectivity and utilization alarms. We will then end the chapter by discussing how to monitor performance.

CERTIFICATION OBJECTIVE 10.01

Basic Troubleshooting for ESX/ESXi

In this section we will review basic troubleshooting for ESX/ESXi Hosts. We will look at some general troubleshooting guidelines for Hosts and discuss common installation issues. We will then look at how to monitor the health of our Hosts and finally how to export diagnostic data to send to VMware if there are issues we can't resolve on our own.

General ESX Server Troubleshooting Guidelines

Like any other operating system, ESX Server and ESXi Server occasionally experience issues. VMware has tried to keep the size of the kernel small so that there would be fewer issues, but some do still come up. To troubleshoot general issues with your ESX and ESXi Servers, follow the same methodology that you use when troubleshooting other operating systems. Here are a few steps you should follow to help resolve your issues:

- Gather information.
    - Record any error messages that appear.
    - Write a description of exactly what was happening on the system when the issues occurred.
    - Review the log files.

- Research possible solutions.
  - Use a search engine to search the web for the error messages you recorded earlier or for the conditions of the issue.
- Ask for help.
  - VMware maintains a forum that can be a very valuable tool for researching issues. Remember to search the forums first before posting a question to see if it has already been asked and answered.
  - Contact VMware Support.

on the
O o b

Many companies have a support agreement with VMware that will allow them a certain number of troubleshooting calls. It is sometimes more cost-effective to involve VMware support early in the troubleshooting process even if there is a cost to call VMware support. This cost can easily be made up by more quickly resolving an issue and reducing lost productivity due to system downtime.

Troubleshoot Common Installation Issues

There are a number of issues that can occur during the installation of an ESX/ESXi Server or immediately after the first reboot. The following is a list of common problems and how to begin resolving them:

- Installation fails.
  - **Bad media** If the DVD you are using to install your server is damaged, the install may fail when it is trying to read from the media. To resolve this type of issue, you will need new installation media.
  - **Unsupported hardware** This is the most common installation issue. Your hardware may not be compatible with ESX/ESXi. To resolve this issue, make sure all of your hardware is on the Hardware Compatibility List.
  - **Hardware failure** If your server has hardware issues, they can prevent ESX/ESXi from loading. You will need to replace any hardware that has failed before installing the Host.

- ESX/ESXi Host will not boot correctly.
  - **LUN-related issues**   If you are using FC LUNs on your ESX Host and the server will not boot up, you may have inadvertently installed ESX to one of the FC LUNs instead of to the local disk. To correct this issue, you will need to reinstall ESX to the local disk.
  - **BIOS boot configuration errors**   If the boot order that is configured in the BIOS is set to boot from either the CD drive or an existing drive other than the ESX/ESXi drive, the server may not boot up properly. To resolve this type of issue, enter the system configuration of your server and check the boot order.
- ESX/ESXi Server is not available on the network.
  - **Configuration issue**   If the IP configuration of the Host is not set correctly, it may not be able to communicate on the network. To resolve this type of issue, confirm that the IP address, subnet mask, and default gateway are set correctly.
  - **Hardware issue**   If there is a physical network issue between your ESX/ESXi Host and the rest of the network, you will not be able to communicate with it. To resolve these types of issues, confirm that the network cable is plugged in to the Host and to your switch, check for link lights on the switch, and possibly replace the network cable if you think it may be defective.

e x a m
w a t c h

For the exam you will need to understand the basic issues that can occur on a Host. You should expect to see *a question that will give you a symptom and ask which of the answers could be a possible cause.*

Monitor ESX Server System Health

The hardware health of your ESX/ESXi Hosts can be monitored by using the vCenter Hardware Status plug-in. If your hardware supports it, this plug-in will provide CIM Monitoring for your physical Host. It will provide hardware statistics such as drive failures and system temperature. These statistics can help you to anticipate hardware failures before they occur and to troubleshoot issues after they occur.

To access the vCenter Hardware Status information, follow these steps:

1. Launch the vSphere Client and connect to your vCenter Server.
2. Confirm that the Plug-in is enabled in the Plug-in Manager.
3. In the navigation bar select Home | Inventory | Hosts And Clusters.
4. Select the Host that you wish to see statistics for from the inventory on the left and select the Hardware Status tab from the window on the right.
5. You will be presented with the Hardware Status window. On this window you can choose to see statistics from the hardware sensors, alerts and warnings, or the system event log. You can also export this information.

Export Diagnostic Data

If you are unable to resolve an issue with your ESX/ESXi Hosts, you can contact VMware for help. In many cases they will ask you to export diagnostic data from the Host and send it to them.

To export diagnostic logs for an ESX/ESXI Host, follow these steps:

1. Launch the vSphere Client and connect to your Host or vCenter Server.
2. From the File menu select Export and then Export System Logs.
3. If you connected to the Host, you will be presented with the Export System Logs window. In the window browse to a location on your client PC where you want to save the diagnostic data and click OK to create the export file.
4. If you connected to the vCenter Server, you will be presented with a different Export System Logs window. In this window select the Host you want to generate diagnostic data for and browse to a location on your client PC where you want to save the diagnostic data. You may also choose to include diagnostic logs for the vCenter Server and Client. Make these selections and click OK to create the export file.

Once you have created this export file, you can send it to VMware and they will analyze it to try to help resolve your issues. Now that you have an understanding of basic troubleshooting for ESX/ESXi Servers, let's take a look at troubleshooting Fault Tolerance.

CERTIFICATION OBJECTIVE 10.02

Basic Troubleshooting for VMware FT and Third-Party Clusters

In this section we will discuss troubleshooting issues that arise when using Fault Tolerance and third-party clusters. We will start by looking at maintenance mode considerations for Hosts with Fault-Tolerant virtual machines. Next we will discuss third-party failover processes for high availability. We will finish the section by troubleshooting partial or unexpected failovers when using Fault Tolerance.

Analyze and Evaluate the Virtual Machine Population for Maintenance Mode Considerations

Before you can place a Host into maintenance mode you must review the virtual machines that are running on it to see if any are running as part of a Fault-Tolerant pair. If you have virtual machines that are running as part of a Fault-Tolerant pair, you will need to move them to another Host that is compatible with the Host containing the other member of the pair before putting the original Host into maintenance mode. If you do not have another compatible Host, you should make sure that only secondaries are on the Host you wish to put into maintenance mode. You can achieve this by failing over any primaries that are on the Host in a controlled manner one at a time. This will help to prevent multiple failovers from occurring at the same time when you put the Host into maintenance mode.

Understand Microsoft Clustering Services Failover/Failback

Microsoft Cluster Services uses two or more similarly configured servers to provide high availability for cluster-aware applications. These servers must all share the same storage and have a heartbeat network connection that is used to monitor members of the cluster. When cluster-aware applications are installed on the cluster, their services are installed onto multiple member servers and any files that are required for them to operate are installed on the shared storage. When it is determined that a member of the cluster has failed, another member will start the services that are required for the application to operate and will take control of the shared storage. Unlike under VMware Fault Tolerance, there is an application outage between the time that the initial server fails and the new server has started the application services.

on the Job

Microsoft Cluster Services is heavily used by a large number of companies for application high availability. By leveraging Fault Tolerance to replace some of these clusters, many companies can see a significant cost savings in hardware as well as reduced application downtime, since FT does not require an outage when failovers occur.

Troubleshoot Fault Tolerance Unexpected Failovers

An *unexpected fault tolerance failover* is when the secondary virtual machine takes over as the primary and redundancy is reestablished but the Host containing the primary machine has not failed. These failovers can be caused by any of the following:

- **Storage issues**   If one of the Hosts containing a member of a Fault-Tolerant pair experiences very slow access to the storage containing the virtual machine or an inability to reach the storage, a failover can occur. To resolve this type of issue, you will need to identify why the storage is slow or inaccessible.

- **Network issues**   If the network connection that is being used by the FT Logging NIC is down or slow or the Host is unable to communicate with the other Host containing a member of a Fault-Tolerant pair, a failover may occur to ensure redundancy of the FT virtual machine. To resolve this type of issue, a separate dedicated network connection should be used for Fault-Tolerant logging.

- **Excess logging NIC traffic**   If too much traffic is being generated by Fault-Tolerant logging for the network connection to adequately handle, failovers may occur. To resolve these types of issues, the number of Fault-Tolerant virtual machines running on a Host should be reduced to reduce the traffic, or additional network resources should be added to handle the load.

■ **VMotion failures of FT virtual machines** If a Fault-Tolerant virtual machine is being migrated using VMotion and the VMotion operation fails, a failover may occur. To prevent this type of issue, Fault-Tolerant virtual machines should be migrated during times they are not busy to reduce the chances of VMotion failures.

■ **Excess activity on a VMFS volume** If there is a large amount of activity on a VMFS volume that contains a Fault-Tolerant virtual machine such as large number of snapshots being taken at the same time, a failover may occur. To resolve these types of issues, migrate the virtual machine to a different VMFS volume.

<table>
<tr><td>For the exam, you will need to understand the basic issues that can cause an unexpected failover. You should</td><td>expect to see a question that will describe a failover scenario and ask you which of the answers could be a possible cause.</td></tr>
</table>

CERTIFICATION OBJECTIVE 10.03

Basic Troubleshooting for Networking

In this section we will discuss how to troubleshoot common networking issues. We will start by confirming that a virtual machine is connected to the correct port group and verifying that the port group settings are correct. We will then confirm that a virtual machine has a proper network connection. We will then verify that the physical NIC settings on our Host are configured correctly. We will end the section by verifying that the vSphere network management settings are correct.

Verify a VM Is Connected to the Correct Port Group

Virtual machines store the names of port groups they are connected to in their configuration files. If a port group that already has virtual machine attached to it is renamed, the virtual machines will no longer be able to connect to it. Virtual machines that are already running and connected will be able to continue to function until they are restarted because they already have a connection. To resolve this issue, you will need to verify that the port group connection for each virtual machine is reassigned to the renamed port group.

To verify the port group setting of a virtual machine, follow these steps:

1. Launch the vSphere Client and connect to your vCenter Server.

2. In the navigation bar select Home | Inventory | VMs And Templates if you connected to the vCenter Server or Home | Inventory | Inventory if you connected to the Host.

3. Right-click the virtual machine you wish to verify and select Edit Settings from the drop-down menu.

4. You will be presented with the Virtual Machine Properties window. Select the Network Adapter from the Hardware list on the left to show the NIC properties. Under Network Connection on the right side of the window make sure the proper Network Label is selected. If not, select the proper network from the drop-down menu. Click OK to save your changes and exit.

on the job *Renamed port groups can be a significant problem for less experienced administrators. It is very easy to rename a port group, and since there are no immediate ramifications, the issue can go uncaught for some time. Be extremely careful when renaming production port groups.*

Verify Port Group Settings Are Correct

You can experience networking problems if the settings on your port groups are not what you expect them to be. If you are experiencing unexplained networking issues for virtual servers that are all on the same port group, verify the port group settings are correct.

To verify the port group settings, follow these steps:

1. Launch the vSphere Client and connect to your vCenter Server.

2. In the navigation bar select Home | Inventory | Hosts And Clusters.

3. Select the Host that you wish to check from the Inventory on the left and click the Configuration tab.

4. Click Networking from the Hardware list.

5. You will be presented with the Networking window. Select Virtual Switch from the View menu at the top and then click Properties for the virtual switch that contains the port group you want to verify.

6. You will be presented with the vSwitch Properties window. Select the port group you want to verify from the Ports list on the left and click Edit.

7. You will be presented with the Properties window for the port group as shown in Figure 10-1. Check the settings on all four tabs—General, Security, Traffic Shaping, and NIC Teaming—to make sure they are set properly.

8. Once you have verified the settings click OK and then Close to exit.

FIGURE 10-1

The Port Group
Properties
window

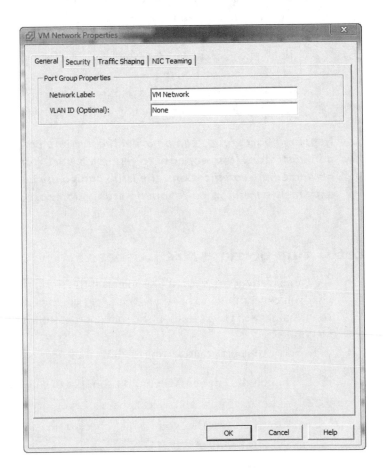

Verify That the Network Adapter Is Connected Within the VM

If you experience an issue where a virtual machine will not connect to the network, a good first step is to ensure that the network adapter for the virtual machine is connected.

To verify that a virtual machine's NIC is connected, follow these steps:

1. Launch the vSphere Client and connect to your vCenter Server.
2. In the navigation bar select Home | Inventory | VMs And Templates if you connected to the vCenter Server or Home | Inventory | Inventory if you connected to the Host.
3. Right-click the virtual machine you wish to verify and select Edit Settings from the drop-down menu.
4. You will be presented with the Virtual Machine Properties window. Select the Network Adapter from the Hardware list on the left to show the NIC properties. Under Device Status confirm that Connected is checked if the virtual machine is powered on and confirm that Connect At Power On is checked if the virtual machine is powered off.
5. Click OK to exit.

Verify VM Network Adapter Settings

You can experience network issues on a virtual machine if you are attempting to use a virtual network adapter that is not compatible with your environment. VMware allows you to manually set the MAC address for your virtual network adapter. This can lead to a possible issue with duplicate MAC addresses. To resolve these types of issues, you will need to confirm the virtual NIC that is configured for your virtual machine and confirm the MAC address that is configured for it.

To verify a virtual machine's NIC network adapter settings, follow these steps:

1. Launch the vSphere Client and connect to your vCenter Server.
2. In the navigation bar select Home | Inventory | VMs And Templates if you connected to the vCenter Server or Home | Inventory | Inventory if you connected to the Host.

3. Right-click the virtual machine you wish to verify and select Edit Settings from the drop-down menu.

4. You will be presented with the Virtual Machine Properties window. Select the Network Adapter from the Hardware list on the left to show the NIC properties. Under Adapter Type confirm that you are using a supported adapter for your environment. Under MAC Address make sure that if you are using Manual MAC address assignments, you do not have a duplicate address configured.

5. Click OK to exit.

Verify Physical Network Adapter Settings

Network issues can often be the result of improperly configured physical network adapters in your Hosts. The symptoms of improperly configured network adapters range from extremely slow network performance to a complete inability to connect to the network. To resolve these types of issues you will need to confirm that the settings for the physical adapter are set properly.

To verify physical network adapter settings, follow these steps:

1. Launch the vSphere Client and connect to your vCenter Server.

2. In the navigation bar select Home | Inventory | Hosts And Clusters.

3. Select the Host that you wish to check from the Inventory on the left and click the Configuration tab.

4. Click Network Adapters from the Hardware list.

5. You will be presented with the Networking Adapters window. On this window you can confirm the following information:

   ■ The type of network card you are using

   ■ The configured speed, duplex setting, and MAC address

   ■ The vSwitch it is attached to

   ■ The observed IP ranges

   ■ Wake on LAN support

CERTIFICATION OBJECTIVE 10.04

Basic Troubleshooting for Storage

In this section we will discuss how to troubleshoot common storage issues. We will start by looking at storage contention and storage over-commitment. We will then discuss storage connectivity issues and identify potential issues with the iSCSI software initiator. We will end the section by discussing storage reports and storage maps.

Understand Storage Contention Issues

Storage contention occurs when multiple Hosts are requesting access to the same storage at the same time and there is not enough bandwidth to satisfy all of the requests. Some of the symptoms include slow performance for virtual machines when accessing storage and temporary Host disconnects from the storage. To resolve these types of issues, you should more evenly disperse virtual machines across different storage locations.

Understand Storage Over-Commitment Issues

Storage over-commitment can occur when using Thin-provisioned disks on virtual machines. Thin provisioning allows you to specify that a virtual disk will start out small and grow up to a specified maximum size as the virtual machine needs additional space. If a large number of virtual machines are configured with Thin-provisioned disks and the total of all of the maximum sizes exceeds the available space on a storage device, you can experience over-commitment issues. If you begin to experience issues with storage over-commitment, you should move one or more virtual machines with Storage VMotion to another datastore to free up space on the original datastore.

Understand Storage Connectivity Issues

Storage connectivity issues occur when a Host is unable to connect to its storage. Storage connectivity issues can occur for a number of reasons:

- **Physical issues** Physical issues can include defective storage systems or defective components that connect the Host to the storage. These can be resolved by identifying and replacing the defective equipment.

- **Configuration issues** ESX Hosts must be correctly configured before they will be able to access network-based storage or storage on an FC SAN. If you are initially unable to connect to a storage location, there is a good possibility that the configuration is your issue. If you lose a connection to storage that you were previously able to access, it is more likely a different issue, but you should still check your configuration to make sure nothing was inadvertently changed.

- **Permission issues** Much of the storage that is used in a vSphere environment is located on a different device than the Host, such as an iSCSI or FC SAN. Before a Host will be able to connect to this storage, it will need to be granted permission either by directly assigning it permission in the case of iSCSI or through zoning in the case of FC LUNs. If you are initially unable to connect to a storage location, there is a good possibility that the Host does not have permission to access the storage. If you lose a connection to storage that you were previously able to access, it is more likely a different issue, but it is possible that the permissions could have been changed.

Identify iSCSI Software Initiator Configuration Issues

As we discussed in Chapter 6, the iSCSI software initiator is used to allow a Host to connect to iSCSI Storage over a network connection. If this initiator is not configured correctly, you will not be able to connect to iSCSI Storage. The configuration of the iSCSI software initiator will need to be checked in two different locations: the VMkernel Port under Networking and the iSCSI Software Adapter under Storage.

To verify VMkernel Port settings, follow these steps:

1. Launch the vSphere Client and connect to your vCenter Server.
2. In the navigation bar select Home | Inventory | Hosts And Clusters.

3. Select the Host that you wish to check from the Inventory on the left and click the Configuration tab.

4. Click Networking from the Hardware list. You will be presented with the Networking window.

5. Click Properties next to the Virtual Switch that contains the VMkernel Port.

6. You will be presented with the Properties window for the virtual switch. Select the VMkernel Port from the Ports list and click Edit to view the settings.

7. You will be presented with the Properties window for the VMkernel Port. On the General tab make sure you have the correct VLAN ID set, and on the IP Settings tab make sure you have the correct IP Address and Subnet Mask.

8. Once you have confirmed these settings, click OK to exit.

To verify iSCSI Software Adapter settings, follow these steps:

1. Launch the vSphere Client and connect to your vCenter Server.

2. In the navigation bar select Home | Inventory | Hosts And Clusters.

3. Select the Host that you wish to check from the Inventory on the left and click the Configuration tab.

4. Click Storage Adapters from the Hardware list. You will be presented with the Storage Adapters window.

5. Highlight the iSCSI HBA under Storage Adapters and then click Properties under Details.

6. You will be presented with the iSCSI Initiator Properties window. If you are using Dynamic Discovery, confirm that the correct iSCSI Server and Port are defined on the Dynamic Discovery tab. If you are using Static Discovery, confirm that the correct iSCSI Server, Port, and iSCSI Target Name are defined on the Static Discovery tab.

7. Once you have confirmed these settings, click OK to exit.

A number of issues outside of the configuration of the iSCSI software initiator can cause a Host to be unable to access iSCSI Storage. Examples are network connectivity issues and permission issues.

Interpret Storage Reports

Storage reports are spreadsheet-like reports that can be generated on Datacenters, Clusters, or Hosts that show various data related to the storage that is being used. A number of different types of storage reports can be generated:

- **Show all Virtual Machines**   This storage report displays information about the virtual machines that are contained under the object you selected.
- **Show all Datastores**   This storage report displays information about the datastores that are contained under the object you selected.
- **Show all Hosts**   This storage report displays information about the Hosts that are contained under the object you selected.
- **Show all Resource Pools**   This storage report displays information about the resource pools that are contained under the object you selected.
- **Show all SCSI Volumes**   This storage report displays information about the SCSI volumes that are contained under the object you selected.
- **Show all SCSI Paths**   This storage report displays information about the SCSI paths that are used by the SCSI volumes that are contained under the object you selected.
- **Show all SCSI Adapters**   This storage report displays information about the SCSI adapters that are used by Hosts that are contained under the object you selected.
- **Show all SCSI Targets**   This storage report displays information about the SCSI targets that are defined on the Hosts that are contained under the object you selected.
- **Show all NAS Mounts**   This storage report displays information about the NAS mounts that are used by the Hosts that are contained under the object you selected.

To access storage reports, follow these steps:

1. Launch the vSphere Client and connect to your vCenter Server.
2. In the navigation bar select Home | Inventory | Hosts And Clusters.
3. Select the Datacenter, Cluster, or Host that you wish to generate a storage report for and click the Storage Views tab.
4. You will be presented with the Storage Views window. Under the View section click Reports.

5. You will be presented with the Storage Report view as shown in Figure 10-2.

6. From the drop-down menu at the top of the view select the type of storage report you would like to see.

You can use storage reports to help you to understand how storage is being used in your environment and to troubleshoot storage-related issues. Now that you understand storage reports, let's take a look at storage maps.

For the exam you may be presented with a storage report and asked various questions about the data it shows. **You should become familiar with these reports both for the exam and for use in your vSphere environment.**

Interpret Storage Maps

Storage maps are visual representations of vSphere components and how they are attached to storage devices. They can be configured to show any of the following items:

- Datacenters
- Clusters
- Hosts
- Virtual machines
- Datastores
- SCSI volumes
- NAS mounts
- SCSI adapters
- SCSI targets

FIGURE 10-2	The Storage Report view

View: Reports Maps

Last Update Time: 2/7/2010 8:30:54 AM   Update...

Show all Datastores ▾

Datastore, File system type or Connectivity Status contains: ▾ [   ]   Clear

Datastore	File system type	Connectivity Status	Multipathing Status	Capacity	Free Space	Space Used	Snapshot Space	Number of Virtual Disks
Storage1	VMFS	Up	Partial/No Redundancy	10.75 GB	9.94 GB	2.00 GB	0.00 B	3
Storage2	VMFS	Up	Partial/No Redundancy	9.75 GB	9.31 GB	102.69 MB	0.00 B	1

To view storage maps, follow these steps:

1. Launch the vSphere Client and connect to your vCenter Server.
2. In the navigation bar select Home | Inventory | Hosts And Clusters.
3. Select the Datacenter, Cluster, or Host that you wish to generate a storage report for and click the Storage Views tab.
4. You will be presented with the Storage Views window. Under the View section click Maps.
5. You will be presented with the Storage Maps view as shown in Figure 10-3.
6. Under the Controls section select the devices you would like to see on the storage map and then click Update View to generate the map. You can use the Zoom slider to increase or decrease the size of the storage map.

Once you have configured the storage map to show all of the devices you would like, you can export them to a file that you can use when writing reports by right-clicking the Map and selecting Export Map.

FIGURE 10-3   The Storage Maps view showing a Host, two Datastores, and four SCSI adapters

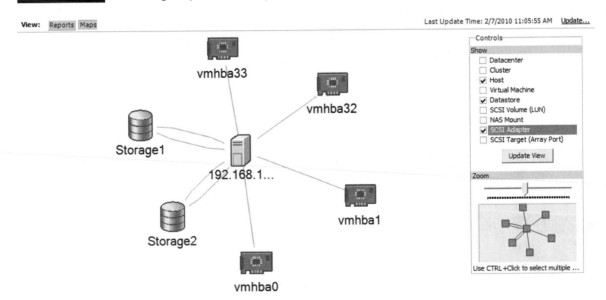

CERTIFICATION OBJECTIVE 10.05

Basic Troubleshooting for HA/DRS and VMotion

In this section we will discuss how to troubleshoot High Availability (HA), Dynamic Resource Scheduler (DRS), and VMotion issues. We will start by looking at the requirements for HA, DRS, and VMotion and verify that they are configured correctly. We will then discuss DRS Resource Distribution Graphs and Topology Maps. We will then end the section by reviewing HA capacity and redundancy issues.

Requirements for HA/DRS and VMotion

Many of the issues that occur with HA/DRS and VMotion are caused by a failure to meet their requirements. The requirements for HA/DRS and VMotion are as follows:

- Each Host in the Cluster must have access to the same shared storage.
- Each Host in the Cluster must have compatible processors.
- The Hosts must be connected by a Gigabit Ethernet connection.
- The Hosts must have identically named virtual machine port groups.

Verify VMotion Functionality Is Enabled

One potential problem with VMotion is that it may not be enabled. If all of the requirements for VMotion are met and you are still having issues, you should check to make sure that VMware is enabled on each of your Hosts.

To verify VMotion is enabled for a Host, follow these steps:

1. Launch the vSphere Client and connect to your vCenter Server.
2. In the navigation bar select Home | Inventory | Hosts And Clusters.

3. Select the Host that you wish to check from the Inventory on the left and click the Summary tab.

4. You will be presented with the Host Summary view. Under the General section locate the VMotion Enabled key and confirm that it is set to Yes.

If VMotion is not enabled for the Host, you will need to go into the VMkernel port configuration and enable VMotion.

Interpret the DRS Resource Distribution Graph and Target/Current Host Load Deviation

The DRS Resource Distribution Graph is a bar chart that shows how CPU and memory resources are distributed across the Hosts in a DRS cluster. These charts can be used to make sure that load balancing is occurring between all of the Hosts in a DRS cluster.

To view a DRS Resource Distribution Graph, follow these steps:

1. Launch the vSphere Client and connect to your vCenter Server.

2. In the navigation bar select Home | Inventory | Hosts And Clusters.

3. Select the DRS Cluster that you wish to check from the Inventory on the left and click the Summary tab.

4. You will be presented with the Cluster Summary view. Under the VMware DRS frame click View Resource Distribution Chart.

5. You will be presented with the DRS Resource Distribution Chart. To view CPU resource distribution, click the CPU button, and to view memory resource distribution, click the Memory button.

By default, DRS evaluates the loads on each Host in a cluster every five minutes to determine if virtual machines should be moved between Hosts to improve load balancing. To make this determination, the cluster uses the values of the "Target host load standard deviation" and the "Current host load standard deviation." The "Current host load standard deviation" is equal to the standard deviation of the sum of all of the virtual machine workloads on a Host divided by the available resources on the Host for all of the Hosts in the cluster. If the "Current host load standard deviation" is higher than the "Target host load standard deviation," the cluster will either make recommendations for virtual machines to be migrated or migrate the machines automatically, depending on the automation level.

To view a DRS Resource Distribution Graph, follow these steps:

1. Launch the vSphere Client and connect to your vCenter Server.
2. In the navigation bar select Home | Inventory | Hosts And Clusters.
3. Select the DRS Cluster that you wish to check from the Inventory on the left and click the Summary tab.
4. You will be presented with the Cluster Summary view. Under the VMware DRS frame you can see the Current and Target host load standard deviation as shown in Figure 10-4.

Troubleshoot VMotion Using Topology Maps

Topology maps show a graphical display of inventory objects and the relationships they share. You can use a topology map to verify that virtual machines meet the following requirements for VMotion:

- Each Host in the Cluster must have access to the same shared storage.
- The Hosts must have identically named virtual machine port groups.

Figure 10-5 shows a topology map for a resource pool. From this map you can see that both Hosts share the storage location Storage2 and that both Hosts have a port group named VM Network.

FIGURE 10-4	
The VMware DRS frame	

VMware DRS

Migration Automation Level:	Fully Automated
Power Management Automation Level:	Off
DRS Recommendations:	0
DRS Faults:	0
Migration Threshold:	Apply priority 3 or higher recommendations
Target host load standard deviation:	<= 0.2
Current host load standard deviation:	0 (⊘ Load balanced)

View Resource Distribution Chart

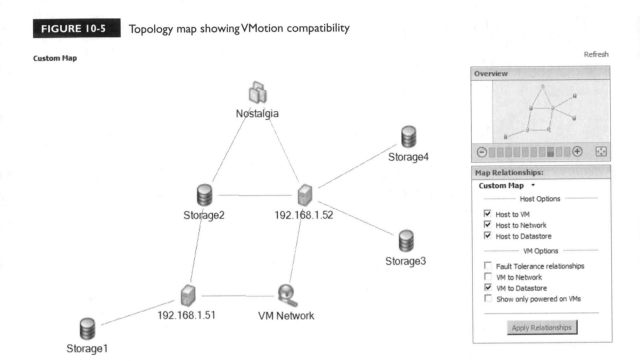

FIGURE 10-5 Topology map showing VMotion compatibility

Understand HA Capacity Issues

As we discussed earlier, High Availability (HA) is the ability of vSphere to restart virtual machines from a failed Host or number of Hosts on other available Hosts. In order to be able to provide this capability, there must be enough available resources in the remaining Hosts to handle the loads that were contained on the failed Hosts. If your cluster is configured to use strict admission control, you will not be able to start virtual machines that would cause there to be insufficient resources in the event of Host failures. If you do not use strict admission controls, you can run into a situation where Host failures can result in insufficient resources in the remaining Hosts to handle all of the virtual machines from the failed Hosts. In these instances the highest-priority virtual machines will be restarted and those with a lower priority will not. To avoid these types of issues, it is recommended that strict admission controls should be used or additional capacity should be added to make sure there will be sufficient resources for Host failures.

CERTIFICATION OBJECTIVE 10.06

Create and Respond to vCenter Connectivity Alarms

In this section we will look at creating and responding to vCenter connectivity alarms. Connectivity alarms are used to alert administrators to different conditions that are occurring in their vSphere environment. Connectivity alarms are triggered when connectivity to an object is lost or restored. We will start by reviewing the default connectivity alarms that come with vCenter. We will then look at the actions that can be taken when an alarm goes off. We will finish the section by creating a new connectivity alarm.

List vCenter Default Connectivity Alarms

vCenter Server comes preconfigured with a number of connectivity alarms that you will need to know for the exam:

- **Cannot Connect to Network**   This alarm monitors the object's connectivity to a virtual switch.
- **Cannot Connect to Storage**   This alarm monitors a Host's ability to connect to a storage device.
- **Host Connection and Power State**   This alarm monitors the ability of the vCenter Server to communicate with a Host and monitors changes in a Host's power state.
- **Host Connection Failure**   The alarm monitors a Host for connection failures with the vCenter Server.
- **Host Storage Status**   This alarm monitors a Host's connectivity to the storage devices that are defined for it.

List Possible Actions for Connectivity Alarms

For each connectivity alarm you can define an action that should be taken when the alarm is triggered. The following actions are available in vSphere for connectivity alarms:

- **Enter maintenance mode**   This action causes a Host to be placed into maintenance mode. This action can be set for alarms on the following objects: Host.

- **Enter standby**   This action causes the operating system of a virtual machine to enter standby mode. This action can be set for alarms on the following objects: Host.

- **Exit maintenance mode**   This action causes a Host to exit maintenance mode. This action can be set for alarms on the following objects: Host.

- **Exit standby**   This action causes the operating system of a virtual machine to exit standby mode. This action can be set for alarms on the following objects: Host.

- **Reboot host**   This action causes a Host to reboot. This action can be set for alarms on the following objects: Host.

- **Run a command**   This action runs a single command or script that you provide. It can be used to run a script that can resolve common issues or perform other actions. This action can be set for alarms on the following objects: Datacenter, Datastore, Cluster, Host, Resource Pool, and Virtual Machine.

- **Send a notification email**   This action sends a notification e-mail via SMTP to notify administrators of the alarm. This action can be set for alarms on the following objects: Datacenter, Datastore, Cluster, Host, Resource Pool, Virtual Machine, Network, dvSwitch, and dvPort Group.

- **Send a notification trap**   This action sends an SNMP notification trap to a monitoring system such as HP Openview or SIM. This action can be set for alarms on the following objects: Datacenter, Datastore, Cluster, Host, Resource Pool, and Virtual Machine.

- **Shutdown Host**   This action causes a Host to shut down. This action can be set for alarms on the following objects: Host.

Create a vCenter Connectivity Alarm

You can use the default vCenter connectivity alarms to monitor your vSphere environment, or you can create custom connectivity alarms.

To create a custom vCenter connectivity alarm, follow these steps:

1. Launch the vSphere Client and connect to your vCenter Server.

2. In the navigation bar select Home | Inventory | Hosts And Clusters.

3. Select the vCenter Server from the inventory.

4. From the File menu select New and then Alarm. You will be presented with the Alarm Settings window as shown in Figure 10-6.

5. On the General tab enter a name for the alarm and a description. Under the Alarm Type section select the object type that you want to monitor and use the radio buttons to select whether you are monitoring for conditions or events. You can also choose to have the alarm Enabled or Not Enabled.

6. On the Triggers tab enter conditions or events that would cause the alarm to be triggered. You can also choose whether you want the alarm to be triggered if any of the conditions or events occurs or only if all of the conditions or events occur.

7. On the Reporting tab you can specify how often an alert should be triggered if it is not resolved and if the alarm should be triggered if the condition increases by a certain percentage.

8. On the Actions tab you can specify the actions that should be taken when the alarm is triggered.

9. Once you have configured the information on each tab, click OK to create the new alarm.

FIGURE 10-6

The Alarm
Settings window

CERTIFICATION OBJECTIVE 10.07

Create and Respond to vCenter Utilization Alarms

In this section we will look at creating and responding to vCenter utilization alarms. Utilization alarms are used to alert administrators to different conditions that are occurring in their vSphere environment. Utilization alarms are triggered when the utilization of a resource hits a certain level. We will start by reviewing the default utilization alarms that come with vCenter. We will then look at the actions that can be taken when an alarm goes off. We will finish the section by creating a new utilization alarm.

List vCenter Default Utilization Alarms

vCenter Server comes preconfigured with a number of utilization alarms that you will need to know for the exam:

- **Datastore Usage on Disk**   This alarm monitors the percentage of a datastore that is currently being used.
- **Host CPU Usage**   This alarm monitors the percentage of CPU resources that are currently being used on a Host.
- **Host Memory Usage**   This alarm monitors the percentage of memory resources that are currently being used on a Host.
- **Virtual Machine CPU Usage**   This alarm monitors the percentage of CPU resources that are currently being used on a virtual machine.
- **Virtual Machine Memory Usage**   This alarm monitors the percentage of memory resources that are currently being used on a virtual machine.

List Possible Actions for Utilization Alarms

For each connectivity alarm you can define an action that should be taken when the alarm is triggered. The following actions are available in vSphere for Connectivity Alarms:

- **Enter maintenance mode**   This action causes a Host to be placed into maintenance mode. This action can be set for alarms on the following objects: Host.

- **Enter standby**   This action causes the operating system of a virtual machine to enter standby mode. This action can be set for alarms on the following objects: Host.

- **Exit maintenance mode**   This action causes a Host to exit maintenance mode. This action can be set for alarms on the following objects: Host.

- **Exit standby**   This action causes the operating system of a virtual machine to exit standby mode. This action can be set for alarms on the following objects: Host.

- **Migrate VM**   This action causes a virtual machine to be powered down and migrated to another Host. This action can be set for alarms on the following objects: Virtual Machine.

- **Power on VM**   This action causes a virtual machine to be powered on. This action can be set for alarms on the following objects: Virtual Machine.

- **Power off VM**   This action causes a virtual machine to be powered off. This action can be set for alarms on the following objects: Virtual Machine.

- **Reboot Guest on VM**   This action causes the guest operating system of a virtual machine to be gracefully rebooted. This action can be set for alarms on the following objects: Virtual Machine.

- **Reboot Host**   This action causes a Host to reboot. This action can be set for alarms on the following objects: Host.

- **Reset VM**   This action causes all activity on a virtual machine to be paused. This action can be set for alarms on the following objects: Virtual Machine.

- **Run a command**   This action runs a single command or script that you provide. It can be used to run a script that can resolve common issues or perform other actions. This action can be set for alarms on the following objects: Datacenter, Datastore, Cluster, Host, Resource Pool, and Virtual Machine.

- **Send a notification email**   This action sends a notification e-mail via SMTP to notify administrators of the alarm. This action can be set for alarms on the following objects: Datacenter, Datastore, Cluster, Host, Resource Pool, Virtual Machine, Network, dvSwitch, and dvPort Group.

- **Send a notification trap**   This action sends an SNMP notification trap to a monitoring system such as HP OpenView or SIM. This action can be set for alarms on the following objects: Datacenter, Datastore, Cluster, Host, Resource Pool, and Virtual Machine.

■ **Shutdown Guest on VM** This action causes the guest operating system of a virtual machine to be gracefully shut down. This action can be set for alarms on the following objects: Virtual Machine.

■ **Shutdown Host** This action causes a Host to shut down. This action can be set for alarms on the following objects: Host.

■ **Suspend VM** This action causes a virtual machine to be suspended. This action can be set for alarms on the following objects: Virtual Machine.

Create a vCenter Utilization Alarm

Just as you can with connectivity alarms, you can use the default vCenter utilization alarms to monitor your vSphere environment, or you can create custom utilization alarms.

To create a custom vCenter utilization alarm, follow these steps:

1. Launch the vSphere Client and connect to your vCenter Server.

2. In the navigation bar select Home | Inventory | Hosts And Clusters.

3. Select the vCenter Server from the inventory.

4. From the File menu select New and then Alarm. You will be presented with the Alarm Settings window.

5. On the General tab enter a name for the alarm and a description. Under the Alarm Type section select the object type that you want to monitor and use the radio buttons to choose whether you are monitoring for conditions or events. You can also choose to have the alarm Enabled or Not Enabled.

6. On the Triggers tab enter conditions or events that would cause the alarm to be triggered. You can also choose whether you want the alarm to be triggered if any of the conditions or events occurs or only if all of the conditions or events occur.

7. On the Reporting tab you can specify how often an alert should be triggered if it is not resolved and whether the alarm should be triggered if the condition increases by a certain percentage.

8. On the Actions tab you can specify the actions that should be taken when the alarm is triggered.

9. Once you have configured the information on each tab, click OK to create the new alarm.

Monitor vSphere ESX/ESXi and Virtual Machine Performance

In this section we will look at various metrics that you can use to determine how well your ESX Hosts and virtual machines are performing. We will start by looking at memory over-commitment techniques and memory metrics. We will then discuss network and storage metrics. We will then review overview and advanced charts. We will finish the section and the chapter by looking at using the Perfmon utility within Windows guests.

Explain Memory Metrics

vSphere uses a number of techniques that allow you to over-commit the amount of memory you have in your Host compared to the memory you have defined for your virtual machines. You will need to understand the following techniques for the exam:

- **Ballooning** Ballooning is a memory management technique that allows an ESX Host to reclaim some memory from a virtual machine to be used by another virtual machine. The technique uses the vmmemctl driver that is installed with the VMware Tools to convince a virtual machine that some of its memory is already being used so that it will start using swap space. Once the virtual machine has stopped using the memory, the Host will then use it to allow other virtual machines to meet their memory reservations. The performance of the virtual machine that has given up some of its memory is only slightly affected.

- **Page sharing** Page sharing is a technique that allows virtual machines to transparently use a single copy of memory page data when they are identical, reducing the need to maintain multiple copies of the same page data. Page sharing is enabled by default.

- **Swapping** ESX Hosts can use Host-level swapping to reclaim additional memory from virtual machines. This allows some of the active memory pages to be swapped out to disk and swapped back into memory as needed. Because the disk storage is slower, there can be a notable performance issue if an ESX Host is performing excessive swapping.

In addition to these memory over-commitment techniques there are a number of memory metrics that you will need to understand:

- **Memory Usage**   This counter shows the memory usage as a percentage of available memory.
- **Swap Out**   This counter shows the amount of memory that is currently being swapped out to disk.
- **Shared**   This counter shows the total amount of shared memory that is being used.
- **Memory Used by VMkernel**   This counter shows the amount of memory that is being used by the VMkernel.
- **Balloon**   This counter shows the amount of memory that is being used by the ballooning memory control.
- **Consumed**   This counter shows the amount of memory that is being consumed by virtual machines.

Now that you have an understanding of memory metrics, let's move on and look at CPU metrics.

Explain CPU Metrics

A large number of CPU metrics can be monitored using vSphere Performance Monitoring. The following are the more important CPU metrics and what they mean:

- **CPU Usage**   This counter shows the total CPU usage as a percentage during a specified time interval.
- **CPU Idle**   This counter shows the total time that a CPU stayed in the idle state and did not perform work.
- **CPU Ready**   The counter shows the percentage of time that a virtual machine was ready to use a CPU but could not be scheduled to run on a physical CPU. A high CPU Ready value could indicate that the Host does not have sufficient CPU resources.

Explain Network Metrics

In the same way that vSphere monitors a large number of CPU metrics, there are also a large number of network metrics that can be monitored. The following are the more important network metrics:

- **Network Usage** This is an aggregated statistic for overall network performance.
- **Packets Transmitted** This counter shows the total number of packets that were transmitted during a specified time interval.
- **Received Packets Dropped** This counter shows the total number of received packets that were dropped during a specified time interval.
- **Transmitted Packets Dropped** This counter shows the total number of transmitted packets that were dropped during a specified time interval.

Explain Storage Metrics

In addition to memory, CPU, and network metrics, vSphere also provides counters for storage metrics. The following are the more important storage metrics:

- **Read Latency** This counter shows the average amount of time it takes for a read from storage to be completed by the guest operating system.
- **Write Latency** This counter shows the average amount of time it takes for a write to storage to be completed by the guest operating system.
- **Disk Usage** This is an aggregated statistic for overall storage performance.
- **Bus Resets** This counter shows the total number of bus resets during a specified time interval. A large number of bus resets can indicate storage connectivity issues.
- **Queue Read Latency** This counter shows the average amount of time a read request spends in the VMkernel queue.

Compare and Contrast Overview and Advanced Charts

Now that you understand some of the performance metrics that are available in vSphere, let's take a look at how to display them using charts. There are two different types of charts that can be used to gather performance data from your vSphere environment: overview and advanced charts.

- **Overview charts** Overview charts are meant to give you a quick look at the overall performance of your environment. Using overview charts, you can quickly review total CPU, disk, memory, and network usage metrics. These charts show the following information: percentage CPU usage, CPU usage in MHz, memory ballooning, memory swap-out rate, disk latency, percentage memory usage, disk usage in KBps, network usage in Mbps. You can view this information in real time or as a defined time range.

■ **Advanced charts** Advanced charts are meant to give you a more in-depth look into the various metrics that make up the total CPU, disk, memory, and network usage metrics. Using advanced charts, you can specify a large number of different metrics. You can also choose the type of chart you wish to see: Line Graph, Stacked Graph, or Stacked Graph (per VM).

Create an Advanced Chart

Now that you know the differences between overview and advanced charts, let's go ahead and create a custom advanced chart for a Host.

To create a custom advanced chart for a Host, follow these steps:

1. Launch the vSphere Client and connect to your vCenter Server.

2. In the navigation bar select Home | Inventory | Hosts And Clusters.

3. Select the Host from the inventory that you wish to create an advanced chart for and select the Performance tab.

4. You will be presented with the Performance window. Click Advanced to view Advanced Charts.

5. You will be presented with the Advanced Charts window. At the top of the chart click Chart Options.

6. You will be presented with the Customize Performance Chart window as shown in Figure 10-7.

7. From the Chart Type frame select the type of chart you wish to generate.

8. From the Chart Options frame select the class of metrics you want to include in the chart (such as CPU or Disk) and the time frame you wish to use.

9. From the Counters frame select the counters that you wish to include in your chart. If you use a time frame other than real time, not all of the counters will be available.

10. Repeat Steps 8 and 9 for each class of metrics you wish to include and then click Save Chart Settings and enter a name for the new chart.

11. Click Apply to see the new custom chart.

FIGURE 10-7

The Customize
Performance
Chart window

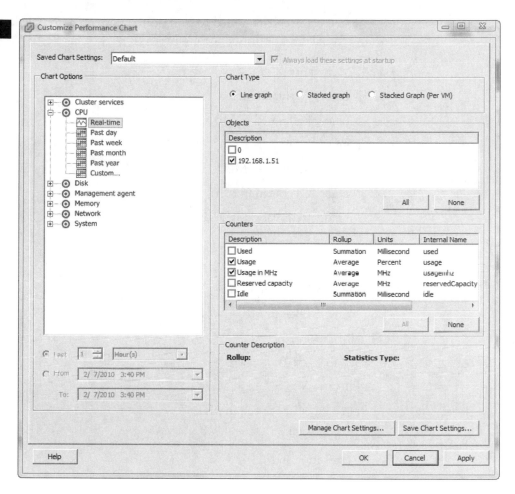

Determine Performance Metrics Using Perfmon in a Guest

In previous versions of VMware's virtual infrastructure, obtaining accurate
metrics for virtual machines using Perfmon could be very difficult. A new
feature has been added with vSphere that will make it much easier. When
VMware Tools is installed on a Windows guest, customized virtual machine

performance counters are added to Perfmon. There are two new keys that each contain a number of performance counters:

- VM Memory

  Memory Active in MB

  Memory Ballooned in MB

  Memory Limit in MB

  Memory Mapped in MB

  Memory Overhead in MB

  Memory Reservation in MB

  Memory Shared in MB

  Memory Shares

  Memory Swapped in MB

  Memory Used in MB

- VM Processor

  % Processor Time

  Effective VM Speed in MHz

  Host Processor Speed in MHz

  Limit in MHz

  Reservation in MHz

  Shares

Using these metrics, you can determine if you have the proper configuration for your virtual machine and review its performance. You can also utilize these metrics to get a decent picture of how the Host that the virtual machine is running on is performing. A high Memory Ballooning metric would indicate that the Host may not have sufficient memory for the virtual machines running on it, and a low Effective VM Speed metric may indicate that the Host does not have sufficient CPU resources for all of its virtual machines.

INSIDE THE EXAM

Using Perfmon Within a Guest

To test your knowledge of the new features of vSphere, you should expect to see a question about using Perfmon within a guest to gather performance metrics. In previous versions of

Virtual Infrastructure there were significant issues with using Perfmon to gather metrics. These issues have now been resolved with the addition of new virtual machine counters for Perfmon.

CERTIFICATION SUMMARY

We started this chapter by reviewing some basic troubleshooting techniques for ESX/ESXi Hosts. We looked at how to troubleshoot common installation issues and how to monitor the health of our Hosts. We finished the section by discussing how to export diagnostic data for our Hosts that can be used when working with VMware to resolve Host issues.

In the next section we discussed basic troubleshooting for VMware Fault-Tolerant virtual machines and looked at the basics of third-party failover systems. We started by discussing maintenance mode considerations when using Fault Tolerance. We then looked at the Microsoft Clustering Services and compared it to Fault Tolerance. We finished the section by reviewing Fault Tolerance partial and unexpected failovers.

In the third section we discussed basic troubleshooting for networking. We started by verifying that a virtual machine was connected to the correct port group and that the port group settings were configured correctly. We then confirmed that the network adapter of a virtual machine was configured to be connected and that the network adapter settings were configured correctly. We finished the section by verifying that the physical network adapter of a Host was correctly configured.

Next we discussed basic troubleshooting for Storage. We started the section by discussing the concepts of storage contention and storage over-commitment. We then discussed storage connectivity issues and potential issues with the iSCSI software initiator. We finished the section by working with storage reports and storage maps.

The fifth section was all about troubleshooting HA/DRS and VMotion. We started the section by reviewing the requirements for HA/DRS and VMotion. We then confirmed that VMotion functionality was enabled for a virtual machine. Next we discussed the DRS Resource Distribution Graph and target and current Host load deviations. We then discussed using topology maps to help troubleshoot VMotion, and we finished the section by discussing potential HA capacity issues.

In the sixth and seventh sections we looked at connectivity and utilization alarms. We started each section by listing the default alarms that are provided by vCenter Server and the possible actions for each type of alarm. To end each section we created a custom alarm.

In the final section we discussed ESX/ESXi and virtual machine performance monitoring. We started the section by looking at the important metrics for memory, CPU, network, and storage performance. We then looked at overview and advanced charts to display these metrics and created a custom advanced chart. We ended the section and the chapter by reviewing a new feature of VMware Tools that allows the Windows Perfmon utility to gather accurate metrics from within a virtual machine.

TWO-MINUTE DRILL

Basic Troubleshooting for ESX/ESXi

❑ The three basic steps for problem resolution are gather data, research solutions, ask for help.

❑ Installation failures can be caused by bad media, unsupported hardware, and hardware failures.

❑ Host boot failures can be caused by LUN-related issues and BIOS boot configuration issues.

❑ Host network problems can be caused by configuration issues or hardware issues.

❑ The hardware health of your ESX/ESXi Hosts can be monitored by using the vCenter Hardware Status plug-in.

Basic Troubleshooting for VMware FT and Third-Party Clusters

❑ Fault Tolerance must be taken into account before placing a Host into maintenance mode.

❑ Microsoft Clustering Services requires an application outage during failovers.

❑ Fault Tolerance failovers can occur unexpectedly because of: storage issues, network issues, excess logging NIC traffic, VMotion failures of FT virtual machines, and excess activity on a VMFS volume containing FT virtual machines.

Basic Troubleshooting for Networking

❑ When troubleshooting virtual machine network connectivity issues, confirm that the virtual machine is connected to the correct port group.

❑ When troubleshooting virtual machine network connectivity issues, confirm that the port group settings are correct.

❑ When troubleshooting virtual machine network connectivity issues, confirm that the network adapter is connected within the virtual machine and is correctly configured.

❑ When troubleshooting virtual machine network connectivity issues, confirm that the physical network adapter in the Host is configured correctly.

Basic Troubleshooting for Storage

❑ Storage contention occurs when multiple Hosts are requesting access to the same storage at the same time and there is not enough bandwidth to satisfy all of the requests.

❑ Storage over-commitment can occur when using Thin-provisioned disks on virtual machines.

❑ Storage connectivity issues occur when a Host is unable to connect to its storage.

❑ Storage connectivity issues can be caused by: physical issues, configuration issues, and permission issues.

❑ Storage reports are spreadsheet-like reports that can be generated on Datacenters, Clusters, or Hosts that show various data related to the storage that is being used.

❑ Storage maps are visual representations of vSphere components and how they are attached to storage devices.

Basic Troubleshooting for HA/DRS and VMotion

❑ When troubleshooting VMotion issues, confirm that it is enabled for the VMkernel port group of each Host.

❑ The DRS Resource Distribution Graph is a bar chart that shows how CPU and memory resources are distributed across the Hosts in a DRS cluster.

❑ The current Host load standard deviation is equal to the standard deviation of the sum of all of the virtual machine workloads on a Host divided by the available resources on the Host for all of the Hosts in the cluster.

❑ Topology maps can be used to help diagnose issues with VMotion.

Create and Respond to vCenter Connectivity Alarms

❑ Connectivity alarms are triggered when connectivity to an object is lost or restored.

❑ You can use the default connectivity alarms, or you can create custom connectivity alarms in vCenter Server.

Create and Respond to vCenter Utilization Alarms

❑ Utilization alarms are triggered when the utilization of a resource hits a certain level.

❑ You can use the default utilization alarms, or you can create custom utilization alarms in vCenter Server.

Monitor vSphere ESX/ESXi and Virtual Machine Performance

❑ Ballooning is a memory management technique that allows an ESX Host to reclaim some memory from a virtual machine to be used by another virtual machine.

❑ Page sharing is a technique that allows virtual machines to transparently use a single copy of memory page data when they are identical, reducing the need to maintain multiple copies of the same page data.

❑ ESX Hosts can use Host-level swapping to reclaim additional memory from virtual machines.

❑ The CPU Ready counter shows the percentage of time that a virtual machine was ready to use a CPU but could not be scheduled to run on a physical CPU.

❑ Overview charts are meant to give you a quick look at the overall performance of your environment.

❑ Advanced charts are meant to give you a more in-depth look into the various metrics that make up the total CPU, disk, memory, and network usage metrics.

❑ When VMware Tools is installed on a Windows guest-customized virtual machine, performance counters are added to Perfmon.

SELF TEST

The following questions will help you measure your understanding of the material presented in this chapter. Read all the choices carefully and remember that there is only one best answer for each question.

Basic Troubleshooting for ESX/ESXi

1. Which of the following utilities can be used to monitor the health of ESX/ESXi Host hardware?
   A. vCenter Guided Consolidation
   B. vCenter Hardware Status
   C. vCenter Update Manager
   D. vCenter Hardware Monitor

Basic Troubleshooting for VMware FT and Third-Party Clusters

2. When using Microsoft Clustering Services to provide application failover, in which location are the application files stored?
   A. On each node of the cluster
   B. On the primary node of the cluster
   C. On shared storage
   D. On the secondary node of the cluster

Basic Troubleshooting for Networking

3. If the name of a port group is changed, what will happen to virtual machines that are currently attached to the port group?
   A. They will continue to function normally.
   B. They will continue to function normally until they are restarted.
   C. They will lose their network connection to the port group.
   D. They will lose their network connection until they are restarted.

Basic Troubleshooting for Storage

4. Which of the following occurs when multiple Hosts are requesting access to the same storage at the same time and there is not enough bandwidth to satisfy all of the requests?
   A. Storage contention
   B. Storage over-commitment
   C. Storage connectivity issues
   D. None of the above

Basic Troubleshooting for HA/DRS and VMotion

5. Which of the following charts show how CPU and memory resources are distributed across the Hosts in a DRS cluster?
   A. Storage maps
   B. Topology reports
   C. DRS Resource Distribution Graph
   D. None of the above

Create and Respond to vCenter Connectivity Alarms

6. Which of the following default alarm actions uses SMTP?
   A. Send a notification e-mail
   B. Send a notification trap
   C. Enter standby
   D. Shutdown Host

Create and Respond to vCenter Utilization Alarms

7. Which of the following is not a default vCenter Server alarm?
   A. Host CPU Usage
   B. Host Memory Usage
   C. Host Storage Usage
   D. Datastore Usage on Disk

Monitor vSphere ESX/ESXi and Virtual Machine Performance

8. Which of the following is a memory management technique that allows an ESX Host to reclaim some memory from a virtual machine to be used by another virtual machine?

   A. Ballooning

   B. Page sharing

   C. Swapping

   D. None of the above

9. Which memory counter shows the amount of memory that is being swapped to disk?

   A. Memory Usage

   B. Consumed

   C. Swap Out

   D. Disk Swap

10. Which CPU counter shows the percentage of time that a virtual machine was waiting to use a CPU but could not be scheduled to run on a physical CPU?

   A. CPU Idle

   B. CPU Ready

   C. CPU Wait

   D. CPU Usage

SELF TEST ANSWERS

Basic Troubleshooting for ESX/ESXi

1. ☑ **B.** The vCenter Hardware Status plug-in is used to monitor the hardware health of ESX/ESXi Hosts.

   ☒ **A, C,** and **D** are incorrect. vCenter Guided Consolidation is an additional module for vCenter Server that allows an administrator to virtualize an existing physical datacenter. vCenter Update Manager is an additional module for vCenter Server that can be used by administrators to simplify the process of patch management for ESX Hosts as well as Windows and Linux virtual machines. vCenter Hardware Monitor is not an actual VMware tool.

Basic Troubleshooting for VMware FT and Third-Party Clusters

2. ☑ **C.** When using Microsoft Clustering Services, the files that make up an application must be kept on shared storage to allow all of the nodes of the cluster to access them.

   ☒ **A, B,** and **D** are incorrect. When using Microsoft Clustering Services, the files that make up an application must be kept on shared storage. If they were located on only a primary or secondary node of a cluster, a failure of that node would make the files unavailable. If they were maintained on multiple nodes, it would be difficult to keep the copies in sync.

Basic Troubleshooting for Networking

3. ☑ **B.** If the name of a port group is changed, currently running virtual machines will continue to function until they are restarted. After a restart, they will no longer be connected to the port group.

   ☒ **A, C,** and **D** are incorrect. The virtual machines will only continue to run correctly until they are restarted. Running virtual machines will not lose their connection to the port group until they are restarted. Restarting a virtual machine without changing its network configuration will not resolve the renamed port group issue.

Basic Troubleshooting for Storage

4. ☑ **A.** Storage contention occurs when multiple Hosts are requesting access to the same storage at the same time and there is not enough bandwidth to satisfy all of the requests.

   ☒ **B, C,** and **D** are incorrect. Storage over-commitment occurs when using Thin-provisioned disks on virtual machines. Storage connectivity issues occur when a Host is unable to connect to its storage.

Basic Troubleshooting for HA/DRS and VMotion

5. ☑ **C.** The DRS Resource Distribution Graph is a bar chart that shows how CPU and memory resources are distributed across the Hosts in a DRS cluster.

   ☒ **A, B,** and **D** are incorrect. Storage maps are visual representations of vSphere components and how they are attached to storage devices. Topology maps show a graphical display of inventory objects and the relationships they share.

Create and Respond to vCenter Connectivity Alarms

6. ☑ **A.** The "Send a notification email" action sends a notification e-mail via SMTP to notify administrators of the alarm.

   ☒ **B, C,** and **D** are incorrect. The "Send a notification trap" action sends an SNMP notification trap to a monitoring system. The "Enter standby" action causes the operating system of a virtual machine to enter standby mode. The "Shutdown Host" action causes a Host to shut down.

Create and Respond to vCenter Utilization Alarms

7. ☑ **C.** Host Storage Usage is not a default vCenter Server alarm.

   ☒ **A, B,** and **D** are incorrect. Host CPU Usage monitors the percentage of CPU resources that are currently being used on a Host. Host Memory Usage monitors the percentage of memory resources that are currently being used on a Host. Datastore Usage on Disk monitors the percentage of a datastore that is currently being used.

Monitor vSphere ESX/ESXi and Virtual Machine Performance

8. ☑ **A.** Ballooning is a memory management technique that allows an ESX Host to reclaim some memory from a virtual machine to be used by another virtual machine.

   ☒ **B, C,** and **D** are incorrect. Page sharing is a technique that allows virtual machines to transparently use a single copy of memory page data when they are identical, reducing the need to maintain multiple copies of the same page data. ESX Hosts can use host-level swapping to reclaim additional memory from virtual machines.

9. ☑ **C.** The Swap Out counter shows the amount of memory that is currently being swapped out to disk.

   ☒ **A, B,** and **D** are incorrect. The Memory Usage counter shows the memory usage as a percentage of available memory. The Consumed counter shows the amount of memory that is being consumed by virtual machines. Disk Swap is not a valid counter.

10. ☑ **B.** The CPU Ready counter shows the percentage of time that a virtual machine was ready to use a CPU but could not be scheduled to run on a physical CPU.

☒ **A, C,** and **D** are incorrect. The CPU Idle counter shows the total time that a CPU stayed in the idle state and did not perform work. CPU Wait is not a valid counter. The CPU Usage counter shows the total CPU usage as a percentage during a specified time interval.

A

Run vSphere in a Virtual Environment for Testing

I n this appendix we will cover installing vSphere in a virtual environment. We will discuss the reasons you would want to install vSphere in a virtual environment and the hardware and software requirements to do so. We will then look at installing an ESX 4.0 Host, a vCenter Server, and an iSCSI storage appliance. Once you know how to do the installs, we will discuss the different types of scenarios you should run in the test environment when preparing for the VCP exam.

Why Should You Run vSphere in a Virtual Environment?

You might want to run vSphere in a virtual environment for a number of reasons. Since you are currently preparing for the VCP exam, the most obvious reason is to learn about vSphere by installing and running it. The best way to do this would be to have a large test lab with multiple servers and a SAN available for you to experiment with. Unfortunately, most of us do not have this type of test lab to use. The next best thing would be to have a virtual test lab running on one or two well-equipped workstations. You could then use this virtual test lab to study for the exam and to simply learn more about vSphere.

Another reason you might want to run vSphere in a virtual environment is to provide demonstrations of its capabilities to your management. Many companies will want to perform a limited pilot project of vSphere to make sure it meets their needs before deciding to move forward with a full-scale vSphere deployment. By running this pilot project in a virtual environment, you may be able to demonstrate that vSphere does what it says and can meet your company's requirements. Using the virtual environment would reduce the amount of time and expense associated with deploying a limited pilot vSphere project.

You may also want to run vSphere in a virtual environment to test some of its features before deploying them into your existing vSphere production environment. You can increase your knowledge about these features before you deploy them and give management a better comfort level by showing them how features will work before deploying them.

Performance Expectations

Most of vSphere features can be deployed in a virtual environment, but it is important to have realistic expectations about how they will perform. Each layer of virtualization adds some performance overhead, so running vSphere under

VMware Workstation will be noticeably slower than running it on physical servers. Even though the performance will be significantly slower, it is still adequate for a test lab. For the most part, it will not be practical to run vSphere under a virtual environment for production systems.

Now that you know why you would want to run vSphere under VMware Workstation and what kind of performance to expect, let's take a look at the hardware and software requirements for the test lab.

Virtual Lab Hardware and Software Requirements

In this section we will discuss the hardware and software requirements for running vSphere in a virtual environment. Let us start by taking a look at the hardware requirements.

Hardware Requirements

The hardware requirements for the virtual lab will depend on the number of components you wish to install. You will need to have a CPU that has virtualization technology built in, that is, an Intel VT or AMD-V 64-bit processor. You will also need enough memory for all of the virtual machines you wish to create as well as some left over for the Host operating system. You will also need to have enough hard drive space available for all of the virtual machines. VMware Workstation allows you to allocate hard drive space to a virtual machine as needed, but this does further reduce performance.

To configure a decent test lab on a single workstation, you will need the following hardware:

- An Intel VT or AMD-V 64-bit CPU
- As much RAM as possible (minimum 6GB)
- Approximately 100GB of hard drive space

To configure a more robust test lab on multiple workstations, you will need the following hardware:

- An Intel VT or AMD-V 64-bit CPU for each workstation
- As much RAM as possible (minimum 4GB)
- Approximately 100GB of hard drive space
- A switch to enable IP connectivity between the workstations

The more memory you have available, the more functionality you will have with your test lab. Now that you know the hardware requirements, let's take a look at the software requirements.

Software Requirements

The software requirements for the virtual lab will depend on what you are trying to install and test. In general we will need to have a 64-bit operating system that is running VMware Workstation 6.51 or later. ESX 4.0 requires a 64-bit operating system to run in a virtual environment, and it will not install correctly on older versions of VMware Workstation.

To fully install the virtual lab, you will need to have the following software:

- A 64-bit operating system
- VMware Workstation 6.5 or later
- An ISO image of ESX 4.0
- An ISO image of ESXi 4.0
- An ISO image of ESX 3.5
- An ISO image of vCenter Server
- An ISO image of Windows Server 2003 or Windows Server 2008

Most of these ISO files and VMware Workstation can be downloaded as trial versions from VMware. Windows Servers can also be downloaded as trial versions from Microsoft.

Configuring the Virtual Lab

In this section we will look at configuring each component of the virtual lab. We will discuss the requirements for ESX 4.0 Hosts, a VMware vCenter Server, and an iSCSI Storage virtual machine. Once you know how to create these three different components, you can create a large number of lab scenarios to test your abilities with vSphere. Let's start by looking at an ESX 4.0 Host.

Installing an ESX 4.0 Host in the Virtual Lab

As long as your workstation meets the minimum hardware requirements, it will be able to run multiple instances of ESX 4.0 Server. These hosts will not perform as well as those installed on physical hardware, but they are adequate for testing vSphere features and for studying for the VCP exam.

To create a virtual machine for an ESX 4.0, follow these steps:

1. Launch VMware Workstation.

2. From the Edit menu select Preferences and then select the Memory tab.

3. Select the "Allow most virtual machine memory to be swapped" radio button as shown in Figure A-1. Selecting this option will allow more virtual machines to run with the limited memory of the workstation. It will affect performance if the virtual machines are memory intensive. Click OK to continue.

4. From the File menu select New and then Virtual Machine. The New Virtual Machine Wizard will be launched.

5. You will be presented with a window asking you to create a Typical or Custom virtual machine. Select Custom and click Next to continue.

6. You will be presented with a window asking you to set the compatibility level for the virtual machine. Click Next to continue and accept the default of Workstation 6.5.

7. You will now see the Guest Operating System Installation screen. On this screen select the radio button for "I will install the operating system later" and click Next to continue.

8. You will be presented with the Select A Guest Operating System window. On this window select the radio button for Linux and then use the drop-down to select Red Hat Enterprise Linux 5 64-bit. Click Next to continue.

9. You will now see the Name The Virtual Machine window. On this screen enter a name for the virtual machine and select the folder where you want to create the virtual machine. Click Next to continue.

10. On the next screen you will be asked to select the number of processors for the virtual machine. Select the radio button for One and click Next to continue.

11. You will be presented with the Memory for the Virtual Machine screen. ESX 4.0 will not install without a minimum of 2GB of memory. Enter a minimum of 2048MB and click Next to continue.

12. You will now see the Network Type window. On this screen select the radio button for Use Bridged Networking and click Next to continue.

13. You will be presented with the Select I/O Adapter Type window. Click Next to continue and accept the default of LSI Logic.

14. You will now see the Select A Disk window. Click Next to continue and accept the default of Create A New Virtual Disk.

15. You will be presented with the Select A Disk Type window. Click Next to continue and accept the default of SCSI.

16. You will now see the Specify Disk Capacity window. On this screen select a Maximum Disk Size of 16GB and check the boxes for "Allocate all disk space now" and "Store virtual disk as a single file." Click Next to continue.

17. You will be presented with the Specify Disk File window. On this screen enter a name for the virtual disk and click Next to continue.

18. You will now see the Ready To Create Virtual Machine window. On this screen click Customize Hardware to continue.

19. You will be presented with the Hardware window. On this screen remove the Floppy, USB Controller, and Sound Card, since they are not needed by ESX 4.0.

20. Select CD/DVD and on the right side select Connect At Power On and Use ISO Image File. Under Use ISO Image File enter the path to your ESX 4.0 ISO image.

21. Select Network Adapter and on the right side check Replicate Physical Network Connection State.

22. Select Display and on the right side uncheck Accelerate 3D Graphics.

23. Select Processors and on the right side set the Preferred Mode to Intel VT-x or AMD-V. Click Next to continue.

24. You will be presented with the Ready To Create Virtual Machine window. Click Finish to create the virtual machine. The creation will take a few minutes or longer, depending on your hardware.

25. Once the virtual machine is created, close VMware Workstation.

26. Navigate to the folder where you created the virtual machine and locate the disk file you named in Step 17.

27. Edit this file and add the line **monitor_control.restrict_backdoor=true** as shown in Figure A-2.

28. Restart VMware Workstation and power on the virtual machine.

29. Install ESX 4.0 as if you were on a physical server.

Allow most
virtual machine
memory to be
swapped.

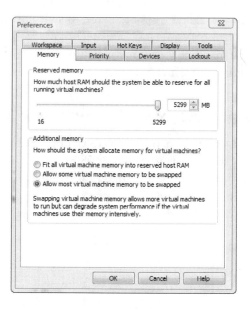

Add a line to the
virtual disk file of
an ESX 4.0 Host.

```
ESX40 - Notepad
File  Edit  Format  View  Help
.encoding = "windows-1252"
config.version = "8"
virtualHW.version = "7"
vcpu.hotadd = "TRUE"
maxvcpus = "4"
scsi0.present = "TRUE"
scsi0.virtualDev = "lsilogic"
memsize = "2048"
mem.hotadd = "TRUE"
scsi0:0.present = "TRUE"
scsi0:0.fileName = "ESX40.vmdk"
ide1:0.present = "TRUE"
ide1:0.fileName = "C:\Users\Rob\Downloads\esx-DVD-4.0.0-171294.iso"
ide1:0.deviceType = "cdrom-image"
floppy0.present = "FALSE"
ethernet0.present = "TRUE"
ethernet0.virtualDev = "e1000"
ethernet0.wakeOnPcktRcv = "FALSE"
ethernet0.linkStatePropagation.enable = "TRUE"
pciBridge0.present = "TRUE"
pciBridge4.present = "TRUE"
pciBridge4.virtualDev = "pcieRootPort"
pciBridge4.functions = "8"
pciBridge5.present = "TRUE"
pciBridge5.virtualDev = "pcieRootPort"
pciBridge5.functions = "8"
pciBridge6.present = "TRUE"
pciBridge6.virtualDev = "pcieRootPort"
pciBridge6.functions = "8"
pciBridge7.present = "TRUE"
pciBridge7.virtualDev = "pcieRootPort"
pciBridge7.functions = "8"
vmci0.present = "TRUE"
monitor.virtual_mmu = "software"
monitor.virtual_exec = "hardware"

monitor_control.restrict_backdoor=true

roamingVM.exitBehavior = "go"
displayName = "ESX40"
```

You should now be able to use this virtual machine the same way you would a physical ESX 4.0 Host. This technique will also work for creating an ESX 3.5 virtual machine. Now that you know how to install an ESX Host, let's take a look at installing a vCenter Server.

Installing VMware vCenter Server in the Virtual Lab

In most environments VMware vCenter Server is installed as a service on a Windows 2003 or Windows 2008 Server. The basic process of installing vCenter Server in a virtual environment is to create a Windows Server virtual machine and then install vCenter Server onto it.

To create a virtual machine for a vCenter Server, follow these steps:

1. Launch VMware Workstation.
2. From the File menu select New and then Virtual Machine. The New Virtual Machine Wizard will be launched.
3. You will be presented with a window asking you to create a Typical or Custom virtual machine. Select Custom and click Next to continue.
4. You will be presented with a window asking you to set the compatibility level for the virtual machine. Click Next to continue and accept the default of Workstation 6.5.
5. You will now see the Guest Operating System Installation screen. On this screen select the radio button for "I will install the operating system later" and click Next to continue.
6. You will be presented with the Select A Guest Operating System window. On this window select the radio button for Microsoft Windows and then use the drop-down to select Windows Server 2003 Standard Edition. Click Next to continue.
7. You will now see the Name the Virtual Machine window. On this screen enter a name for the virtual machine and select the folder where you want to create the virtual machine. Click Next to continue.
8. On the next screen you will be asked to select the number of processors for the virtual machine. Select the radio button for Two and click Next to continue.

9. You will be presented with the Memory for the Virtual Machine screen. Enter a minimum of 3072MB and click Next to continue.

10. You will now see the Network Type window. On this screen select the radio button for Use Bridged Networking and click Next to continue.

11. You will be presented with the Select I/O Adapter Type window. Click Next to continue and accept the default of LSI Logic.

12. You will now see the Select A Disk window. Click Next to continue and accept the default of Create A New Virtual Disk.

13. You will be presented with the Select A Disk Type window. Click Next to continue and accept the default of SCSI.

14. You will now see the Specify Disk Capacity window. On this screen select a Maximum Disk Size of 8GB and check the boxes for "Allocate all disk space now" and "Store virtual disk as a single file." Click Next to continue.

15. You will be presented with the Specify Disk File window. On this screen enter a name for the virtual disk and click Next to continue.

16. You will now see the Ready To Create Virtual Machine window. On this screen click Customize Hardware to continue.

17. You will be presented with the Hardware window. On this screen remove the Floppy, USB Controller, and Sound Card, since they are not needed by vCenter Server.

18. Select CD/DVD and on the right side select Connect At Power On and Use ISO Image File. Under Use ISO Image File enter the path to your Microsoft Windows 2003 Server ISO image. Click Next to continue.

19. You will be presented with the Ready To Create Virtual Machine window. Click Finish to create the virtual machine. The creation will take a few minutes or longer, depending on your hardware.

20. Power on the virtual machine and install Windows Server 2003.

21. Once Windows Server is created, you will need to redirect the CD/DVD setting to point to an ISO image of vCenter Server. Click Edit Virtual Machine Settings.

22. You will be presented with the Virtual Machine Settings window. On this screen select CD/DVD and then on the right select the box for Use ISO

Image File and enter the path to the ISO image for vCenter Server. Click OK to continue.

You are now ready to install vCenter Server just as if you were on a physical server.

Using iSCSI Storage in the Virtual Lab

To use many of the advanced features of vSphere, we need to have a shared SAN solution for our ESX Hosts. Since a Fibre Channel SAN would be cost prohibitive for most people, we will use a freeware iSCSI virtual appliance called Openfiler. Openfiler is available as a downloadable virtual appliance and will run under VMware Workstation.

To configure Openfiler on VMware Workstation, follow these steps:

1. Use a web browser to go to www.openfiler.com and download the x86 VMware ESX Virtual Appliance for Openfiler.

2. Save the Virtual Appliance to a separate directory.

3. Launch VMware Workstation.

4. From the File menu select Open and then navigate to the newly saved virtual appliance.

5. Before powering on the virtual machine, select Edit Virtual Machine Settings and add an additional 24GB SCSI drive to the virtual machine.

6. Once the new drive is created, power on the virtual machine.

7. Once the virtual machine has finished booting, connect to it using a web browser pointed to the IP address that is shown on the console screen of the Openfiler virtual machine.

8. You will be presented with a logon screen. The default username is "openfiler," and the default password is "password." Enter the userid and password and click Log On to continue.

9. The first step to configuring Openfiler is to create a new volume. Click the Volumes tab at the top of the page. You will see that there are no volumes currently defined.

10. Click Create New Physical Volumes.

11. You will be presented with the Block Device Management window. Click /dev/sdb to begin creating a new volume.

12. You will be presented with the Create A Partition In /dev/sdb window. On this window click Create to continue.

13. The next step is to create a volume group. Click the Volumes tab at the top of the page. Select Volume Groups on the right side of the screen.

14. You will be presented with the Create A New Volume Group window. Enter a name for the new volume group that contains no spaces and check the box next to /dev/sdb1. Click Add Volume Group to continue.

15. The next step is to add a volume to the volume group. Select Add Volume on the right side of the screen.

16. You will be prompted to select the volume group you wish to add a volume to. Select the volume group you just created. Enter a name for the new volume, add a brief description, select all of the available space, and select iSCSI as the volume type. Click Create to continue.

17. The next step is to create a share for the volume. Click the System tab at the top of the page.

18. Under Network Access Configuration enter the name of the volume group you created, the IP Address of the Openfiler Server, and the subnet mask for the Openfiler Server. Click Update to Continue.

19. The last step is to enable the iSCSI target. Click the Services tab at the top of the page.

20. Locate the iSCSI target server service and click Enable to enable the target.

You should now have a functioning shared iSCSI SAN available for testing vSphere functions like vMotion and HA. In the next section we will discuss some of the testing scenarios you may want to set up in your test lab.

Recommended Test Lab Scenarios

Now that you know how to install ESX Hosts, vCenter Servers, and shared iSCSI Storage in our virtual lab, let's discuss some of the scenarios you should set up in the test lab. You can use this section as a checklist to make sure you are getting the most from your test lab, but do not treat it as exhaustive.

You can perform the following tasks in your test lab:
❏ Install ESX 4.0 on a virtual machine.
❏ Install ESX 3.5 on a virtual machine.
❏ Install the vSphere Client on your Host workstation and use it to connect to an ESX 4.0 Host.
❏ Use the vSphere Host Update Utility to upgrade an ESX 3.5 Host to ESX 4.0.
❏ Install virtual machines on an ESX Host running on a virtual machine. These will need to be 32-bit VMs, since 64-bit VMs do not run correctly on a virtualized ESX Host.
❏ Create a template of a virtual machine and deploy another virtual machine from the template.
❏ Configure an ESX Host to use iSCSI SAN storage using the Openfiler virtual appliance.
❏ Install vCenter Server on a virtual machine.
❏ Connect to a vCenter Server using the vSphere Client.
❏ Add Hosts to a vCenter Server.
❏ Experiment with virtual switches and vNetwork Distributed Switches.
❏ Deploy a virtual machine using VMware vCenter Converter Enterprise.
❏ Install Update Manager on your vCenter Server.
❏ Create Baselines of ESX Hosts and virtual machines.
❏ Create, delete, import, and export Host Profiles.
❏ Apply a Host Profile to a new ESX Host.
❏ Create a VMware Cluster and add Hosts to it.
❏ Perform a vMotion of a virtual machine from one ESX Host to another ESX Host.
❏ Configure and test HA.
❏ Create a Resource Pool and add virtual machines to it.
❏ Create, delete, and restore Snapshots.
❏ Install and test the vCenter Data Recovery plug-in.

Hopefully you have managed to install a functional test lab. Use it to gain experience working with all of the different functions of vSphere.

B

About the CD-ROM

The CD-ROM included with this book comes complete with MasterExam, an electronic version of the book, and electronic flash cards. The software is easy to install on any Windows 2000/XP/Vista computer and must be installed to access the MasterExam feature. You may, however, browse the electronic book and flash cards directly from the CD without installation. To register for the bonus MasterExam, simply click the Bonus MasterExam link on the main launch page and follow the directions to the free online registration.

System Requirements

Software requires Windows 2000 or higher and Internet Explorer 6.0 or above and 20 MB of hard disk space for full installation. The electronic book and flash cards require Adobe Acrobat Reader.

Installing and Running MasterExam

If your computer CD-ROM drive is configured to auto run, the CD-ROM will automatically start up upon inserting the disk. From the opening screen you may install MasterExam by clicking the MasterExam link. This will begin the installation process and create a program group named LearnKey. To run MasterExam use Start | All Programs | LearnKey | MasterExam. If the auto run feature did not launch your CD, browse to the CD and click on the LaunchTraining.exe icon.

MasterExam

MasterExam provides you with a simulation of the actual exam. The number of questions, the type of questions, and the time allowed are intended to be an accurate representation of the exam environment. You have the option to take an open book exam, including hints, references, and answers, a closed book exam, or the timed MasterExam simulation.

When you launch MasterExam, a digital clock display will appear in the bottom right-hand corner of your screen. The clock will continue to count down to zero unless you choose to end the exam before the time expires.

Electronic Book

The entire contents of the Study Guide are provided in PDF format. Adobe's Acrobat Reader is also included on the CD.

Flash Cards

Also included on the CD are 350 study questions for the VCP410 Exam, in PDF format. These questions are presented as flash cards that can be printed or used electronically to help you memorize the facts that you will need to know to pass the exam. Many of the questions you will encounter on the exam require you to know a maximum or minimum value, or to be able to name a specific technology based on a description of its functionality. These cards will help you quickly memorize these important values and technologies, allowing you to devote more of your study time to learning and understanding the concepts of vSphere, without having to worry about memorizing all the little details.

Help

A help file is provided through the help button on the main page in the lower left-hand corner of the CD user interface. An individual help feature is also available through MasterExam.

Removing Installation(s)

MasterExam is installed to your hard drive. For best results removing programs, use the Start | All Programs | LearnKey | Uninstall option to remove MasterExam.

Technical Support

For questions regarding the content of the electronic book, flash cards, or MasterExam, please visit http://www.mhprofessional.com/techsupport/. For customers outside the 50 United States, email: international_cs@mcgraw-hill.com.

LearnKey Technical Support

For technical problems with the software (installation, operation, removing installations), please visit www.learnkey.com, email techsupport@learnkey.com, or call toll free at 1-800-482-8244.

INDEX

F

O

P